God and Popular Culture

God and Popular Culture

A Behind-the-Scenes Look at the Entertainment Industry's Most Influential Figure

Volume 2

Stephen Butler Murray and
Aimée Upjohn Light, Editors

 PRAEGER™

An Imprint of ABC-CLIO, LLC
Santa Barbara, California • Denver, Colorado

Library of Congress Cataloging-in-Publication Data

God and popular culture : a behind-the-scenes look at the entertainment industry's most influential figure / Stephen Butler Murray and Aimée Upjohn Light, editors.
     volumes cm
   Includes the following: GOD AND FILM, GOD IN TELEVISION, GOD AND MUSIC, GOD AND SPORTS, GOD AND POLITICS AND COMMERCE, GOD AND POPULAR CULTURE.
   Includes bibliographical references.
   ISBN 978-1-4408-0179-2 (print : acid-free paper) — ISBN 978-1-4408-0180-8 (e-book)
1. Popular culture—Religious aspects—Christianity.   2. Popular culture—Religious aspects.   I. Murray, Stephen Butler.   II. Light, Aimée Upjohn.
   BR115.C8G634 2015
   261—dc23   2014045168

ISBN: 978-1-4408-0179-2
EISBN: 978-1-4408-0180-8

19 18 17 16 15   1 2 3 4 5

This book is also available on the World Wide Web as an eBook.
Visit www.abc-clio.com for details.

Praeger
An Imprint of ABC-CLIO, LLC

ABC-CLIO, LLC
130 Cremona Drive, P.O. Box 1911
Santa Barbara, California 93116-1911

This book is printed on acid-free paper ∞

Manufactured in the United States of America

Contents

Introduction

*Stephen Butler Murray and
Aimée Upjohn Light*

Contemporary culture simultaneously is increasingly secular and religiously pluralistic, but it cannot get over or get past the desire to know God. References to God permeate every aspect of media, providing us with an ongoing societal meditation on theological themes, imagining and reimagining encounters between the divine and the mundane. Humanity is defined, time and again, by a relationship with God that is interactive, mutually compelling, and dramatically active in the present day. God in contemporary culture takes on traditional roles and wildly new ones, cast in imagery straight from the Bible and right out of a music video. God is a burning bush and a cartoon CPU; an immense thundercloud rolling over a city; and George Burns, Morgan Freeman, and Alanis Morissette. The singer Joan Osborne ponders what if God was one of us, and the television show *Joan of Arcadia* presents God as a stranger on a bus.

Our cultural craving for connection with the divine presents a conversation between belief and creativity on the nature of God and the repercussions of that nature on what it means to be human. We wonder through different forums whether God is absent or present, utterly beneficent or casually indifferent. Artists present God not merely through the Trinitarian lens of Western Christianity, but also through the perspective of Judaism's monotheism and Hinduism's nearly infinite representations of God. Filmmakers explore the nature of evil and goodness, prosperity and despair through God as an actor, a participant in the narrative. We watch sports on television in which football players kneel in prayer upon scoring a touchdown, and on C-SPAN as chaplains pray at the beginning of congressional meetings for a nation that proclaims the value of the separation of church and state.

God is an important and inextricable part of contemporary popular culture, which addresses notions of divinity and morality through the use of "God" to develop extraordinary narratives that allow explorations of morality, responsibility, consequence, and ultimate meaning. Religious depictions of God as mediated by culture have a profound influence on politics, art, and culture, but also provide themes of meaning-making without necessarily advancing a theological argument. God has appeared in the culture of every era, whether we are discussing the architectural genius of a great cathedral or the music of Mozart or the writings of Tolstoy. What is it about culture that seeks and maybe even needs God as an objective, a character, a narrative twist, and a moral compass? How do individual artists embrace and utilize this concept of God to provide a weight and importance to their stories, which otherwise could not be achieved?

We have invited not only scholars within religious studies, but also artists and attorneys, businessmen and puppeteers, filmmakers and philosophers to discuss the role of God in popular culture. Each of the two volumes is divided into three main sections, each examining the phenomenon of God and popular culture as articulated through a particular medium. The first series of essays in Volume 1 examines how God is portrayed in film, with a number of essays exploring engagements with science fiction and fantasy engagements. Danielle Elizabeth Tumminio grapples with whether love itself serves as a form of divinity in the *Harry Potter* series, and Gregory W. Carmer ponders the zombie-apocalypse subgenre as a discourse on the transcendence of humanity and the very question of God. Thomas Cattoi investigates themes of grace and forgiveness in Terrence Malick's remarkable *The Tree of Life*, as Ronald W. Baard inquires as to the inner healing of men in contemporary film. John Bechtold discusses misrepresentations of the Christ-figure in popular film, and Ian McCausland uncovers issues concerning Christianity and subjectivity in *Alien3*. Richard O'Connell offers a compelling theological and cinematic reading of two biblically based movies, *The Greatest Story Ever Told* and *The Passion of the Christ*; Jari Ristiniemi grapples with love as portrayed through religion and emotion in cinema; and Matthew Lon Weaver offers an analysis of the spirit of healing in *Harold and Maude* through the theological perspective of Paul Tillich, the 20th-century theologian who first observed the importance of how culture affects theology and how theology affects culture.

The second section in Volume 1, God in Television, begins with Valerie Elverton Dixon's observations regarding the role of technology as God in the dramatic *Person of Interest*, and Michelle J. Morris provides acute insights into how Chris is skewered and evolves in the comedic cartoon *South Park*. Rachel Wagner delves into the complex metaphorical narratives of *The*

Twilight Zone, Hannah Adams Ingram investigates the increasing religious pluralism of the United States as seen through prime-time network television, and Alicia Vermeer offers *Joan of Arcadia* as a view into the religiosity of youth and young adults in America. God and Music is the final section in Volume 1 beginning with Courtney Wilder's Tillichian meditation on Pink and Lady Gaga, and continuing with T. Mark McConnell's Kierkegaardian observations on Arcade Fire. Echol Nix, Jr. offers an overview of gospel music as literally singing the "good news" of God.

God and Sports, the first section in Volume 2, provides the reader with four fascinating perspectives on both conventional and unconventional athletic competitions. Rebecca A. Chabot and Jason Neal examine the global cultural sports phenomenon of soccer as a religion, arguing that the stadium itself serves as a church. The religious motivation of athletes provides Carmen Celestini with an intense tableau in the sports of cage fighting and mixed martial arts. In a similar vein, B. J. Parker, Rebecca Whitten Poe Hays, and Nicholas R. Werse discover the world of evangelical fight clubs; and Brian Cogan and Jeff Massey inquire into "Python wrassling" as a form of religious observance in the quest for the reality of God.

The next section in Volume 2, God and Politics and Commerce, offers five essays on how God is depicted and utilized within government, business, and media imagery. The legal scholar and religious ethicist Jeremy G. Mallory wrestles with the role of God in the U.S. Senate, and the business scholar Robert Brancatelli provides important parallels between the evangelist and the venture capitalist and Andris Berry focuses on the spiritual language of trade and advertising. Paula J. Lee makes an important critique about the role of media as the common mediatory of theological meaning-making, and Jann Cather Weaver develops a shared critical ethic for media images and liturgy.

The final section in Volume 2 examines God and Popular Culture, a series of essays that do not fit within the forums on specific media. Joyce Ann Konigsburg reaches into the pocket of society and takes out the religious dimensions of the smartphone. David Beard and David Gore explore the project of the theorist Marshall McLuhan with regard to the claim that "In Jesus Christ, the medium and the message are fully one and the same." The poet-pastor Steven E. Berry argues for the prophetic power of poetry, and Paul H. Carr finds God in near-death experiences, art, and science. Amitabh Vikram Dwivedi plays with the role of gods in Indian popular jokes, Andriette Jordan-Fields inquires into the presence of the cross in popular culture, and Guido Oliana sees African language, drum, and dance as symbols of God's saving mystery. Carolyn D. Roark explores the divine/human relationship within puppetry, and Carlos Vara Sánchez examines the *Via Negativa* as aesthetic experience.

In many cultures today, God appears differently and sometimes is forbidden from being represented at all. Popular culture has been at play with the different ways of representing God and has even bucked the theologies that would argue that God should not be depicted at all. Do such "appearances" of God in popular culture bring honor or defame that which some people find holy? God appears throughout television and film, on FOX News and in *The New York Times*, on Twitter and beliefnet.com. In nearly every aspect of popular culture, God plays an unparalleled role in determining the importance of storylines and moral reflection. Why do authors and directors use God as a vehicle to examine the human condition? What about God sparks such strong concern in news reports and political commentary? Who is the God depicted in comic books and music videos? Contemporary popular culture is fascinated by God at a time when mainstream churches are failing. Do we rely on culture to feed our imagination of the divine and discuss matters of ultimate meaning, rather than depend on doctrine and theology to determine the course of cultural expression? This set of volumes explores why popular culture needs God and why, in fact, God might need popular culture.

God and Sports

CHAPTER ONE

Soccer Is My Religion, the Stadium Is My Church: Soccer and/as Religion

Rebecca A. Chabot with Jason Neal[1]

Though certainly not the only athlete to publicly speak about his faith, Tim Tebow has come to serve as the shining example of the intersection between sport and faith, between sport and God. In the world of professional club soccer, Tebow's equivalent would be AC Milan forward and Brazilian international Ricardo Izecson dos Santos Leite, better known as Kaka. Kaka has been equally vocal about his faith and its importance in his life and career. He attributes his success on the pitch to God in postmatch interviews, just like rappers and actors do at awards shows. He is certainly not the only soccer player to be vocal about his faith or to be demonstrative about faith on the pitch, but he is (at present) the only player to take off his jersey to reveal a t-shirt that read, "I belong to Jesus."

If one is lucky enough to be able to watch a match live in a stadium, it is inevitable that one will see some sort of a religious display from a player or players. Many players cross themselves before they step onto the pitch; others cross themselves after scoring a goal. The diversity of religions and religious practice in the world of professional soccer is vast and is something about which more and more players and teams are becoming aware. In 2010, the Deutscher Fußball-Bund, the German football association, published a series of videos in which members of Die Mannschaft, the German

National Football Team, shared their own rituals and superstitions. Some were entirely football related, like stepping onto the pitch last, but others wove religious practices into their stories.

When FC Bayern München was celebrating their Bundesliga (German premiere league) title in 2013, some were outraged that defender Jérôme Boateng poured beer over the head of midfielder Franck Ribéry. Ribéry, a practicing Muslim, was initially upset about the incident, until he learned that it had been nonalcoholic beer. This small moment illustrated that soccer is adaptable to differing religious practices and that the world's largest clubs are microcosms of the religiously cosmopolitan societies in which they are usually situated: A German player consistently thought of the identity of the other and adapted a traditional German ritual accordingly so that his teammate could still be a full participant in the celebrations.

There is, however, another level to the interplay between soccer and religion. For many people around the world, soccer has come to function as a kind of religion. It is the locus of their meaning-making, the source of their connection to something beyond themselves. This is not true of all fans, but soccer understood as a religion does not make the same universalist claims that other religions do. In fact, soccer as religion has both a theist and a nontheist articulation; some fans bridge their traditional practices with their fandom, praying before matches or lighting candles, and others come with no religious tradition and see no connection between the game and a higher power. For those who practice a theistic brand of soccer, God's favor is tied directly to on-pitch results, the signing of high-quality players, and the winning of trophies; God's disapproval comes in the form of losses, poor managers, players failing to live up to their potential, and injuries. The most important thing, though, is that the Club is the way by which fans engage with the sport and experience transcendence for both soccer theists and nontheists.

One could use any number of religious theorists to make the argument that soccer functions as a religion, but for the sake of brevity, here we will use one of the most famous definitions of religion, that of Clifford Geertz. Geertz famously defined religion as "a set of symbols which acts to establish powerful, pervasive and long-lasting moods and motivations in men by formulating conceptions of a general order of existence and clothing these conceptions with such an aura of factuality that the moods and motivations seem uniquely realistic."[2] To help explain this further, we have developed a set of Eleven Commandments that articulate the major tenets of soccer when it is understood as a religion.

Eleven Commandments[3]

Commandment the First: You Will Have No Other Clubs Before This One

The idea of sports loyalty is fairly familiar to an American audience. However, when it comes to professional club soccer, in many parts of the world, we need to talk about something that goes deeper than loyalty. Club allegiance is hereditary.[4] It is handed down from parents and grandparents, siblings, cousins, and so on. To change allegiance would be analogous to leaving one's tradition for another, to become a Lutheran after having been raised Catholic, or, in some cases, to convert from Christianity to Islam. In some cases this is true even in more traditional senses of religion. To trade allegiance, say, from Glasgow's Celtic FC to Glasgow's Rangers FC is quite literally to cross social and religious lines defined by Scottish sectarian religious strife. This is not to place a value judgment upon conversion or suggest that one club or religion is superior to others (though, in the soccer world, we certainly have our biases, as do all fans). Rather, this is to say that there is a deeper significance to club loyalty than merely supporting a team: It is constitutive of personal identity, the source of profound (and often religious) experiences. In modern and secularized societies, Club allegiance serves as the locus for engagement within the broader community, occasionally fulfilling the role that a church or synagogue or mosque filled in other contexts.

Much like religious conversion, defection from team loyalty strains social bounds and ties. John Oliver, formerly the Senior British Correspondent for *The Daily Show* and one of the hosts of the weekly podcast *The Bugle*, has joked that his father would rather see him dead than cheer for a team other than Liverpool.[5] When Simon Critchley's first son, Edward, was born, his "first violent patriarchal act was to decorate his room with Liverpool pennants and other paraphernalia. Like me, he would have had no choice but to support Liverpool."[6] Likewise, in his memoir Fever Pitch, novelist Nick Hornby shares his childhood memories of attending Arsenal matches with his father, which led to a lifelong love of the Club. To cheer for an opposing team would be blasphemy. Hornby says, "There must be fathers around the country who have experienced the cruelest, most crushing rejection of all: their children have ended up supporting the wrong team."[7] For, Matt Burnett, a 30-plus-year Arsenal supporter, he has seen his teenage son's adolescent rebellion take the shape of cheering for Chelsea; although Matt agrees it could be worse, "still, I wish it weren't Chelsea."[8] Crucially, these remarks are only partially ironic; the Club matters enough that defection can place real strain on family and social relationships. It is also important to note that, even though geography may play a role in how someone comes to claim a club, Club trumps geography: No self-respecting FC Dallas fan who moves to Houston will suddenly begin cheering for the Dynamo.

Commandment the Second: Honor the Match Day and Keep It Holy

Saturdays and Sundays are the traditional match days. However, for the clubs involved in pan-European competition, like the Champions League or the Europa League,[9] and those still in the running for their country's Cup often have midweek matches. Whenever possible, the match takes priority in scheduling. Classes are scheduled around them (or skipped if they happen to conflict with a Champion's League knockout stage match). We adjust our work schedules, finding people to cover shifts, in order to watch our team. Nick Hornby says it well:

> As I get older, the tyranny that football exerts over my life, and therefore over the lives of people around me, is less reasonable and less attractive. Family and friends know, after long years of wearying experience, that the fixture list always has the last word in any arrangement; they understand, or at least accept, that christenings or weddings or any gatherings, which in other families would take unquestioned precedence, can only be plotted after consultation. So football is regarded as a given disability that has to be worked around. If I were wheelchair-bound, nobody close to me would organize anything in a top door flat, so why would they plan anything for a winter Saturday afternoon?[10]

Yet it is not just the effort made to watch the match that renders the match day holy. It is also the rituals in which we participate that sanctify and honor the day.

Our rituals are equally important to the liturgical sense of the match. Whether in the stands, having made the pilgrimage from home to the "cathedral," or at home or a pub, watching alone or with friends, often over beers, our rituals matter. We wear our "lucky" jerseys, believing that our choice of attire can in some way influence the outcome of the match. We surround ourselves with talismans, with objects that we associate with the team. They decorate their rooms with posters and scarves. We write for blogs and use social media to comment on the match, to be able to claim a small piece of it for ourselves. We cross their fingers and clutch rosaries, refuse to sit or pace restlessly, feeling a physical connection to the action of the match. Whether or not this is literally the case matters little; these rituals enable us to be a part of things. They enable us to participate in the ritualization and the liturgical rhythms of the match. Budweiser has pitched an entire marketing campaign on this idea during the NFL season: "it's not weird if it works." And so we keep to our rituals because they are not weird; they work.

Commandment the Third: You Will Not Take the Name of the Club in Vain

Bad things happen in soccer. As Simon Critchley says, "Football is all about the experience of failure and righteous injustice. It is about hoping to win and learning to accept defeat. But most importantly, it is about some experience of the fragility of belonging: the enigma of place, memory and history."[11] The team that deserves to win does not always win, people get injured, and sometimes, your coach is a complete and total idiot who is destroying your team. And we, as fans, are vocal about our feelings on these things. And players, managers, other teams, referees, the club's board of directors—all of these things are fair game for our anger and frustration. We can curse them, we can malign them, we can publicly denounce them on social media and draw attention to their failings. Those of us who write for blogs know how difficult it can be sometimes to be charitable to that one player who gets under our skin or to not eviscerate the hope of others in our treatment of a match.

But under no circumstances, at no time, are we ever allowed to bad-mouth the club itself. All else is fair game, but the club itself is not. This is, in large part, because the club is not just the team; the club is the team, the reserves, the coaches, the trainers, the physicians, the board of directors, the front office staff, and the fans who claim allegiance to the club. The club is the thing that transcends boundaries and it is the club to whom we have pledged our loyalties. Although we can trash talk a rival, and by that we mean the ENTIRE Club, I cannot ever say that about my own Club. Apostasy is not tolerated in the world of football and that means you never demean your own club. Go after the people involved, yell at the players, but never, ever talk badly about the club or besmirch its name.

Commandment the Fourth: You Will Not Make Graven Images (Until They Either Retire or Officially Sign with Another Club)

Throughout the world, we like to make statues that honor celebrities and politicians, people who have gained fame through their prowess on the pitch or in music or elsewhere. And even though the statue of Michael Jackson that graced Craven Cottage in London is a little creepy, they did at least wait until he died to erect it; it was taken down in 2013 after two years of display.[12] Manchester United fans learned this lesson the hard way. When it looked like their star striker Wayne Rooney would likely leave the club, and quite possibly for cross-town rivals Manchester City, fans constructed an effigy of the United striker as Shrek.[13] Shortly after the effigy was burned, and after fans had rallied in front of Rooney's house, he resigned with United. And the fans felt a bit foolish for having made assumptions about the fate of their star. Jumping the gun and turning a player into a martyr or a hero or a villain too quickly happens often in soccer, but it also speaks to the importance that this holds in people's lives. The very fact that people feel the need to make giant signs with players' faces on them, that they make effigies of them when they are playing badly or thinking of leaving the club, indicates the deep seriousness with which many fans take even a potential betrayal of the club. And, once retired, bronzing players is part of the indispensable process of creating the cult of the club's history. But statues are best left until after a player retires or passes away . . . it helps prevent embarrassment later.

Commandment the Fifth: You Will Honor Your Mother and Father

Soccer, like society as a whole, struggles with social issues like homophobia, sexism, and racism. Intriguingly, the response to these issues has leveraged respect for the game as a mechanism to correct social ills. Initiatives such as You Can Play, Kick It Out, and the Respect Campaign have all presumed a shared sense of deep value of the game such that sport officials have assumed that attachment to soccer itself is a powerful enough attachment to be used to push back against the divisive forces of prejudice and fear within the sport.[14] It shows the power of the game over the imagination of the people that respect for the game is not just a sporting value, but a social one. In 2010, soccer fans from around the world came together on LiveJournal, a blogging site, and created Red Card Homophobia, an organization aimed at rooting out homophobia in the game. After its creation in 2010, Red Card Homophobia began reaching out to clubs with some success, including a 2011 photo shoot with the Dutch club Ajax.[15]

All of these organizations use belief that sport should be free of discrimination as a shared ideal from which to act. Given that there are still no openly gay players playing soccer in most countries and only one in a major league worldwide, and the fact that players of color are routinely subjected to racist abuse during European matches, there is still much work to be done and fans are helping to lead the way. Some clubs have implemented zero-tolerance policies, where fans who use homophobic or racist language are immediately removed from the stadium, but the institutional culture of the game still has a long way to go to catch up with many fans around the world.

Commandment the Sixth: You Will Not Commit Bad Fouls

Of course, what constitutes a bad foul is a matter of profound disagreement. Was an injury-inducing tackle careless? Malicious? Or something in between? Was a trip on the edge of the penalty box a matter of tactical savvy or cynical unfair play? Was he playing the ball or playing the man? Arguments about fouls are not simply a matter of advantage to one team or another or even a matter of disagreement about a particular event; rather, disagreements about bad fouls can define club cultures, regional cultures, even national cultures. What does or does not constitute a bad foul can expose passionately held values about the game.

In every league, there's at least one team with a reputation for intentionally tackling for injury. In the English Premiere League, the mere mention of Stoke will cause fans of rival clubs to curse them. In Germany, a match against Dortmund will inherently mean that fans will be sympathetically rubbing their shins at various points during the game. In Major League Soccer, the mention of San Jose Earthquakes' defender Victor Bernárdez and forward Alan Gordon draws grumbling and comments about "knuckle draggers" from opposing fans. Regardless of league or club, the teams that play in this chippy style are reviled by all but their own fans, as bad fouls violate the spirit of the game.

Commandment the Seventh: You Will Not Bear False Witness

For fans and nonfans alike, one of the most common complaints relates to diving. When the Canadian writer Adam Gopnik watched the World Cup of 1998 on TV for the New Yorker, he as an outsider to soccer immediately focused on this problem. The "more customary method of getting a penalty" he wrote "is to walk into the 'area' with the ball, get breathed on hard, and then immediately collapse . . . arms and legs splayed out while you twist in agony and beg for morphine, and your teammates smite their foreheads at the tragic waste of a young life. The referee buys this more often than you might think. Afterward the postgame did-he-fall-or-was-he-pushed argument can go on for hours."[16] Perhaps more than any other sport, soccer has an ability to be understood as a "sport para joder," a phrase drawn from ethicist Miguel De La Torre's work that means intentionally screwing with the system. In short, there is a tension between those who view diving as legitimate trickery and those who perceive it as a betrayal of the game; between those who value the pragmatic outcome and those who see simulation as a betrayal of fair play. Debates about whether a specific incident constituted a dive can be interminable, as can debates about the ethics of diving in general. Our point is not to favor one argument or another; our point is that ideas about diving evoke deep passions and can form divisive and constitutive components of different soccer cultures.

Commandment the Eighth: You Will Not Steal

In soccer, unlike in other sports, the club owns a player's contract and the way that players transfer from one team to another is by a club buying that player's contract. Fans of smaller clubs hate it, because they see their favorite players snapped up by the biggest clubs in Europe; fans of bigger clubs hate being accused of stealing. Some clubs develop player-related rivalries with clubs in their country and others develop these rivalries with clubs hundreds or thousands of miles away, based on nothing more than economic jousting. For example, London's Arsenal FC and Barcelona's FC, who have no natural sporting rivalry, have developed an animosity based on the economics of transfer. Arsenal often signs players out of Barcelona's youth academy. And after Arsenal has developed them and given them experience in big matches, Barcelona swoops in and buys them (or any other player they decide they want). The ethics of transfers can generate lingering hostility that supersedes both national and sporting boundaries.

Commandment the Ninth: You Will Not Commit Club Adultery

There are some clubs that give the phrase "bitter rivals" new meaning. In Spain, the match between the two biggest Spanish clubs, Barcelona and Real Madrid, is called "El Classico," the Classic. Adultery in soccer comes in two forms: cheering for a rival club and, in the case of players, playing for the rival club. Very few players have managed to successfully play for rival clubs without backlash from both sides. Some fans try and split the difference, cheer for both clubs, and then find that they are brutally mocked and abused by both sides. The depth of club passion can make adultery an unpleasant, even dangerous act.

In the last two years, FC Bayern München has signed two players who played for rival Borussia Dortmund. The signing of Mario Götze in 2013 was announced ahead of the 2013 Champion's League Final, which featured both clubs, and led to accusations that Bayern had intentionally leaked the news in order to psych out their opponents ahead of the final. Götze, who was injured at the time of the 2013 CL Final and who struggled to break into the first team at Bayern, now regularly features in the starting 11 for the Bavarian squad and has been embraced by Bayern fans; when Götze, a product of Dortmund's academy, returned to the club of his youth in the fall of 2013 for a Bundesliga match, the Dortmund fans gave him a hard time until Götze opened the scoring in the 66th minute and silenced the fans. The signing of Polish international and Dortmund striker Robert Lewandowski in 2014 did not help to ease tensions between the two clubs. And one need only listen to an Arsenal match to know when Emmanuel Adebayor (now playing for Arsenal's bitter North London rivals Tottenham Hotspur) or Robin van Persie (now playing for Manchester United and referred to by fans as "Robin van Pursestrings") touch the ball; all one can hear is booing. Cheating on one's club in any manner is considered extremely bad form.

Commandment the Tenth: You Will Not Covet Your Neighbor's Striker

For the fan of soccer, the excellence of one's neighbor is an opportunity for exercising resentment.[17] In short, one's ability to see and appreciate skill is colored almost entirely by club or team loyalty. Barcelona, therefore, does not covet Cristiano Ronaldo, the star striker for Real Madrid. They hate him. You never covet the player who is beating you; you hate him. You do not lament that he plays for another club; you wish ill health and prolonged contract negotiations upon him. Regardless of the brilliance of a player, if they play for your rivals, they are off-limits.

However, sometimes circumstances present you with challenges that force fans to rethink this, to learn to love an enemy as one of their own. In 2011, it was announced before the end of the Bundesliga season that Bayern Munich had signed German number one goalkeeper Manuel Neuer from their rivals Schalke 04. Although many Bayern fans were either cautiously optimistic about the signing or quiet about their ambivalence, some Ultras made their displeasure in signing a player who had been a Schalker his entire life known; they showed up to Bayern's second match against Schalke that spring with signs that read "Koan Neuer," Bavarian for "No Neuer." The club's response was to kick those fans out and revoke their season tickets unless they apologized and agreed not to protest against one of their own players. The fans had to remember that it is no longer coveting when the player joins your team.

Similarly, when Borussia Dortmund striker and Polish international Robert Lewandowski informed Dortmund that he would not be signing a new contract with them, rumors began to fly about where he would sign a contract and to what team he would be lending his considerable talents. Bayern Munich was mentioned as the frontrunner and during the winter transfer window in 2013–2014, Bayern and Lewandowski announced the deal he had signed, to go into effect upon the termination of his contract with Dortmund. As one Bayern fan explained, it was not that the team was actively recruiting him or that fans were all that excited to have him on the team; it was that a player of high caliber made it clear that Bayern was where he wanted to play, despite knowing that he would have to earn a spot in the starting 11 and would not be guaranteed the stardom of his previous team. Coveting players while they play for your rival is off-limits, and because of that, sometimes it takes a paradigm shift to accept a once-enemy as a friend.

Commandment the Eleventh: You Will Have Hope, for There Is Always Next Season

Hope is the only way to survive a bad season. Following the distinction drawn by Gustavo Gutierrez,[18] we must always remain hopeful that our team will win, but that does not mean that we have to be optimistic about their chances; hope and optimism are not the same thing. In other words, I believe that my team can win, not that they necessarily will win. Hoping takes us beyond ourselves and encourages us to imagine a better world; it allows us to see what is possible and not be trapped solely with what is practical. Optimism comes and goes, but hope remains. Hope is the certainty that things will get better; optimism is the belief that they will get better sooner rather than later. Critchley puts it this way: "Football is all about an experience of disappointment in the present that is linked to some doubtless illusory memory of greatness and heroic virtue. The odd thing is that it isn't the disappointment that is so difficult to bear; it's the endlessly renewed hope with which each new season begins."[19] Maintaining hope that the future will be different is perhaps the most vital tenet of soccer-as-religion; without hope of victory, there is no purpose in supporting a team or watching matches.

Fan Typology

In the same way it is impossible to paint all Christians or all Muslims with the same brush, it is impossible to explain all soccer fans in any kind of typology. However, there are certain types of fans that one is likely to encounter in the soccer world that are also found in religions or in other sports. This is not meant to be an exhaustive list, but is meant to help explain some of the typical fans that one would be likely to encounter amongst any group of hard-core fans. There are two subdivisions within this typology. The Major Types (Evangelist, Systematician, Sacristan, Choir Director, Faithful Dissident, and Mystic) are found in every club, but they are found in particular individuals and are not as common as the Minor Types. The Minor Types (Creaster Crowd, Initiate, Church Shopper, Apostate) are found in every club as well, but in larger groups of people, not a single individual. That is to say, if one takes one particular supporters' group as your place of departure, one is likely to find one or two of each of the Major types and many folks who fall somewhere within the Minor types.

The explanation of each type follows, accompanied by examples from the ethnographic research carried out for a doctoral dissertation.[20] Because of the level of access granted to the PI by the Dallas Beer Guardians (DBG), whenever possible, an example from within that group is used and supplemented by the additional anecdotes gathered during the interviews. The typology was developed during the time spent with DBG while looking at the various ways that fans relate to their clubs and attempting to be somewhat systematic about it. Not everyone will neatly fit into a type, just as no typology perfectly encompasses anything. Rather, this typology is intended to serve as a guide to assist with understanding the importance of soccer in the lives of its faithful; it is not intended to define or limit fans to only these modes of interaction.

The Evangelist

The minute a person meets Aaron Willis, it is clear that he is an ambassador of soccer.[21] His passion for it is unrivaled and FC Dallas is his club. From the moment you meet him, you can see how much he cares, not just about his club, but also how much he cares about sharing that passion with others. Willis is an Evangelist; one could see him standing on a street corner in another setting, sharing his love with all those who pass by. Whether or not Aaron sets out to convert you, you cannot help but be drawn in by his love and passion and desire. He is one of the leaders of Dallas Beer Guardians, and if you ask his colleagues who has the most passion for FCD, they will all point in his direction.

Key characteristics: Tries to convert everyone; hard to bring down, eternally optimistic; spends time and money to distribute tickets, invite people, etc; bribes people to watch matches, will bend over backwards to make sure they have access to the game; mix of street-corner prophet and charismatic preacher, their enthusiasm is both compelling and frustrating.

Motto: "There's nothing like the real thing. I remember my first time . . ."

According to a Systematician: "Unbridled enthusiasm for the game. Eternally optimistic that friends' interest will last beyond world cup. Ready and willing with clips, diagrams, and relentless acts of explanation."

According to a Sacristan: "Will tell you every reason that you should be a fan of their team. Lives by example. Believes that they can lift everyone's passion by showing it themselves, and expects the same from those they recruit."

The Systematician

When one meets a Systematician, it is apparent right away. Systematicians know more about the game, its technical and financial sides, and players than anyone. They are truly scholars of the game, devouring any information that they can find about their club. They watch matches with their web browser open to the salaries of their team, they draw up tactical formations on napkins in pubs to explain a key moment to someone else, and they have a steel-trap memory for the history of their club, on and off the pitch. Kenny Price is the Dallas Beer Guardians' resident Systematician. Kenny and his wife moved to Dallas because they wanted to live in a city that had both a professional soccer team and an Ikea; Dallas won over Kansas City because it was slightly closer to their home in Alabama. It only took one match before Kenny knew he had found his home and his colleagues routinely call upon his encyclopedia-like knowledge to supplement their own. While prepping the opening day tifo at Toyota Stadium, Kenny was called upon no fewer than four times in the course of an hour to settle disagreements or debates between others gathered; the Systematician is the one to whom everyone else looks when there is a question about the game.

Key characteristics: Someone who's a scholar of the game; obsesses over theory, strategy, tactics; devours abstract Grantland-style articles in whatever medium they can find them; passion is tempered with obsessive tendencies to try to digest and an understanding of what happened; knows the salary and stats of every player.

Motto: "I'm telling you! 4-3-3 formation is the future of the sport."

According to a Mystic: "Knows everything. Has read and forgotten more about the team than most fans will ever know. Able to remember who scored which goal and in what order during a match that happened three years ago. Can name just about every player who has ever worn the uniform of the team, knows which coach prefers what formation, and has strong opinions about everything. Has an enviable memory and can explain the finer points of just about everything in a way that makes sense."

According to a Sacristan: "This is the person that can tell you what the formation of the youth team of your squad's newest addition was in the mid-1990s. This person is more likely to get upset with their team's Technical Director than their head coach."

The Sacristan

If one wants to find the Sacristan in the run-up to a match, one should start by looking at the people running around like crazy at the tailgate, making sure that everything is set up properly and that everyone who attends will have a great time. If it is not a match day, the Sacristan is the person organizing service projects for his or her supporters' group, working to facilitate away-match travel, or recording a podcast. There are few people who are willing to do that much behind-the-scenes work and even fewer who are intent on making sure that the hard work of others (and occasionally themselves) is acknowledged by the community. Jay Neal's entire existence embodies the Sacristan. He writes for a blog and cohosts a soccer podcast, but he is also in charge of service and outreach for the Dallas Beer Guardians. Yet his commitment does not stop there. He is one of the first to volunteer to help create a banner for a match or to coordinate with visiting supporters to make sure that the environment on match day is as awesome as possible. Having a conversation with Jay at the stadium can be difficult, because he is constantly getting pulled away to help with various things or, more often, is volunteering to assist someone with something. For Jay, service and Club dedication are inseparable.

Key Characteristics: Has their hands in everything, behind-the-scenes kind of person; want to see credit given where it is due, whether it is their work or the work of others; first one there, last to leave; volunteer for everything; set up, take down, assist however they can to make sure that the experience is incredible for all involved; able to see the big picture, but focused on the details needed for it.

Motto: "Man, Dailymotion has started enforcing copyright? Back to the Russian feed . . ."

According to a Systematician: "Organizer of local fan groups, administrator of fan twitter accounts, relentless poster of video clips of dubious copyright legality, insatiable editor of highlight reels."

According to a Mystic: "Super helpful, totally understands that the community is vital to appreciating soccer. Willing to do whatever is needed.

Often the fan who would love nothing more than to work for the club, in any capacity, in order to help facilitate the experience for others."

The Choir Director

The head cheerleader, the Choir Director, is the person constantly rallying support behind their fans. They are the ones in the stadium who lead the chants and songs; they are the ones on Twitter who attempt to keep spirits lifted before, during, and after the match. They are one side of the supporter's coin (the other side being the Faithful Dissident); they are the kind of fan who has the best experience when they are creating a welcoming and cheerful environment with others. Jennie Killion, a die-hard FC Bayern fan who is also an FC Dallas supporter, is a Choir Director.[22] Every match, her Facebook status is "Auf geht's Bayern" and she is unfailingly positive about her club, its chances every season, and her favorite players. Her elementary students know that, if Ms. Killion has used a jeans pass and is wearing a jersey, it is a match day. Her neighbors all know when she is watching a match, as her yelling can be heard through her open back door, with her neighbors occasionally asking follow-up questions; when she yelled, "That's a card!" during a Bayern match against Leverkusen, her neighbor yelled back "Yellow or red?!"

Key characteristics: Leads congregation (both in person and online); part cheerleader, part organizer; wants to make everyone feel included; finds creative ways to react to things both on and off the pitch.

Motto: "Come on Arsenal! #aft #COYG #FACup #Gooners #winning."

According to a Systematician: "In public, a singer and song leader. The one at a fan section or at the bar with her back to the game leading chants and cheers. For the choir director, Club-centeredness can mean that the game itself takes backstage to the spectacle, the song, the noise, the commotion of being part of a Club. In a digital age, leads the way with jokes, tweeted fan chants, and memes."

According to a Sacristan: "Not only are they the cheerleader but sometimes the driver of positive morale. After a bad loss they are the person smiling and finding a silver lining to everything in order to keep supporter morale high."

The Faithful Dissident

There is always at least one fan who loves his or her Club as much as one possibly can, but shows that love through constantly being frustrated with their team. The Faithful Dissident is a fan who demands perfection, is willing to point out how and why a club might not be as invincible as they think they are, and utters the phrase "no lead is safe" at least four or five times in a single match. One would think that a history of winning and an excellent current record would silence them, but the Faithful Dissident always wants more for the Club, always wants that next trophy or win or key signing. It is precisely because of their hope in the team that the Faithful Dissident fights against optimism. By preparing for the worst and (secretly) hoping for the best, even the Faithful Dissident will show emotion when the Club wins a major trophy. Fans who are introduced to the game by Faithful Dissidents will often pick up a bit of their cynicism, but their critiques of their team should not be seen as disinterest or apathy; it is because they care that they kvetch.

Key characteristics: A true blue, dyed-in-the-wool fan, but hypercritical of the club; often spends time going off on the manager, a particular player, the board, etc; never satisfied with less than perfection; thinks the world of the club and thus wants the club to be the best it can be; somewhat pessimistic, even in times of triumph; loves their club enough to give it hell, even when it maybe does not need it.

Motto: "Apathy is a lack of love, not kvetching. Kvetching is the highest sign of affection."

According to a Systematician: "Think of Piers Morgan (who claims credit for Özil—he critiqued Wenger and Wenger changed, allegedly). Insists the best for the club, unwilling to settle for less. Harsh on players, owners, and especially managers. Frequently results driven."

According to a Sacristan: "There's a great line in an Eli Young Band song that really encapsulates this person, 'If you start out depressed then everything comes as a pleasant surprise.'"

The Mystic

As this typology began to develop, it became clear that there needed to be a hybrid type that consolidated many of the characteristics of the Major Types in a way that allowed for some flexibility. Enter the Mystic. The Mystic blends together various parts of the other Major Types in his or her own unique way and no two Mystics look the same. Some, like Samantha, blend the cynicism of the Faithful Dissident with the Evangelist; others are a prophetic creation of their own devising that less obviously reflects the other Major Types.[23] Samantha, an American studying in Berlin whose family spent seven years living in Munich, has recruited many fans to the FC Bayern camp through her blend of cynicism and enthusiasm. At once one of the team's biggest fans and one of their harshest critics, Samantha shows that Mystics are able to accomplish the work of the Evangelizer and convert people, all while still retaining their innate skepticism and dark sense of humor about their team's chances. Mystics tend to be easy to find, though, because they all have a set of rituals that they follow and they have a tendency to adapt their fandom to different circumstances. A Mystic may appear to be a Systematician in some settings, but in others, they come across as a Choir Director; the Mystic relies on an ability to meet people where they are and yet still challenges and calls people to a deeper engagement with their Club.

Key characteristics: Hard to pin down, seems to vacillate between Types; blends aspects of other Major Types into something unique; all embody some sort of superstition or ritual into their practice of fandom.

Motto: "It's not superstition. Superstition suggests it's not real."

According to a Systematician: "A Mystic may have the proclivities of the Systematician, in terms of reading style and understanding. On game day, though, the Mystic is like the prophetess in a black parish, all up in the front waving hands and s——. A little bit Choir Director-ish. It's soccer's Anna in the temple night and day, with a hefty dash of Systematician. The soccer version of an amma/abba."

According to a Sacristan: "This person is hard to pin down, an enigma of sorts. You can't necessarily peg them as a specific type but you know them when you meet them."

The Initiate

Perhaps the favorite type of the Major Types, the Initiate is someone who is just learning the ropes of their new Club. Often, they have had a sense of coming home when they find the right Club, but the process of learning the ropes and rituals can be intimidating. Some fans stay in this stage precisely because they are overwhelmed by the level of devotion exhibited by the Major Types or fear that they will never be able to learn enough to be respected as a true fan of the game. For Jeff Culver, a high-school teacher from Highlands Ranch, Colorado, his interest in soccer grew out of having played it as a child and coming to a point where continuing to support the violence of professional (North American) football had become untenable.[24] Convinced by a former student and a close friend that Arsenal was the team to watch, he has become a Gunner, but is still very much in the initial stage. He has yet to adjust to watching games via online streams because he cannot yet identify players when they are small or blurry or both.

Key characteristics: The newbie; impressionable, easily influenced as they learn the game and club; other types adore Initiates because they think they can bend them to fit their mold of how to be a proper fan; perhaps has not made a full commitment to a team or is in the beginning stages; has yet to take the full plunge, but is attracted to a club/team for reasons they may not yet be able to articulate.

Motto: "Wait, what countries are in the Champions League again?"

According to a Systematician: "May like the idea of soccer better than the 7 a.m. kickoff. They are still unsure about confusing league schedule, how exactly transfers work, not to mention utterly lost in the history of the sport or the various implications of declaring loyalty to one club or another."

According to a Sacristan: "New to the game yet tends to be hungry for more information about it. Supporters Groups, like DBG, love these types."

The Church Shopper

The Church Shopper is the fan that drives most of the other fan types a little bit crazy. Church Shoppers do not have any real kind of club affiliation; they have yet to find their home Club or they refuse to choose sides for whatever reason. As such, they tend to jump on whatever bandwagon is popular at the time. This is different from those fans who jump on a bandwagon and are immediately at home within their Club; their flakiness means they are able to flit from team to team. They bring genuine excitement and passion to whatever club it is that they are supporting at that moment, but they are often misunderstood by other fans who do not understand how you can possibly care equally for clubs that are bitter rivals and each other's antithesis. They are the fair weather fans of the soccer world.

Key characteristics: Has no real affinity for a professional club; may just love the game, but likely hasn't found a bandwagon that is comfortable; will blow with the wind toward popular teams/players/coaches; often referred to by other fans as "typical Chelsea" after the English side, they're viewed as wishy-washy and noncommittal.

Motto: "I haven't had a win this big since I was a City fan!"

According to a Systematician: "Glory hunter. Attracted to big name, big money signings and recent track records of success. Nowhere to be found after losses or falls from grace. Enjoy a complicated relationship with the fan bases of large clubs, who appreciate revenue streams and loathe plastic fandom."

According to a Sacristan: "Often looking for a home but can't seem to find a team where they feel settled. They like the glitz and glam of flashy players and clubs but can't deal with the hard times."

The Creaster Crowd

Just like Christians who show up to services only on Christmas and Easter, these fans make appearances for league finals, cup finals, things like that. It is not that they do not care about the team, it is that, for whatever reason, they are just not able to revolve their lives around it at a given time. Creaster Crowd fans will still proudly claim allegiance to their club, but they are also able to laugh at the fact that they are rarely around. Charyse Diaz, an FC Bayern München fan and a third-year medical student, is able to laugh at the fact that the only match she has watched in the last year was about 15 minutes of the Champions League Final, but she does wish that she were able to keep up with matches and the team more.[25] These fans would never deny the importance of the Club in their lives, nor would they ever consider that their lack of engagement somehow makes them less of a fan; they simply are practicing their fandom in a manner that appears disengaged, save for the occasions when they are able to join others in celebration.

Key characteristics: Somewhat flaky, they are rarely in attendance for matches, whether it is watching online or going to the pub; fans whose real lives have impacted their ability to be present to the Club.

Motto: "Well, obviously I'm here! It's the final! Now, remind me, who did we beat again to get here?"

According to a Systematician: "A declared fan unwilling/unable/or simply uninterested in committing to fits of mania of the above types. May or may not know preferred team's position in various competitions. Finds the mania of the evangelist or mystic to be off-putting."

According to a Sacristan: "A fan for sure but nowhere close to a diehard. 'But I was here for the important match!' This type of fan drives the Evangelist crazy."

The Apostate

In some ways, the Apostate is the rarest kind of fan, in that they are not really considered fans by others. The Apostate is someone who, whether in a fit of emotion or in a calculated decision, blasphemes the club and violates

Commandment Three. They attack the Club itself, not just the players who made mistakes or the manager who chose a poorly timed substitute. They are reviled and hated, rejected by those who consider themselves true fans, and are often mocked. However, even though most people would say that they have met an Apostate, asking them for examples becomes extremely tricky, as they have been somewhat removed from the crowd and are therefore fair game because they have been deemed an "outsider."

Conclusion

Soccer is the world's most popular sport, the only one that can be played anywhere and at any time; all one needs is something round with which to play. Because it is accessible to all people, and most countries have some sort of institutional soccer, the Eleven Commandments and the typology explored above are both applicable outside of a North American or European context. Whether one holds to the theistic version or not, God in soccer is more about the importance of the Club than about the relationship with a higher power. For soccer fans, the Club is the locus of religious experience, communion with others, and, for many, a chance to experience transcendence.

Notes

1. This work would not have been possible, were it not for the collaboration of Matthew Spotts, SJ. His contributions to this piece, especially the Eleven Commandments, were numerous and vital.

2. Clifford Geertz, *The Interpretation of Cultures* (New York: Basic Books, 1973).

3. The Eleven Commandments found here were first presented at the 2013 Rocky Mountains-Great Plains Regional AAR Meeting in Denver, Colorado, a presentation coauthored with Matthew Spotts, SJ.

4. When used with a lowercase "c," the term "club" refers to the organization itself and its official staff. This limits it to the players, coaches, trainers, physicians, board of directors, and employees of the particular corporation. When used with an uppercase "C," the term "Club" refers to the club, as well as its fan base, its sponsors, and those who hold some sort of allegiance to the club. It is inclusive of local fans and globalized or cosmopolitan fans; it represents the entirety of the club's reach and scope. When used with both the uppercase "C" and the lowercase "c," the term "C/club" refers to both of the above, recognizing that there are different demands placed on the Club and the club, but both understandings of the term should be considered within a particular discussion. That is to say, "C/club" is used when there is an issue at hand that would be considered differently based on whether one is looking at it through the lens of Club or the lens of

club; despite their different perspectives, this use helps to illustrate the complexity of this issue as a whole.

5. *The Bugle,* July 2010.

6. Simon Critchley, "Working Class Ballet." Text of talk provided to authors on February 12, 2014.

7. Nick Hornby, *Fever Pitch* (New York: Riverhead Books, 1998), 130.

8. Matt Burnett, interview with author, Castle Rock, CO, February 17, 2014.

9. The Champions League is a Europe-wide competition between the top clubs in each country's league. The biggest leagues, like the English Premier League, get four spots on the Champions League; some countries only get one space. Competition begins in a Group Stage, with the 32 clubs playing in groups of four. The top two finishers from each group move on to the knock-out Round of 16. Matches through the Round of 16, the quarterfinals, and the semifinals are played in pairs, with each team having a home match and an away match. The final is a single match, played in a stadium determined years ahead of time as host, with the winner taking the title.

10. Hornby, *Fever Pitch*, 213.

11. Critchley, "Working Class Ballet."

12. "Michael Jackson Statue Removed from Outside Craven Cottage Ground," *The Telegraph,* accessed March 14, 2014, http://www.telegraph.co.uk/sport/foot ball/teams/fulham/10333725/Michael-Jackson-statue-removed-from-outside Fulhams-Craven-Cottage-ground.html.

13. "Up in Smoke: Effigy of £200k-a-Week Wayne Rooney Clutching Bag Full of Money Is the Star Attraction on Bonfire Night," *The Daily Mail Online,* accessed March 14, 2014, http://www.dailymail.co.uk/news/article-1327411/ Wayne-Rooney-effigy-burnt-Bonfire-Night-Fans-furious-quit-threat.html.

14. More information on these campaigns is available at http://youcanplay project.org, http://www.kickitout.org, and at http://www.ussoccer.com/community/ respect-campaign.aspx.

15. For more information about Red Card Homophobia, see http://redcard homophobia.wordpress.com.

16. Simon Kuper and Stefan Szymanksi, *Soccernomics: Why England Loses, Why Spain, Germany, and Brazil Win, and Why The U.S., Japan, Australia, Turkey—and even Iraq—Are Destined to Become the Kings of the World's Most Popular Sport* (New York: Nation Books, 2009), 114.

17. "To relieve the tension, the common man seeks a feeling of superiority or equality and he attains his purpose by an illusory devaluation of the other man's qualities or a specific "blindness" to those qualities. But secondly—and here lies the main achievement of ressentiment—the falsities the values themselves which could bestow excellence on any possible object of comparison." Max Scheler, *Ressentiment,* trans. Lewis B. Coser and William W. Holdheim (Milwaukee, WI: Marquette University Press, 2003), 34.

18. Gustavo Gutiérrez, "The Meaning and Scope of Medellín" in *Density of the Present* (Maryknoll, NY: Orbis Books, 1999), 59–100.

19. Critchley, "Working Class Ballet."

20. Over the course of February 2014, I (Rebecca Chabot) conducted an ethnography to examine practices and beliefs of professional club soccer fans. The ethnography was composed of two parts: online fan surveys in English, French, German, and Spanish and a series of 15 interviews conducted by the Primary Investigator (hereafter PI); it also involved some participant observation with the Dallas Beer Guardians. All of the quotations from the various types stem from this ethnography and are purposely left unattributed so as to allow for an honest appraisal of the various types, as viewed by three specific types, without the potential to cause issue.

21. Aaron Willis, interview with author, Plano, TX, February 22, 2014.

22. Jennie Killion, interview with author, Plano, TX, February 22, 2014.

23. Samantha, interview with author, Denver, CO, February 15, 2014.

24. Jeff Culver, interview with author, Castle Rock, CO, February 17, 2014.

25. Charyse Diaz, interview with author, Denver, CO, February 15, 2014.

CHAPTER TWO

Cage Fighting for Jesus

Carmen Celestini

The term "muscular Christianity" was coined in the 1850s to describe the novels of Thomas Hughes and Charles Kingsley.[1] Thomas Hughes's *Tom Brown's School Days* was influential in the United States, even finding a supporter in Theodore Roosevelt. When the book first reached the U.S.'s shores it was received with mixed reviews, because the central premise of the book, that sports builds Christian character, was completely foreign to American Protestants.[2] Colonial and antebellum Protestants viewed artificial exercise as an immoral waste of time.[3] The economy in the United States at this time was still primarily agricultural, unlike that of England,[4] and the emphasis was on hard work, not recreation (which was perceived as sinful). Muscular Christianity encountered resistance in the United States, particularly before 1880. This resistance came from many factors, but the most prevalent was the Civil War, the act of war itself had certified the manliness of many American men.[5] Hughes's book was not something Americans could easily relate to, because the private school setting in the book did not exist in the United States in the 1850s.[6] Muscular Christianity did not take off in the United States until the end of the 19th century,[7] and when it did, Americans took what they wanted and needed from the book. They were looking for confirmation, not direction, and what they adopted were the concepts of a healthy boy's life, the healthier, stronger, freer soul and body.[8]

The philosophy of muscular Christianity promoted the idea that competitive sports, or team games, were composed of an ethical basis and that the training in moral behavior on the field was transferable to other aspects of a man's life.[9] With its biblical origins traceable to the New Testament, where 1 Corinthians 6:19–20[10] promotes physical health,[11] the four core characteristics of muscular Christianity, then and now, are manliness, morality, health, and patriotism.[12] As a philosophy, it is defined as a Christian commitment to health and manliness.[13]

With the Victorian muscularity movement Jesus became the ideal of manhood and commensurate with this ideal, both artistic depictions of Jesus, and his perceived age were criticized as misconceptions to be dispelled. Most images of Jesus were either of him as a baby, or as a venerable sage, and the men's groups believed that the image portrayed of Jesus was of a subdued and weak man, depicted in robes, almost like women's dresses or skirts,[14] who was weighed down with the sins of humanity. Jesus had to be personalized as men wanted someone they could respect, not someone who was seen as a gentle visionary, but a man who dominated with force. To change the image of Jesus and the perception of him as weak and effeminate, men's groups focused on Jesus being a carpenter and the muscular, manly physique that would have been attained from that profession. They promoted an image of Jesus as a young man who perished before the effects of old age were upon him.[15] Although Jesus had consideration for females, especially his mother, he was pitched as a rugged man who was homeless and a nomad.[16] There were calls for manlier depictions of Jesus, which led to art exhibits and the creation of muscular and domineering Jesus images in stained glass in churches.[17]

In the late 20th and early 21st centuries the same issues can be seen at work, leading to the acceptance of a modern version of the movement, or as it is referred to: neo-muscular Christianity. The neo-muscular Christianity movement still endorses some of the ideals of the Victorian era movement: manliness, morality, and health.[18] Just as Hughes's book was the impetus to a movement in the 1800s, John Eldredge in his 3 million-selling *Wild at Heart* (2001) started a revival by stating that the church encourages "good boys" to attend church. The church, by promoting a discipleship of becoming a nice guy, keeps men from embodying their God-given maleness. Eldredge and his book sowed the seeds of a new masculinity movement to remasculinize the church.[19]

Mixed martial arts (MMA) and its largest promotion company the Ultimate Fighting Champion (UFC) have responded to this movement by marketing an image of hyper-masculinity. This is defined as "characterized by the idealization of stereotypically masculine or macho traits and the rejection of traits perceived as the antithesis of machismo."[20] With this contested concept of hyper-masculinity there is a cultural mandate that real men control their fear and other emotions starting from childhood. If a boy expresses fear, pain, empathy or sadness, their peers, parents, and coaches ostracize them. These childhood lessons are manifested in adulthood with men not allowing fear to be shown, and with this indoctrination it has morphed into a culturally revered quality of manhood.[21] "Fearlessness" and how a man responds to fear and pain is encapsulated in hyper-masculinity, and the MMA not only creates the conditions that fighters experience and manage fear, it also primes people to view fighters' management of fear as well as their violence through the lens of gender definitions perpetuating the cultural manifestation of hyper-masculinity.[22]

This call for a vision of Jesus as manly has been reestablished with the neo-muscularity movement by celebrity ministers who use their fame within the Christian community to affect the perception of masculinity. Mark Driscoll, pastor of Seattle's Mars Hill Church, is infamous for speaking out about the weakness of the men in contemporary church culture.[23] Driscoll in a sermon in 2006 mimicked those from the Victorian era when he referred to the contemporary image of Jesus as a long-haired hippie, effeminate, queer, but insists that in fact Jesus was a man with callused hands and big biceps, a man that other men would be drawn to. Driscoll calls this stronger image of Jesus "Ultimate Fighting Jesus."[24] Some Christian men such as Driscoll believe that women have created Jesus in their image and have emasculated him and regaining a "true" biblical image of Jesus, as Driscoll and other neo-muscular Christian males envision him, will be all that is needed to remasculinize him.[25]

Feminist scholars have identified practices in mainstream sports as critical in promoting a patriarchal ideology that is reproduced and celebrated. This ideology is based on the belief that males and females have distinct characteristics. Males are characteristically defined as having superior physical and psychological capabilities (aggression, strength, and mental toughness)[26]—characteristics typically needed to excel in sports. Female characteristics are viewed as lacking in these capabilities as evidenced by their inability to compete with men. Public celebrations of these gender characteristics (sporting events) are used to unify and rally a variety of men under the ideal of male superiority.[27] Sports provide a sphere where masculinity is presumed to be essential and patriarchy is natural. Young men and boys learn how and what it is to be a man and their place in society as a man.[28] With this current call to remasculinize evangelical Protestant churches and the social and economic changes that are being faced, again we see a stronger shift toward sports. In this modern context though, few are mentioning the connection between Christianity and health reform, but are still responding to the connection between Christianity and sport.

Prior to the rise of the MMA within neo-muscular Christianity, boxing was both championed and despised in the evangelical Protestant world. In the mid-1890s boxing clubs and advocates argued that prizefights should be viewed as scientific exhibitions of technical skill and physical discipline. The idea of the discipline of the body was central to the Victorian belief in the educational value of sport, which allowed the promoters to associate the sport with the new religion of an industrializing society.[29] For urbanites in the 1800s as well as today, boxing is vigorously promoted as a manly art[30] and a forum whereby shear force of will, one can rise above poverty and discrimination. It was believed that boxing served the moral and social purposes of the muscular Christianity movement through its promotion of manliness, character, morality and patriotism.[31]

In the mid-1800s everyone appeared to oppose prizefighting, yet the matches routinely attracted large crowds of men. Prizefighting, much like religion, was able to transcend social status with pre-Civil War bare-knuckle prizefighting attracting, through controversy, the complete social spectrum of classes and media. Before the 1840s, English immigrants were the leaders of the sport, and the half-million Irish immigrants to the United States between 1845 and 1850 soon provided competition to the English.[32] By the midcentury, New York had become the center of prizefighting with New Orleans and St. Louis also having thriving pugilistic centers. With this as a backdrop, Christian criticism of prizefighting consisted of a combination of class prejudice and religious piety.[33]

Once the churches had been more masculinized there was less interest in the Social Gospel activities, and sports were used as a lure to bring men and boys into the church.[34] In England, muscular Christianity was influencing youth and boys' groups such as the YMCA (founded 1844), the Boys' Brigade (founded 1883), and the Boy Scouts (founded 1907). Christianity and church worship were an essential aspect of the Boys' Brigade where military-like drills were used to indoctrinate boys into Christian manliness.[35] The muscular Christianity movement believed that they could change and cure the feminization problem by reversing the feminization of religion. By the early 1880s, American Protestants were beginning to try to align Christianity with manliness through boys' groups as well. Organizations such as the American Boys' Brigade and the Knights of King Arthur promoted boys' activities in religion through sports, whereas organizations such as the YMCA linked sports and business to religion.[36] Conversely, the Boy Scouts was not founded to bring boys to Christ but to promote wholesomeness and a reverence for king and country.[37] Churches brought men into the church by associating masculine leisure activities with church activities. They started men's groups, boys' sports groups, intrachurch league sports, and installed billiards and bowling alleys in clubhouses.[38] Religious leaders (clergy) believed that they needed to take a leadership role in sports to promote the mentality of the body as a temple[39] and many clergy themselves became amateur athletes.[40] Christian athletes were celebrated by the ministry and used in homilies and sermons to promote manliness to boys.[41] Churches made alliances with athletic organizations building a brand that religion and recreation belonged together, ensuring that they helped mold and shape sports and recreation morally throughout the United States.[42]

WWI helped sports' acceptance across the United States. For morale and training purposes the soldiers boxed, ran track, and played baseball, football, basketball, and volleyball, often under the guidance of YMCA volunteers. The media promoted these activities as an ally in defeating the Germans. Even prizefighting was presented as patriotic and after the war gained some respectability.[43]

As a whole, the Protestant community fully supported the emergence of amateur sport more than professional sports. Amateurs were considered more wholesome than professionals as they did it for the love of the game, not for money.[44] During the last two decades of the 19th century a new kind of urban church emerged. They were referred to as "open" churches, which dispensed with pews and literally never closed. They had kitchens to provide food and drink, rooms for training, and a gym. They provided space, leadership, and institutional support to groups such as the Boys' Brigade, Boy and Girl Scouts, and sponsored sports teams.[45] The neo-muscular Christianity movement is also class specific, appealing to white middle-class males. Social psychologists believe this is due to their perceived deprivation, based on what they have had in the past and led to believe they can expect in their future.[46]

The neo-muscular Christianity movement of the late 20th and early 21st centuries has embraced the sport of MMA and gained a prominent position in both the UFC and amateur MMA worlds. The popularity of the MMA has seen a significant rise in the United States and many Christians, who are fans, love both Jesus and the sport, facing an internal conflict in the process. The community of believers must find justification for their love of the sport within their community, which is divided on the issues of violence and Christianity. Christian MMA supporters find themselves living in a paradox between and within belief systems, and need to find ways to address the internal conflict between their religious beliefs and their leisure.[47]

Muscularity naturally evokes images of competition and dominance together with an inner strength to endure such activities. The inception of the quest to create an "ultimate" fighting style by combining the best aspects of many distinct styles has a convoluted history with little consensus in the relevant literature. A brief listing of the many hybrid techniques include ju-jitsu, boxing, karate, kickboxing, taekwondo, and vale tudo with a variety of origins and are known collectively as mixed martial arts.[48] Some believe it was developed from pankration, a mix of Hellenic boxing and wrestling, which was introduced to the Olympic Games in 649 BCE.[49] Others believe the inception has its roots in the tensions between Eastern and Western fighting styles highlighted in the 1970s Bruce Lee films.[50]

The first cultural commingling happened around the end of the 19th century with the Meiji Restoration increasing Japanese and Western cultural contact. Westerners became more exposed to the Japanese disciplines and the Japanese became more exposed to Western sport forms such as boxing.[51] Martial artists first taught their techniques and sometimes displayed their skills in organized competitions against Western boxers or wrestlers. American merchant sailors coming to Japan took part in contests named "Merikan" where boxers fought against local fighters under event specific rules. These events were seen as exhibitions rather than genuine sporting challenges between fighting disciplines.[52] The hybridization of Asian and Western disciplines started in the 1960s. The contests were decided based on judges' decisions rather than knockout or submission. Speed and technique were the deciding factors rather than strength and aggression. The fighters perceived these contests to be too restrained and an inadequate test of fighting capabilities.[53] In the 1970s the World Karate Association (WKA), an American organization representing full-contact fighters, supported the 1974 *Full Contact Championship* broadcast by Universal Pictures, which evolved into full-contact kickboxing contests from 1977 to 1979.[54]

The competitive or killer instinct in sports is something hard to reconcile for evangelical athletes. The argument for justification, according to Shirl James Hoffman, Professor Emeritus of Exercise and Sport Science at University of North Carolina, is that humans' biological dispositions insist that we give expression to these aspects of ourselves, and that sport is the divinely ordained institution to allow this.[55] Using textbook advertising and marketing strategies, sport evangelism has become focused on parachurch groups, which are not attached to churches or denominations. Through this they are able to refine the gospel message to the pop culture tastes and jargon of their target audiences. There are between 50 and 150 of these parachurch organizations that currently shape their ministries around sports.[56] Sports are not a blank canvas on which to put a Christian message of conversion; the Christian message is also competing with the message of the sport itself. They are not only pitching what Jesus has done in their lives, but they are also pitching some of the not-so-Christian images of the sport itself.[57]

The world of the MMA has developed its own distinctive culture. There is a public image that MMA is dangerous, violent, and only for "real" men.[58] Exhibitions of hegemonic, traditional masculinity (aggressive, confrontational, less intimate physical contact) come from athletes who use striking (punching, kicking) as their main fighting style and identity. In contrast, athletes' whose main fighting style is one of submission (various ways to submit to an opponent using judo and ju-jitsu techniques) exhibit their masculinity on a less confrontational and in a less traditional manner.[59] When fighters use striking techniques, physical contact during matches resembles a bar fight and is limited to brief, fast-paced moments of impact and usually ends in a knockout, referee stoppage, or tap out. When a fight changes from a striking match to a ground match, this is usually greeted with boos from the audience and rarely ends with a knockout,[60] the preferred way to end. Striking matches are considered to be more violent and therefore more manly fights, or a more manly way of fighting.[61] Even if a fighter is knocked out and loses the fight, his masculinity is preserved because he did not quit or tap out.[62] When a fight is decided by a submission technique the opponent is considered a cheater, even though this process is allowed via the rules with the fighters who lose often stating that their opponent "did not fight like a man." Submission is considered a more humiliating way to lose, because the fighter is forced to admit he gives up by tapping out.[63] Some fighters, in trying to avoid the humiliation of tapping out, will simply refuse to tap, and this may cause the loss of consciousness or bodily injury. This has led to a phrase in the MMA "tap or snap," which refers to the choice the fighter has to make when facing voluntary admission of loss. This is not a choice a fighter who is knocked out or defeated through strikes has to make.[64] The MMA is an arena where different types of masculinity compete against each other. Winning a match emasculates the loser and gives the winner the status of being a real man. Grapplers can emasculate the strikers by defeating them through submission. Striking is the most popular form of MMA fighting in North America and men who submit are considered feminized.[65]

The sport now eclipses boxing and wrestling as the favored combat sport of the key television audience demographic of 18–34-year-old men.[66] The UFC is rule bound, although their publicity does not promote this, to add to their cachet.[67] Sports magazines such as *ESPN* and *Sports Illustrated* have also done in-depth reports on MMA events and have featured UFC fighters on their covers. Bud Light and Harley Davidson have become prominent sponsors of events,[68] and to complete the commercialization, the UFC has launched action figures, video games, and sport trading cards.[69] UFC fights are now global events broadcast by such networks as CBS and ESPN.[70] The "UFC: Final Chapter" on October 10, 2006 achieved record ratings for Spike TV and the UFC with the main event on the card in the two-hour broadcast, drawing 1.6 million viewers from this coveted 18–34-year-old male demographic.[71] In conjunction with this success, a humanizing window into this world was opened in 2005 with the inception of a Spike Television reality TV show entitled The Ultimate Fighter. With combatants wearing simply open-fingered gloves and fighting in a locked cage,[72] the efforts of these modern-day gladiators are televised on a weekly basis.[73] UFC television events draw better cable ratings in key demographics than that of NBA, NHL, and MLB games.[74] This popularity is utilized by the neo-muscular Christianity movement to promote Christian fighters, as a conduit to luring men into the movement and the churches. This utilization of sports "heroes" is not a new development and was utilized by earlier Christian movements.

As the MMA presence in society grows, more and more Christians are embracing the sport. Almost 700 churches in the United States have begun incorporating MMA into their ministry in some capacity.[75] Recruitment for the fight ministries, which are predominantly white, include fight-night television-viewing parties and lecture series, which through the use of ultimate fighting, explain how Christ fought for what He believed in. Reminiscent of the movement in the Victorian era, contemporary ministries have gyms where the pastors/ministers train, or they organize fights themselves with other fight club ministries.[76] The ministers of these churches say that the goal of incorporating MMA into their churches is to inject machismo into their ministries and onto the image of Jesus.[77]

The leader of this MMA ministry movement is Brandon Beals, who is best known as "the Fight Pastor."[78] Over 100 young men attend parties at Beals' Canyon Creek Ministries in Seattle but it is his other ministry based in Las Vegas, appropriately named Fight Church, that houses a gym.[79] This latter organization provides pastoral and spiritual care to MMA fighters, coaches, and other members of the MMA community (managers, agents, gym owners, ring girls, and referees).[80] Another vocal supporter of MMA ministries is Ryan Dobson, who is the son of Focus on the Family founder James C. Dobson.[81] Ryan Dobson speaks of the role of the man in the household, stating he should be the leader, and Dobson also suggests that his parent's generation has raised a generation of little boys, meaning the men are not real men.[82] These MMA ministry movement leaders believe
. the MMA can help Christianity reach new demographics and help spread the faith and fight within a secular world.

The Christian MMA community has become active participants in the commodification of the sport. Jesus Didn't Tap, a Christian MMA clothing company, was the first in the market to combine commercialization with a Christian message for MMA. Jason David Frank, one of the co-owners of Jesus Didn't Tap, is better known as Tommy Oliver on the *Mighty Morphin Power Rangers*. Using his recognition as a Power Ranger he has built not only this company, but also a thriving MMA studio for children.[83] The message being conveyed by the clothing company's name is that Jesus never gave up, even while suffering unimaginable pain on the cross.[84] Their product lines represent both the competitiveness of the MMA and honoring God, with imagery such as Jesus choking Satan, and slogans such as "Jesus Loves Me and My New Tattoos" and "Warrior of God."[85] The images within the gallery on the company's website are predominately from MMA bouts, both UFC and amateur, and feature openly Christian fighters wearing their clothing line while in the cage. The fighters' tattoos are positioned to be seen and are religious in nature and feature such symbols as angels, and hands with nails through them. These religious symbols on the bodies of the fighters' are juxtaposed with advertising banners for Hooters in the background,[86] a perfect example of the internal conflict of those involved in the sport. The company's justification for Christian involvement in the sport is best summed up by the following quote by co-owner Patrick Hutton: "Fighting is in the Old Testament; in fact, the Bible is real violent. Everyone struggles within the locked cage of life . . . but Jesus is the only champion. People will say, 'Oh, the only reason Jesus didn't tap was because his hands were nailed to the cross.' But he could have verbally tapped and he didn't."[87]

This commodification of the sport and Christianity within it serves more than one purpose, as it also provides the groundwork to sow the seeds for the next generation. The Christian neo-muscular movement is also active virtually with a Christian social media network www .anointedfighter.com.[88] Throughout the site God is referred to as the "heavenly trainer." Also joining in on the commercialization of the sport and the movement, Anointed Fighter has created a line of training videos and handbooks for children and teens entitled "ChristJitsu."[89] From the cover of one of the videos, the imagery of Christ as muscular is seen "To train Anointed Fighters for Christ in the art of spiritual warfare against the evil forces in spiritual realms, while teaching them how to master and control the most important functions of the brain (intellect, emotions, and will) according to God's divine purpose."[90] The marketing for their Anointed Fighter Handbook and Devotional *The Cage of Life* opens with "This is not the devotional book for sissies to read."[91]

The Anointed Fighter site has a children's section with seven animated children's characters who blog about Christ and scripture. Two of the characters are girls, whose biographies are small in comparison to the boy characters. Whereas the girls' character traits focus on being intellectual, smart, keen witted, practical, and a willingness and loyalty in following others; the boys' traits include athletic strength, strategy, leadership skills, inspiration to rally the community, and promote physical exercise, goal setting, and hard work.[92] Girls represent hope and faith, and the boy characters are named after truth, respect, discipline, perseverance, and courage. In addition to the blogs, the company has created a line of merchandise with these animated characters including toys, clothing, backpacks, sports equipment, and a credit card.[93] This contemporary use of sport to interest young boys and male youths to the neo-muscular Christian movement is not new and is based on the Victorian era where there was a concerted effort to do the same.

The Christian involvement in the MMA and UFC has caught the attention of secular filmmakers. There is a feature film distributed by Lions Gate Entertainment entitled *Warrior,* starring Tom Hardy (*Inception*), Joel Edgerton (*Legend of the Guardians*), and Nick Nolte. It is a Christian family film set on the parable of the Prodigal son from Luke 15 and set in the world of the MMA. The film is also accompanied by a Bible Study created by the distributor.[94] A full-length feature documentary, *Fight Church*, directed by Academy Award winner Daniel Junge and Bryan Storkel follows several pastors and fighters reconciling their faith with a violent sport. A short documentary called *The Saint*[95] is about John Renken, a former Satanist, Army Ranger, and a professional ultimate fighter, who is now a born-again Christian and founder of Xtreme Ministries in Clarksville, Tennessee. *The Saint* won the Best Documentary Short award at the Oxford Film Festival in 2012. Renken in voice-over throughout the film is heard saying that in today's society Jesus is portrayed as a bearded lady, he is feminized, and his manliness is downplayed.[96] Renken asks the viewers and his fellow Christians to recognize that Jesus's strength is seen in his crucifixion by the pain he suffered.[97] Based on this perseverance, Renken believes those who promote Christ as a pacifist, as a man who would not fight, are completely wrong and do not understand the Scriptures, as Jesus came to destroy evil and is the greatest fighter against evil. The Bible commands believers to go where lost people are; it does not matter if it is in the ring or cage. For Renken, MMA is just a tool to bring people into the fold.[98] In an interview on FoxNews,[99] Renken explains that his ministry is in response to the feminization of the church, and through MMA he is attracting men to the church and reaching out to the lost people in the MMA as Scripture directs him to. Much like the original muscular Christianity movement in the Victorian era, Renken's ministry offers a vacation fight school to boys and youth.[100]

Not all of the reactions from the secular world have been positive to the Christian involvement in the MMA. Author Mark Simpson, writing for LGBTQI magazine *Out*, wrote that the MMA "looks remarkably like gay porn for straight men."[101] His one comment was perceived as an attack on the masculinization of both the movement and the sport itself. In direct response to the Christian MMA there is now a small growing movement under the name MMAtheists, who are calling for the "Separation of Church and Cage." This movement is composed of fighters, coaches, doctors, training partners, fans, friends, and family who believe that fighters' religious beliefs have no place in the world of combat sports.

Well-known pastor Mark Driscoll wrote a response to these and other MMA dissenters on his church's website in a piece entitled "A Christian Evaluation of Mixed Martial Arts."[102] Rather than truly responding to the criticisms, he focuses on how prominent Christians in the sport are personifying their faith, such as UFC fighter Ben Henderson. Henderson is a devoted Christian as well as a MMA fighter. Entering the ring to gospel music, he also quotes scriptures after his fights to reporters.[103] A biography on Henderson that aired on Spike TV showed him reading Psalm 23 over workout and fight footage and of him going to church and talking about his faith. Referred by his coach as God's Warrior,[104] Henderson has a tattoo of Psalm 144:1 on his chest. Similarly, fellow Christian and MMA fighter Jon Jones has a tattoo of Philippians 4:13, "I can do all things through Christ who strengthens me." Both fighters' personify the Christian message with tattoos emblazoned across their chests and prominent throughout all fights.

The neo-muscular Christianity movement is becoming commonplace within the secular world of sports. Athletes such as Tim Tebow and his now infamous praying position after throwing a touchdown have become fixtures in mainstream culture. The fluctuations and uncertainty of the current economic climate and the rise in the cultural diversity of the United States, not only in ethical terms, but in religious and nonreligious terms as well, continues to resemble the chaos of the late 1800s. There can be no question that the 9/11 terrorists acts in 2001 helped to instigate questions of the perceptions of strength and safety of all of the United States. As seen in the 1800s, these societal and cultural issues are addressed in terms of gender and gender order. Much like the Victorian-era version of this movement, there is a modern relationship between manhood, sports, the feminized church, and an urgent need to bring a strong manly version of Jesus back into the church. The similarities between the actual movements, such as the reimaging of Christ, calling to men to join the church through sports, the use of sports heroes and using sports to reach out to young boys through camps and clubs, can assist us as academics in following this movement and its implications.

The mediums have changed, as video games, pay-per-view, the Internet, and animations are being used to lure males to the church, but the message has not. This neo-muscular Christian movement presumes that Jesus came to earth to model genuine masculinity, implying that if the church takes on a male psyche it fulfills its purpose, and when it is effeminate and personifying a female psyche, it is not.[105] This view of masculinity is extremely narrow and excludes women from discipleship,[106] coinciding with the original Victorian-era muscular Christianity movement. Through embracing the commercialization and technological advancements, Protestant Christians, then and now, have been able to bring their message to the males in society. The mediums and the sports have changed, but the challenges, the fears of feminization, and societal and economic challenges have remained the same.

Notes

1. C. Putney, *Muscular Christianity: Manhood and Sports in Protestant America, 1880–1920* (Cambridge, MA: Harvard University Press, 2003), 1.

2. Ibid., 20.

3. Ibid., 2.

4. Ibid., 21.

5. Ibid.

6. W. J. Baker, *Playing with God: Religion and Modern Sport* (Cambridge, MA: Harvard University Press, 2007).

7. Putney, *Muscular Christianity: Manhood and Sports,* 3.

8. Baker, *Playing with God,* 36.

9. T. Ladd and J. A. Mathisen, *Muscular Christianity: Evangelical Protestants and the Development of American Sport* (Baker Books, 1999), 15.

10. "Do you not know that your bodies are temples of the Holy Spirit, who is in you, who, you have received from God? You are not your own; you were bought at a price. Therefore honor God with your bodies" (1 Corinthians 6:19–20 [KJV]).

11. Putney, *Muscular Christianity: Manhood and Sports,* 11.

12. Ladd and Mathisen, *Muscular Christianity: Evangelical Protestants,* 16.

13. Putney, *Muscular Christianity: Manhood and Sports,* 2.

14. Ibid., 93.

15. Ibid., 92.

16. Ibid., 93.

17. Ibid., 94.

18. J. Parry, *Sport and Spirituality: An Introduction* (Routledge, 2007), 90.

19. B. O'Brien, "A Jesus for Real Men: What the New Masculinity Movement Gets Right and Wrong," *Christianity Today* 52, no. 4 (2008): 48–52, 49.

20. N. Cheever, "The Uses and Gratifications of Viewing Mixed Martial Arts," *Journal of Sports Media* 4, no. 1 (2009): 25–53, 31.

21. A. Vaccaro, D. P. Schrock, and J. M. McCabe, "Managing Emotional Manhood: Fighting and Fostering Fear in Mixed Martial Arts," *Social Psychology Quarterly* 74, no. 4 (2011): 415.

22. Ibid., 417.

23. O'Brien, "A Jesus for Real Men," 49.

24. Ibid., 49.

25. Ibid., 50.

26. B. Beal, "The Promise Keepers' Use of Sport in Defining 'Christlike' Masculinity," *Journal of Sport and Social Issues* 21, no. 3 (1997): 279.

27. Ibid.

28. Ibid., 278.

29. K. B. Wamsley and D. Whitson, "Celebrating Violent Masculinities: The Boxing Death of Luther McCarty," *Journal of Sport History* 25 (1998): 421.

30. J. T. Sammons, *Beyond the Ring: The Role of Boxing in American Society* (Champaign: University of Illinois Press, 1990), 6–7.

31. Wamsley and Whitson, "Celebrating Violent Masculinities," 420.

32. Baker, *Playing with God*, 26.

33. Ibid., 27.

34. G. Bederman, "'The Women Have Had Charge of the Church Work Long Enough': The Men and Religion Forward Movement of 1911–1912 and the Masculinization of Middle-Class Protestantism," *American Quarterly* 41, no. 3 (1989): 454.

35. Putney, *Muscular Christianity: Manhood and Sports*, 18.

36. Bederman, "'The Women Have Had Charge,'" 438.

37. Putney, *Muscular Christianity: Manhood and Sports*, 18.

38. Bederman, "'The Women Have Had Charge,'" 454; Baker, *Playing with God*, 64.

39. Putney, *Muscular Christianity: Manhood and Sports*, 57.

40. Ibid., 59.

41. Ibid., 61.

42. Ibid., 61.

43. Baker, *Playing with God*, 104.

44. Ibid., 44.

45. Ibid., 73–74.

46. M. S. van Leeuwe, "Servanthood or Soft Patriarchy? A Christian Feminist Looks at the Promise Keepers Movement," *The Journal of Men's Studies* 5, no. 3 (1997): 233.

47. M. I. Borer and T. S. Schafer, "Culture War Confessionals: Conflicting Accounts of Christianity, Violence, and Mixed Martial Arts," *Journal of Media and Religion* 10, no. 4 (2011): 166–67.

48. Ibid.

49. S. M. Kim et al., "An Analysis of Spectator Motives in an Individual Combat Sport: A Study of Mixed Martial Arts Fans," *Sport Marketing Quarterly* 17, no. 2 (2008): 110.

50. R. S. García and D. Malcolm, "Decivilizing, Civilizing or Informalizing? The International Development of Mixed Martial Arts," *International Review for the Sociology of Sport* 45, no. 1 (2010): 43.

51. Ibid.

52. Ibid.

53. Ibid.

54. Ibid., 44.

55. S. J. Hoffman, *Good Game: Christianity and the Culture of Sports* (Waco, TX: Baylor University Press, 2010), 157.

56. Ibid., 223.

57. Ibid., 229.

58. A. Hirose and K. K. Pih, "Men Who Strike and Men Who Submit: Hegemonic and Marginalized Masculinities in Mixed Martial Arts," *Men and Masculinities* 13, no. 2 (2010): 198.

59. Ibid., 192.

60. Ibid., 199.

61. Ibid.

62. Ibid.

63. Ibid., 199–200.

64. Ibid., 200.

65. Ibid., 201.

66. Cheever, "The Uses and Gratifications," 25.

67. García and Malcolm, "Decivilizing, Civilizing or Informalizing?," 41.

68. Ibid., 48.

69. C. H. Lim, T. G. Martin, and D.H. Kwak, "Examining Television Consumers of Mixed Martial Arts: The Relationship Among Risk Taking, Emotion, Attitude, and Actual Sport-Media Consumption Behavior," *International Journal of Sport Communication* 3, no. 1 (2010): 49.

70. García and Malcolm, "Decivilizing, Civilizing or Informalizing?," 45.

71. Kim et al., "An Analysis of Spectator Motives," 109.

72. Vaccaro et al., "Managing Emotional Manhood," 414.

73. Borer and Schafer, "Culture War Confessionals," 167.

74. Kim et al., "An Analysis of Spectator Motives," 109.

75. Borer and Schafer, "Culture War Confessionals," 167.

76. R. M. Schneiderman, "Flock Is Now a Fight Team in Some Ministries," *New York Times,* February 1, 2010.

77. Ibid.

78. Ibid.

79. Borer and Schafer, "Culture War Confessionals," 167.

80. B. Beals, "fightchurch.com," accessed March 12, 2012, http://fightchurch .com.

81. Borer and Schafer, "Culture War Confessionals," 167.

82. Schneiderman, "Flock Is Now a Fight Team."

83. K. Shellnutt, "Jesus as the Ultimate Ultimate Fighter," *Houston Chronicle,* June 24, 2010.

84. Various, "jesusdidnttap.com," accessed July 12, 2012, http://www .jesusdidnttap.com.

85. Ibid.

86. Ibid.

87. B. Bearak, "Ultimate Fighting Dips a Toe Into the Mainstream," *New York Times,* November 11, 2011.

88. Various, "anointedfighter.com," accessed July 12, 2012, http://www .anointedfighter.com.

89. Ibid.

90. Ibid.

91. Ibid.

92. Ibid.

93. Ibid.

94. Lions Gate Entertainment, "Warrior," accessed July 12, 2012, http://www .warriorfilm.com/index2.html.

95. Various, "roryfraser.com," accessed July 12, 2012, http:// http://roryfraser .com/index.php?/documentary/saint/.

96. Ibid.

97. Ibid.

98. Ibid.

99. J. Renken, "FoxNews," accessed September 12, 2012, http://video .foxnews.com/v/4008457/cage-fighting-for-jesus.

100. Various, "cmmaa.com," accessed July 12, 2012, http://cmmaa.com.

101. M. Simpson, "Fight Club: How Gay Is MMA?," *Out Magazine,* June 2008.

102. M. Driscoll, "A Christian Evaluation of Mixed Martial Arts," accessed July 12, 2012, http://pastormark.tv/2011/11/09/a-christian-evaluation-of-mixed -martial-arts.

103. Ibid.

104. Ibid.

105. O'Brien, "A Jesus for Real Men," 50.

106. Ibid.

CHAPTER THREE

Evangelical Fight Clubs and the Power of Religious Metaphor

B. J. Parker, Rebecca Whitten Poe Hays, and Nicholas R. Werse

Metaphors are by nature powerful tools of communication. Religious metaphors adopt further power by assuming a level of religious authority. It goes without saying, therefore, that religious teachers carry a heavy responsibility in the selection and utilization of metaphors for communicating their religious teachings. Such responsibility includes the consideration of how a metaphor will communicate, what it will communicate, and how it could be misunderstood. The subject of this study, however, will be the far greater danger entailed within the world of religious metaphors. In this chapter we will explore the often unrecognized power of religious metaphor to hijack meaning gradually, thereby communicating a message originally absent from the "authorial intent." This danger will be explored in relation to the rise of "Fight Club" metaphors in evangelical men's ministries. Our study will proceed in three parts. First, a preliminary methodological discussion will explore metaphor theory and the capacity for self-inflicted miscommunication. Second, two historical examples will demonstrate this process of hijacking a metaphor. Finally, we will explore the recent appropriation of "Fight Club" metaphors in evangelical men's ministries and conclude with an assessment of the ways in which this metaphor is primed to develop beyond its current intended function.

A Framework for Metaphor: Influence over the User and the Recipient

Humans have been utilizing metaphor and other figures of comparison for thousands of years. Defining exactly what *constitutes* a metaphor and exactly what *contribution* metaphor makes to communication nevertheless remains a complex task. While at its most basic level one can understand metaphor as "[a]ny figure that asserts the equivalence of two or more disparate elements,"[1] recent studies of metaphor, in particular that of Janet Martin Soskice, have demonstrated metaphor's unique capacity to convey ideas and feelings that reach beyond the sum of its parts.[2]

As early as the fourth century BCE, Aristotle had articulated in his *Poetics* a theory of metaphor (μεταφορά) that understood metaphor to involve "the transferred use of a term that properly belongs to something else."[3] Recent literary scholars and philosophers of language hold Aristotle ultimately responsible for the oversimplified, though common, notion that metaphor is merely a matter of substituting the literal with the figurative.[4] Speaking in metaphor involves speaking about one thing when one really means something else. This "substitution" or "decorative" theory of metaphor assumes that metaphorical speech differs from literal speech only in being more interesting: If one removes the metaphor, no aspect of the communication is lost.[5]

An alternative theory of metaphor ascribes to this device greater rhetorical power. Soskice argues that even at the dawn of metaphor studies, Aristotle recognized the potential for metaphor to fill the "lexical gaps" and "name the unnamed."[6] In the 1980s, George Lakoff and Mark Johnson drew attention to the ways in which the metaphors a person employs suggest the underlying thought patterns that govern that person's thinking and behavior.[7] Soskice further developed this work by proposing that metaphor not only *reflects* a cognitive/emotive process but that it actually advances understanding. Metaphor has the ability to communicate that which cannot be communicated in any other way.[8]

If one is to understand a metaphor fully, one must identify both the "tenor" and the "vehicle" involved in the figure and explore their respective connotations. The tenor is the underlying subject of the metaphor; the vehicle is the language/imagery one uses to present the subject. In order for a metaphor to communicate successfully, however, the tenor and vehicle (with their respective associations) must possess the right balance of similarity and dissimilarity. If these elements are too similar, the metaphor will be pointless. If they are too dissimilar, the metaphor will be unintelligible. The ideal metaphorical scenario is for the dissimilarity between the tenor and its vehicle to be as great as possible so as to "push" conceptual boundaries and shock the metaphor's recipient into recognizing something new about the tenor.[9]

Critical for understanding a metaphor is the recognition that the tenor and the vehicle are presenting a single subject.[10] The idea of the tenor suggests the language and imagery one uses to present the idea in the vehicle. Soskice argues that "metaphor is a form of language use with a unity of subject-matter and which yet draws upon two (or more) *sets of associations.*"[11] In many ways, this act of drawing upon associations, connotations, feelings, and assumptions is responsible for imbuing metaphor with its unique communicative power:

> By using metaphors, much more can be conveyed, through implication and connotation, than through straightforward, literal language. Take the case of . . . . that literary metaphor *dolphin-torn*: what exactly is Yeats suggesting about the sea, and how else could this have been expressed? Just as writers express meanings more open-endedly when they use metaphorical language, readers interpret less narrowly than they would literal language. So meaning is communicated between writer and reader in a less precise way, even though metaphors may seem concrete and vivid. It is this imprecision, this 'fuzziness' of meaning, which makes metaphor such a powerful tool in the communication of emotion, evaluation, and explanation too.[12]

Important to recognize at this point is that the "'fuzziness' of meaning" that broadens the communicative possibilities of metaphor also has the potential to widen the gap between what the user of the metaphor intended to communicate and what the recipient of the metaphor understands.

While the value of metaphor is that it can communicate concepts and feelings in a deeper, more cognitively rich way than can literal speech, metaphor also carries with its "fuzzy" meanings the danger of misinterpretation and misapplication. Because metaphor operates by drawing upon the associations of both user and recipient, the respective associations of the user and the recipient may differ enough that what the metaphor communicates to one is not exactly what the metaphor communicates to the other. Metaphor by its very nature stretches meaning, but the recipient of a metaphor may stretch the meaning beyond the intentions of the metaphor's user. When creating and utilizing metaphors, therefore, the user must consider carefully how the recipient will receive the metaphors.

Historical Examples of Hijacked Metaphor

History provides numerous examples of misunderstood and misappropriated religious metaphors. One may observe an example of the former in the accusation that early Christians were cannibalistic on account of their ritualistic consumption of the "body" and the "blood" of Christ in the Eucharist.[13] An example misappropriation is readily apparent in the rhetorical presentation of Native Americans as "Canaanites" by select early European colonists in North America to justify the extermination of the indigenous population.[14] In many instances, however, the metaphor itself contributes to its own misunderstanding. As subsequent generations of recipients receive and interpret the metaphor, it develops a significant reception history, which may gradually replace authorial intention in defining the tenor of the metaphor. Thus the vehicle of the metaphor contains the power to hijack the tenor, resulting in the metaphor contributing an originally unintended meaning. Diachronic studies of the reception history of numerous religious metaphors that changed along with, and often contributed to, the development of Christian doctrine demonstrate this phenomenon.

One such example, is the infamous "marriage metaphor" of Hosea 1–3. The book of Hosea skillfully employs a marriage metaphor to represent the people's betrayal of the Lord. The metaphor presents the relationship with God as a marriage[15] and likens the worship of other deities to adultery. The image powerfully portrays God's heartbreak and anger over the betrayal as he threatens to strip his unfaithful wife, expose her shame, and kill her with thirst. Yet the anger does not win out as the Lord vows that he will do all these things to win the heart of his bride once again. The danger of marriage as a metaphor for the Lord's response to idolatry is that it lends itself to be read as a lesson on marriage as well. Thus God suddenly becomes the model of a husband, which includes the metaphorical abusive language. This association of God with abuse has been a primary critique of feminist biblical interpreters who recognize and call attention to the ways in which the metaphor has become a means of reinforcing the denigration and subordination of women.[16] The reception history of the metaphor disseminated a potentially oppressive teaching concerning marriage when the authorial intent originally condemned idolatry.

A modern example of the unintended growth of a religious metaphor is the "wall" of separation between church and state.[17] The use of a "wall" metaphor to describe church/state relations first appeared in a personal letter from Thomas Jefferson to the Baptist Association of Danbury upon his election to the presidency.[18] By comparing Jefferson's career as a politician in the state of Virginia and his service as president of the United States of America, Daniel Dreisbach argues that Jefferson perceived the "wall of separation" as functioning differently at the local and federal levels. Dreisbach convincingly argues that Jefferson's "wall" was primarily concerned with keeping the church free from the "general" or federal government, leaving matters of local government up to local discretion.[19]

A series of U.S. Supreme Court rulings, however, reveals how the "wall of separation between church and state" grew to become more of a "wall" than Jefferson initially intended. In 1879, *Reynolds v. the United States* interpreted the "wall of separation" as the authoritative declaration of the function of the First Amendment.[20] In *Everson v. the Board of Education* in 1947, the wall metaphor became binding on local state governments as well.[21]

The language of separation of church and state did not come into wide use as a maxim for the First Amendment until the middle of the 19th century.[22] Today, the common interpretation of the "wall" of separation of church and state is that it represents an impenetrable barrier that now prohibits both the government (federal and state) from influencing the church as well as the church (or ecclesial figures) from influencing the government. By nature of being a "wall," the metaphor grew over time to mean something other than what Jefferson originally intended. With this development in mind, we now turn to the recent use of "Fight Club" metaphors in evangelical men's ministries, exploring the ways in which this metaphor lends itself to growth beyond the intended evangelical message.

Fight Club and the Church in the United States[23]

"The place where feet, fists, and faith collide." This motto describes John Renken's mixed martial arts (MMA) academy that doubled as a church for MMA fighters. The church that John Renken founded in 2000 stands at the center of a growing movement in the United States that attempts to leverage America's newfound love of MMA for the regenerative ends of the gospel.[24] More common than churches involved in MMA, however, are churches that borrow language from the film *Fight Club* to represent their men's ministries. Churches across the country as well as parachurch organizations of substantial size are all seemingly joining the ranks of Tyler Durden's recruits. With Mark Driscoll's (in)famous "Fight Club Theology"[25] wrangling its way into the American psyche and numerous "Fight Club" centered men's ministries popping up all over the nation, more traditional approaches to men's ministries such as Promise Keepers look as if they might be on the ropes.[26] The call for men to struggle for their souls, families, and communities certainly has the capacity to engender stronger faith, yet how might the adoption and use of metaphorical language from the film *Fight Club* negatively impact that very call? In this final section of the chapter, we will look at problems that arise when one closely examines the tenor and vehicle of this metaphor as well as potential ways the "Fight Club" metaphor might morph into something unintended.

The foundational nature of a metaphor's tenor makes it the ideal place to begin analyzing the Christian appropriation of the metaphor of "Fight Club." Though admittedly not exhaustive or univocal, a survey of the relevant ministries' websites does present us with general agreement on the intended tenor because so many ministries explicitly state their purposes. Jim Brown, founder of the ministry named "Fight Club," articulates the purpose of his ministry as follows:

> Fight Club is a men's discipleship resource developed by men, for men, to reach men—to turn the tide on mediocrity and cause men to stand and say "not on my watch!" . . . It carries the flavor of what men desire: camaraderie, competition, and challenge. It will push your men to keep up and to reach new levels with Jesus. . . . Men will grow intellectually, spiritually, physically and relationally. You will see immediate impact on the man daring to take this journey . . . [27]

Throughout interviews in an informational video for the ministry, participants claim "'Fight Club' has shown me the importance of showing kindness and compassion to others," made them a "better husband, coworker, friend," and offered "community, brotherhood, and fellowship."[28]

Another men's ministry with the same title claims its purpose is to "encourage, equip, and empower men to be leaders in their home, church, and community."[29] A third church articulates the purpose of its "Fight Club" ministry as "a Christ-based, Christ-centered men's ministry dedicated to raising men to become men after God's own heart. We are focused on teaching men how to apply the Word of God to their everyday lives. Through the Word, FIGHT CLUB teaches men how to walk in the Power and Authority that the Lord has given us."[30]

A final example describes its ministry as follows: "Fight Clubs allow for deep relationship, trust, and accountability for gospel encouragement, healing, and correction. We seek to help each other identify our idols and see God's grace realized in a real, concrete way."[31]

Community, self-improvement, and spiritual formation tie all of these statements of purpose together. Significant dissonance sounds, however, when one examines the vehicle of "Fight Club" and compares it to the tenor of the previous Christian exhortation. Though numerous psychological and religious layers form the whole of the film *Fight Club*, three examples will illustrate well the dissonance between the vehicle and tenor.

The first example comes from fairly early in the film when the narrator and Tyler are riding on a bus and sizing up all the men around them. The narrator spots a Gucci underwear advertisement and asks Tyler, "Is that what a man looks like?" Tyler responds, "Self-improvement is masturbation. Now self-destruction . . ."[32] From this scene the viewer sees one of the underlying principles that the film explores, namely the difference between societal expectations and an individual's core self. Ironically, this line from the movie, crass as it is, fits well within radical Christianity's call to die to self, yet the push of most of the "Fight Club" ministries often centers on self-improvement.

A second example from the movie further illustrates the conflict between the vehicle and tenor. Nearly halfway through the movie, Tyler Durden holds the narrator down and gives him a chemical burn. Through the narrator's pleas for release, the following dialogue ensues: Tyler yells, "Shut up! Our fathers were our models for God. If our fathers bailed, what does that tell you about God? Listen to me! You have to consider the possibility that God does not like you. He never wanted you. In all probability, he hates you. This is not the worst thing that can happen to you." The narrator quivers, "It isn't?" Tyler shoots back: "We don't need him. Fuck damnation, man! And fuck redemption! We are God's unwanted children. So be it!"[33]

Most immediately one sees a stark contrast between the values of *Fight Club* and those of the various men's ministries across the country. Tyler's challenge to the narrator demonstrates a readiness to cast off the relational bonds between them and any existent deity. This readiness, however, emerges from an acknowledgement of what Tyler understands to be the true reality: God does not love humanity; God abhors humanity. Such a statement exposes the vast gulf between men's ministries and *Fight Club's* ideology.

One of the most fundamental convictions of evangelical Christianity— and even Christianity more broadly—is the existence of a loving God who cares about humanity in an active way. While men's ministries found themselves on this conception of divine love for humanity that then inspires an individual's loving action toward family members and others in the community, Tyler Durden's brief monologue demolishes the foundation of these ministries by violently removing divine love. If these ministries' intended tenor involves the notion of a robust relationship with a loving God as their faith statements suggest, then appropriating a vehicle that explicitly rejects the possibility of *any* relationship with God appears highly problematic at best. Whatever the intended associations may be, the *Fight Club* vehicle will carry with it associations related to the film's presentation of God.

Even though the vehicle's lack of divine love obviously conflicts in an undesirable way with the tenor of the metaphor, another nuance further clarifies the point. Not only does Tyler break the bonds between humanity and God in the above quote, he proceeds to shear the ties between humanity and religion more generally. By removing redemption and damnation, arguably two of the most central components of any religion, Tyler thrusts humanity into a sort of religious anarchy in which no system *is* the system. Freed from the constraints of the threat and reward of religion, humanity can then pursue whatever ends it desires. Chaos becomes the only good. Tyler's proposed salvation for humanity drastically diverges from that of the proposed salvation of men's ministries adopting the *Fight Club* metaphor—salvation through the suffering and glorification of Jesus Christ.

The third example of dissonance between the vehicle and tenor in the case of the evangelical appropriation of the "Fight Club" metaphor is the source for the vision of fight club. The "Fight Club" ministries envision a powerful, authentic man who will fight for what is important. More importantly, they understand this model of masculinity to be God's vision for character formation. In their own words, "We believe God dropped this idea like a boulder from heaven."[34] Ironically, the characters in *Fight Club* pursue their quest for raw, powerful, authenticity not because of God but rather in spite of God and any other structuring system in society. The vision for fight club in the film originates with Tyler Durden, who is nothing more than the outworking of the narrator's psychological instability. Although a metaphorical association of Tyler Durden with the divine leads to a Freudian field day in terms of relating faith to the outworking of humanity's neurosis, the evangelical "Fight Club" ministries would hardly endorse such a presentation of God.

Most of the churches and parachurch organizations that employ the "Fight Club" metaphor do so to varying degrees. Jim Brown's "Fight Club" ministry introduced above, for example, claims no direct inspiration from or connection to the film *Fight Club*, rather attributing the metaphor to the biblical verse Nehemiah 4:14.[35] The use of the name, logos, structure of "charters," "homework" assignments handed out at the end of meetings, and famous lines like "you do not talk about fight club,"[36] however, all elicit a connection on some level to the film. Because no ministry embraces the entire metaphor, three reasons seem the most viable for ministries' adoption of "Fight Club." The first is the cultural cachet the film holds among men, and the second is similar: the common link between ministries using the film and the film itself is a drive toward raw, powerful authenticity. The third reason is that *Fight Club* presents a form of powerful masculinity, which ministries hope will appeal to men.

If churches and ministries are merely adopting some of the jargon and cultural cachet of the movie, one might wonder, "What's the worst that could happen? Doesn't the radical nature of the film make it obviously out of bounds for the men participating in the ministries?" We would submit, however, that embracing the rawness of *Fight Club* that appeals to so many men without the movie's fuller implications is simply impossible.

As the movie progresses, the viewer sees a constant back and forth between the narrator and Tyler. The narrator enjoys the thrill and cathartic effect of fight club but remains unwilling to embrace Tyler's ideals fully. Tyler constantly demands that the narrator let go and let chaos ensue. The viewer, then, sees the conflict of the narrator living with the desire for raw, unchecked power, yet not willing to take the desire to its logical end. At the end of the film, the narrator decides to kill Tyler and Tyler's way of life. In essence, he cannot live with the tension of those two forces pulling on him.

If men's ministries adopt the metaphor of "Fight Club," they most likely do so to meet the desire for authenticity and power among men in their congregations. The problem, however, is that using the metaphor without fully embracing its implications leaves the participants in a sort of in-between space like the narrator. The adoption of the "Fight Club" metaphor triggers all of the associations of the *Fight Club* vehicle yet offers a *very* different tenor. No man will likely lament the lack of realization of Project Mayhem in a church. They might, however, still crave some sort of realization of raw power when they receive self-improvement as the primary outcome of a "Fight Club" ministry. The ministry, then, leaves men with self-improvement when they desire power and authenticity. The effects of such dissonance potentially threaten to damage the faith of participants. If men do not find the authenticity and raw power they seek, the tension will force them either to see the religious system as a failure or to push further toward the logical end of the search for power and authenticity. In a way similar to the narrator, they will either have to embrace Tyler Durden or kill him.

Finally, in the context of what many evangelicals perceive as the church's "feminization,"[37] the "Fight Club" metaphor presents a warrior God who is strong, courageous, and victorious over all that oppose him. Although this aspect of the divine character is indeed present in Scripture (Exodus 15:1–7; Joshua 5:13–15; 1 Samuel 17:45; Psalms 124; 1 Corinthians

15:24–28), an overemphasis on this aspect of God's character can result in a skewed understanding of the God whom the biblical texts also present as gentle, nurturing, and at times even explicitly maternal (Deuteronomy 32:11–12; Isaiah 42:14, 49:15, 66:13; Matthew 23:37). Even the book of Hosea, which also depicts God as an angry husband, includes a beautiful description of God in the role of a mother tending to her child (11:3–4). The theological endeavor by nature involves the use of limited words to describe the unlimited, and no metaphor has the capacity to convey the complete idea or truth. Both metaphors—God as warrior and God as mother—are valid. The problem comes when one metaphor becomes dominant at the cost of the others. The overuse of *Fight Club* images and language in reference to God distorts the understanding of what it means for God to be God and for a man to be a man, ultimately at the cost of the evangelical men's ministries' intended tenor.

Conclusion

The natural communicative power of metaphors is clear. The level of religious authority religious metaphors assume invests them with even greater power. In this chapter we have explored the ways in which religious metaphors grow beyond the originally intended meaning. This growth has been demonstrated through both methodological inquiries and historical examples. With these considerations in mind, we then surveyed the rising "Fight Club" metaphor in evangelical men's ministries and the ways in which the vehicle is inclined to transform the tenor. Although the ministries under consideration pursue admirable goals such as community service and family relationships, when a metaphor's vehicle influences and even co-opts the metaphor's tenor, religious authority can become a frightening interpretive partner. Religious teachers, therefore, have a responsibility to consider carefully not just the tenor of a metaphor but also its vehicle *and* the ways in which that vehicle may unintentionally develop the tenor.

Notes

The authors wish to express gratitude to Joshua Hays for his thoughtful feedback on an earlier version of this chapter.

1. William Packard, "Metaphor," in *The Poet's Dictionary: A Handbook of Prosody and Poetic Devices* (New York: Harper and Row, 1989), 121.

2. Though similar, metaphor stands distinct from other figures of comparison. The category of symbol includes the nonlinguistic. Allegory and satire are broader

in scope than metaphor and are intended to "tell two tales" (in which one need not understand both tales) whereas metaphor has only one subject. Synecdoche and metonymy involve a straightforward substitution of a part for the whole (or *vice versa*) while the comparison in metaphor is more complex. The explicit comparisons of simile stand apart from metaphor at a superficial level because of grammar; more significantly, the grammatical dimension of simile prevents it from extending language the way that metaphor can. Linguistic analogy merely stretches the accepted domain of a word/idea's application, but metaphor makes completely new applications. Cf. Janet Martin Soskice, *Metaphor and Religious Language* (Oxford: Clarendon, 1985), 54–66.

3. Aristotle, *Poetics* 1457b [trans. Hubbard], 119.

4. Cf. Max Black, "More About Metaphor," in *Metaphor and Thought,* ed. Andrew Ortony (Cambridge: Cambridge University Press, 1979), 22; Max Black, *Models and Metaphors; Studies in Language and Philosophy* (Ithaca, NY: Cornell University Press, 1962), 31; Andrew Ortony, *Metaphor and Thought* (Cambridge: Cambridge University Press, 1979), 3.

5. Alice Deignan, *Metaphor and Corpus Linguistics* (Amsterdam, NL: John Benjamins, 2005), 2–4; Soskice, *Metaphor and Religious Language*, 24–26.

6. Soskice, *Metaphor and Religious Language*, 8–9. Soskice supports her argument by citing Aristotle: "Sometimes [an idea] has no word to express it, but it can be expressed through a comparison; for example, scattering seed is called 'sowing', but there is no term for the scattering of light by the sun; but as this is related to the sun as sowing is to the scatterer of seed, we have the expression 'sowing the god-created flame'" (*Poetics*, 1457b [Hubbard], 120) and "It is extremely important to use in the proper place each of the kinds [of literary/rhetorical devices] I have mentioned, but by far the most important is to be good at metaphor. For this is the only one that cannot be learnt from anyone else, and it is a sign of natural genius, as to be good at metaphor is to perceive resemblances" (*Poetics*, 1459a [Hubbard], 122). Interestingly, A. Deignan cites the idea of metaphor filling "lexical gaps" as an aspect of the "decorative" view of metaphor that Soskice rejects (Deignán, *Metaphor and Corpus Linguistics*, 2).

7. George Lakoff and Mark Johnson, *Metaphors We Live By* (Chicago: University of Chicago Press, 2003); cf. Deignan, *Metaphor and Corpus Linguistics*, 4.

8. Soskice, *Metaphor and Religious Language*, 43–53 and *passim*. Soskice builds upon the work of I. A. Richards, who views metaphor as being broader than individual words; instead, Richards understands metaphorical speech to involve the "interanimation" of the words in the entire utterance and its surrounding context. Richards is responsible for providing the tenor/vehicle formula laid out in the next paragraph (I. A. Richards, *The Philosophy of Rhetoric* [New York: Oxford University Press, 1936], 3).

9. Cf. Eberhard Jüngel, "Metaphorical Truth," in *Theological Essays,* trans. J. B. Webster (Edinburgh, UK: T. and T. Clark, 1989), 39–46; Soskice, *Metaphor and Religious Language*, 26. G. H. Kreglinger highlights this shocking, subversive dimension of metaphor in her study of the pedagogical strategy behind Jesus's

parables (cf. Gisela H. Kreglinger, *Storied Revelations: Parables, Imagination, and George MacDonald's Christian Fiction* [Eugene, OR: Pickwick, 2013], 14–59).

10. Contra Black, "More about Metaphor," 47.

11. Soskice, *Metaphor and Religious Language*, 49. Emphasis added.

12. Murray Knowles and Rosamund Moon, *Introducing Metaphor* (London: Routledge, 2006), 11–12.

13. Stephen Benko, *Pagan Rome and the Early Christians* (Bloomington: Indiana University Press, 1986), 60–61, 70–72. Some scholars have begun reassessing this accusation as an example of "labeling" or "stereotyping" as opposed to the misunderstanding of the imagery (e.g., Andrew McGowan, "Eating People: Accusations of Cannibalism Against Christians in the Second Century," *Journal of Early Christian Studies* 2 (1994): 413–42). Although stereotyping likely contributed to the accusation, several historical documents still link this specific accusation with the ritualistic language of the "body" and "blood" of the Eucharist. Not all Christian traditions, of course, reduce the Eucharistic language to mere metaphorical significance. The historical defenses against the accusation of cannibalism, however, still indicate a perceived misrepresentation of the sacrament on the part of Early Christianity's critics (e.g., Origen, *Against Celsus*, 6.27; Athenagores, *A Plea on Behalf of Christians*, c31–36; Tertullian, *Apology*, 9; Minucius Felix, *Octavius*, 9).

14. For further discussion, see: Conrad Cherry, *God's New Israel: Religious Interpretations of American Destiny* (Chapel Hill: University of North Carolina Press, 1998), 185; Stephen R. Haynes, *Noah's Curse: The Biblical Justification of American Slavery* (Oxford: Oxford University Press, 2002), 144–45.

15. There is a fair amount of diversity in identifying God's wife in the metaphor. Proposals include the people of God, the land of Israel, and an unspecified city.

16. See, for example, Rut Törnkvist, *The Use and Abuse of Female Sexual Imagery in the Book of Hosea: A Feminist Critical Approach to Hos 1–3* (Uppsala: Acta Universitatis Upsaliensis, 1998), 170. Letty M. Russell, "Introduction: Liberating the Word," in *Feminist Interpretation of the Bible*, ed. Letty M. Russell (Philadelphia: Westminster Press, 1985), 12; Gale A. Yee, "Hosea," in *The Women's Bible Commentary*, ed. Carol A. Newsom and Sharon H. Ringe (London: SPCK, 1992), 195; Renita J. Weems, *Battered Love: Marriage, Sex, and Violence in the Hebrew Prophets* (Minneapolis: Fortress, 1995), 84–110.

17. The following discussion is not intended to advocate for one modern position on church state relations over another. The function of the present section is merely to observe how the metaphor of a "wall" of separation has grown to mean something in modern American society beyond Thomas Jefferson's original intentions. The benefits and challenges associated with the changed perception of the "wall" of separation is a subject for another paper.

18. In this letter Jefferson states, "I contemplate with sovereign reverence that act of the whole American People which declared that their legislature should 'make no law respecting an establishment of religion, or prohibiting the free exercise thereof,' thus building a wall of separation between Church and State." Letter

dated January 1, 1802, as reproduced by Daniel L. Dreisbach, "The Mythical 'Wall of Separation': How a Misused Metaphor Changed Church–State Law, Policy, and Discourse," *First Principles Series* No. 6 (June 23, 2006): 2, accessed December 30, 2013), http://thf_media.s3.amazonaws.com/2006/pdf/fp_6.pdf.

19. Dreisbach, "The Mythical 'Wall of Separation'"; Daniel L. Dreisbach, *Thomas Jefferson and the Wall of Separation Between Church and State* (New York: New York University Press, 2002); Daniel L. Dreisbach, "The Meaning of the Separation of Church and State: Competing Views," in *The Oxford Handbook of Church and State in the United States*, ed. Derek Davis (Oxford: Oxford University Press, 2010), 207–25.

20. *Reynolds v. United States*, 98 U.S. 145, 164 (1879).

21. *Everson v. Board of Education*, 330 U.S. 1, 16, 18 (1947).

22. Dreisbach, "The Meaning of the Separation of Church and State: Competing Views," 215.

23. The following assessment is not intended to be a critique of the ideology, intentions, or effectiveness of religious instruction and spiritual formation of the evangelical men's ministries adopting the fight club metaphor.

24. In his 2010 *New York Times* article that highlights this movement, R. M. Schneiderman puts the number of fighting churches at 700 of the roughly 115,000 white evangelical congregations in the U.S. ("Flock Is Now a Fight Team in Some Ministries," *New York Times*, February 1, 2010, accessed January 12, 2014, http:// www.nytimes.com/2010/02/02/us/02fight.html?_r=0.

25. Mark Driscoll, "Is God a Pacifist?," *Resurgence: A Ministry of Mars Hill Church*, October 22, 2013, accessed January 12, 2014, http://theresurgence. com/2013/10/22/is-god-a-pacifist. For an excellent response, see Jonathon Merritt, "Mark Driscoll Makes Pacifists Fighting Mad," *Religion News Service*, October 24, 2013, accessed January 12, 2014. http://jonathanmerritt.religionnews .com/2013/10/24/mark-driscolls-pansy-post-outrages-christian-pacifists/.

26. For a discussion of the rise and fall of Promise Keepers, see *John P. Bartkowski' Promise Keepers: Servants, Soldiers, and Godly Men* (New Brunswick, NJ: Rutgers University Press, 2004), 1–23. Also, one might notice the current theme of Promise Keepers National Conference: "Unleashing the Warrior." For an example of the prominence of "Fight Club" metaphor being used, see Grace Community Church's ministry "Fight Club," which has spawned nearly 80 "charters" ("Fight Club Charters," *Fight Club*, n.d., accessed January 12, 2014, http://www .FightClub414.com/#/fight-club-charters.

27. Jim Brown, "About Us: Don't Be That Guy," n.d., accessed January 12, 2014, http://www.fightclub414.com/#/about-us/dont-be-that-guy.

28. Fight Club Trailer. *Fight Club*, n.d., accessed January 12, 2014, http:// www.fightclub414.com/#/welcome.

29. "Fight Club (Men's Ministry)," *The Flipside Church*, n.d., accessed January 12, 2014, http://flipsidechurch.com/ministries-2/fight-club-mens-ministry/.

30. "Fight Club Men's Ministry," *In His Presence Church*, n.d., accessed January 12, 2014, https://ihpchurch.org/fight-club.html.

31. "Ministries," *Redeemer Church*, n.d., accessed January 12, 2014, http://www.redeemerlubbock.org/ministries/helping-you/

32. *Fight Club*, directed by David Fincher (1999; Los Angeles: 20th Century Fox Home Entertainment, 2000), DVD.

33. Ibid.

34. Jim Brown, "About Us: Don't Be That Guy," n.d., accessed January 12, 2014, http://www.fightclub414.com/#/about-us/dont-be-that-guy.

35. Nehemiah 4:8 in the Masoretic Text.

36. See the last bullet point of Jim Brown's "Fight Club Creed," accessed on January 13, 2014, http://storage.cloversites.com/gracecommunitychurch21/documents/fc-creed.pdf.

37. See, for example, Leon J. Podles, *The Church Impotent: The Feminization of Christianity* (Dallas, TX: Spence, 1999); Holly Pivec, "The Feminization of the Church," *Biola Magazine* (Spring 2006): 10–17; David Murrow, *Why Men Hate Going to Church* (Nashville, TN: Thomas Nelson, 2011).

CHAPTER FOUR

Python Wrassling: "Is God Really Real, or Is There Some Doubt?"

Brian Cogan and Jeff Massey

Ask your average "Gumby-on-the-street" about the relationship between Monty Python and God, and (assuming said Gumby actually has even *heard* about Monty Python) his answer will likely involve the phrases "utterly blasphemous," "sacrilegious," or "going to hell."[1] And indeed, during the height of their popularity in the 1970s and 1980s, the British comedy troupe—who are, as of this writing, preparing for a reunion "tour"—openly criticized authority, pushed the boundaries of both traditional television and traditional decency, and generally courted controversy whenever comically possible. These are, after all, the fellows who brought us the projectile vomiting of the explosive Mr. Creosote ("Better get a bucket!") and the necro-cannibalistic mourning of "Undertaker's Sketch" (where the best solution to taking care of one's deceased mother is to eat her and then—if you feel bad about it—"vomit her up in the grave"). Along the way, the Pythons stoked religious outrage with films such as *Life of Brian* (which follows the bildungsroman of "a very naughty boy" who—despite his mother's protests—seems very much like the Messiah) and *The Meaning of Life* (which includes such memorable ditties as "Every Sperm Is Sacred" and "Christmas in Heaven"). Fittingly, their off-screen exploits have rivaled the surrealism of their on-screen shenanigans: The Pythons have lobbed Holy Hand Grenades at authority, argued with (real-life) bishops, and hubristically promised to reveal the "meaning of life" to the unwashed masses.[2] They satirized religion and religious figures in every (then currently) known media: television, film, stage, print, and audio.[3] In short, for many casual viewers, they seem to have had a particularly sharp axe to grind against organized religion, especially Christianity.

Yet throughout the years of apparent blasphemy, the Pythons also taught their fans to "always look on the bright side of life," to "never be rude to an Arab," and to "look sharp and wear a tie": all good Christian tenets. In fact, for a troupe once accused of being dangerously irreligious, they dutifully included the Christian Godhead in each of their major films, and the Trinity comes across as a pretty nice fellow in all three. In *Monty Python and the Holy Grail*, an animated God appears (peering down from the clouds) to give helpful direction—indeed, a unifying quest—to a rather disorganized King Arthur and his silly English kuh-nig-guts; in *Life of Brian*, a well-intentioned Jesus is seen (if not exactly heard) giving his famous Sermon on the Mount to a large and largely uncomprehending crowd; and in *The Meaning of Life,* the Christmas Spirit permeates Heaven, while "Tony Bennett" and a host of plastic-titted chorus girls entertain the recently deceased.[4] In the end, Monty Python's relationship with God—especially as He appears as part of their comic portrayal of Christianity—is far more complicated than it appears at first viewing . . . as is so much of their humor, really.

To better understand Monty Python's take on religion, religious figures, and God, it may be useful to examine who the members of the troupe were, where they came from, and why their uniquely British form of humor remains so happily subversive to this day. To that end, this chapter will examine how Monty Python approached the topic of religion and God, from their initial groundbreaking television series, *Monty Python's Flying Circus* (1969–1974), through their three "proper" films:[5] *Monty Python and the Holy Grail* (1975), *Life of Brian* (1979), and *The Meaning of Life* (1983).

The Pythons

Monty Python may be the Western world's most (in)famous purveyors of surrealistic, high-brow humor and its most erudite purveyors of intellectual comedy, but to many average television or film viewers they remain undervalued as social critics and are remembered primarily for being "exceedingly silly." There is sufficient reason for this. From their earliest incarnation, the troupe has consisted of three budding actor/writers from Cambridge (John Cleese, Graham Chapman, and Eric Idle), two similar blokes from Oxford (Palin and Jones), and a lunatic American ex-pat artist-type (Terry Gilliam). If the Pythons were themselves metatheatrically transformed into a joke, it would start: "An upper-class twit, a colonel, a sleazy emcee, a gumby, a pepperpot, and a naked man walk into a pub . . ."

Before officially forming *Monty Python's Flying Circus*, the six members had worked together—in parts and pieces—on several British Television shows (notably, *At Last the 1948 Show* and *Do Not Adjust Your Set*), and, in one odd case, on a *fumetti* (a photo-comic produced by Gilliam and featuring Cleese). Depending on which Python legend you believe, *Monty Python's Flying Circus* was either conceived as a star vehicle for Cleese (until he roped the others into it) or was an inspired producer's bit of ensemble casting; in either case, the BBC had gathered together some of the best young talent in Britain at the time. Whatever the comic superteam's origin story, they were offered their own Sunday night show on BBC, "in a slot usually reserved for religious programmes."[6] Surprisingly, the fledgling comedians were given unprecedented creative control of the show, mostly because the BBC assumed that no one was actually watching the telly at that time of night anyway.

Despite the initially low expectations of the BBC brass, *Monty Python's Flying Circus* soon became renowned—especially among "insomniacs and intellectuals"—for leading a startling new comedic revolution, one based on the surrealistic and bizarre juxtapositions of skits that skewered authority figures of all stripes. From the most famous political, intellectual, and religious leaders (Stalin, Sartre, and Richelieu) to the most mundane bureaucratic micromanagers (a purveyor of cheesy comestibles, a Minister of Silly Walks, a sniffing media critic), the Pythons lampooned establishment figures relentlessly, exposing the inherent pomposity and grandiosity of all undeserved authority. As we argue in our recent book, *Everything I Ever Needed to Know About _____* I Learned from Monty Python,*[7] Monty Python was not only the funniest and most subversive group of comedians on the BBC in the 1970s; Python remains the richest purveyor of cheesy intellectual humor and metatheatrical comedy ever to break out of a cathode tube. It is our learned contention that no other comic troupe has since produced anything as fresh or consistently innovative as *Monty Python's Flying Circus*.

Indeed, one major problem with *Monty Python's Flying Circus* is that it is so dense in erudition and so complex in theoretical and historical reference that no one could ever successfully imitate its content or, for that matter, its format.[8] Even today, *Monty Python* stands out from the rest of the comedic crop, waiting for a new group of equally innovative comedians to complete, or at least compete with, the work they started . . . but sadly, no one has ever truly risen to the challenge. According to Cleese, Python *did* change modern comedy, "but in a rather negative way because instead of people taking our stuff to the next stage, they avoided it. So it had a rather disappointing effect, which was to close off an avenue for a particular type of humor and I'm surprised that's the way it happened."[9]

Others could try and be as shocking as Python but none would dare take on the sacred Establishment cows that Python so effectively butchered, skewered, masticated, and regurgitated. Of course, Python tackled not just philosophy, art, history, literature, poetry, and mass media, but during their initial television run and later films they took on God as well. From the moment the bedraggled "It's" man crawled to the metaphoric shore of the first *Flying Circus* episode (1969) until the curtain fell on the multiple "meanings" of life in *The Meaning of Life* (1983), the Pythons never stopped "wrassling" with God, the Universe, and Everything.

Despite being revered by many as comedic deities, eventually, and for various reasons, the troupe went their separate ways, although "partial Python" projects involving two or more members often popped up throughout the years. Cleese has since carved out a highly successful acting career in television (starring in the BBC's *Fawlty Towers*) and Hollywood (from the lead in *A Fish Called Wanda* to supporting Daniel Craig's James Bond as the new Q); he has also made a mint in commercials and training films. Gilliam has made a career on the other end of the camera as the controversial director of (often surreal) films ranging from *Time Bandits* and *The Adventures of Baron Munchausen*, to *Brazil*, *The Fisher King*, *Twelve Monkeys*, and *Fear and Loathing in Las Vegas*. In addition to support roles in major films (many of them Gilliam's), the affable Palin has starred in a series of equally affable travelogues, including *Great Railway Journeys of the World*, *Michael Palin: Around the World in Eighty Days*, *Pole to Pole*, and *Full Circle with Michael Palin*. The medieval-minded Jones has pursued his interest in history as a writer and documentarian, following up his critically polarizing book, *Chaucer's Knight: Portrait of a Medieval Mercenary*, with historical television series including *Terry Jones' Medieval Lives* and *Terry Jones' Barbarians*; he has also voiced his social criticism in various newspaper editorials (famously declaring "a war on the war on terror" following U.S. political actions after 9/11).[10] Far less controversially, Idle has worked widely in radio, television, and film, provided voice-acting for cartoons and video games, and toured North America performing old Python sketches and songs on his "Greedy Bastard Tour," all before cocreating *Spamalot*. Finally, Chapman (who, *perhaps* significantly, played God in *MPHG* and "not the Messiah" in *Life of Brian*) has since shuffled off this mortal coil, bereft of life, an ex-Python.[11]

But back in the day, when life was, well, life-lier, the British Pythons grew up in a post–World War II Britain, a land that still held onto vestiges of empire, the class system, the importance of the royal family, and the normative presence of the Church of England. All of the British Pythons grew up attending chapel and were expected to be nominally, if not actively, involved in religious ritual; this early indoctrination echoes throughout their many ritual-heavy religious sketches—including the lengthy sermonizing of Palin in *Monty Python and the Holy Grail* and *The Meaning of Life* ("The Holy Hand Grenade of Antioch" and "O Lord! Oh, you are so big! So absolutely huge. Gosh, we're all really impressed down here, I can tell you" skits, respectively). As with others in their generation, the stifling atmosphere of post-war Britain taught the Pythons the opposite of the intended establishment lesson: Instead of accepting social structures and learning to obey authority, they questioned the status quo and subsequently went on to teach others to question authority as well. As Palin has noted, fans of a similar age shared the way in which they systematically dismantled the structure of normal British life; *Python* was "daring, irreverent, therefore only accessible to those of a certain sort of intellectual status."[12]

Just as the Pythons had their comedic way with a wide variety of establishment figures and groups, they frequently targeted organized religion. As noted, the British members had grown up attending private schools where chapel was compulsory and old hymns were half-muttered/half-sung with all the vigor of a Fleet Street scribe turning down one last free G&T at the opening of a Damien Hirst formaldehyde guppy exhibition. It is probable—based on their own statements over the years—that they more-or-less tolerated such normative traditions of British society in the 1950s. In contrast, Gilliam, the lone American, was quite religious as a young man and at one point briefly considered a career as a Presbyterian missionary. But by the time they had all coalesced into the group responsible for *Monty Python's Flying Circus*, it is difficult to say whether any Python member held onto any serious religious belief at all. What is clear, however, is that they were united by one serious social belief: that the normalized empowerment of authority—whether the BBC, the monarchy, or the Church of England—led to the normalized empowerment of . . . how shall we say this . . . decidedly *silly* behavior. But despite what some critics have argued, they harbored no particular animosity toward belief in general, and certainly held nothing against the life and teaching of Jesus in particular. Given their vicious attacks on myriad authority figures, they were practically benign when it came to God.

Monty Python's Flying Circus[13]

Well before they went on to taunt the Catholic Church for the first (and second) time on the big screen, the Pythons lampooned religion and religious figures on the small screen. The troupe's subversive take on the inherent silliness of both the real and mediated world is readily apparent throughout *Monty Python's Flying Circus*. The Pythons didn't simply deflate our accepted notions about the world, class, society and authority; they challenged the way in which we placidly accept the world around us as real. Just as Python gleefully skewered *all* forms of authority, religious authority—whether incarnated in individual figures or seen as an authority unto itself—periodically came under their satiric crosshairs. *Monty Python's Flying Circus*, a milestone in television for so many reasons,[14] was one of the few shows of the 1960s to tackle difficult questions about theology, faith, and even the existence of God. That the Pythons chose to literally tackle—even wrestle—these topics on screen is but one hallmark of their surrealist humor.

Another mark of their avant-garde humor relied on "fish out of water" scenarios, (an early form of the now-popular "mash-up," really), wherein famous historical figures were contextually displaced—Karl Marx displaced as a gameshow contestant, for example, or Greek philosophers cogitating on a football pitch. In this manner, when religious figures appeared on *Monty Python's Flying Circus*, their religious avocation may have been entirely beside the point. For example, in episode 3, Cardinal Richelieu (Palin) is called upon as an expert character witness in a trial over a parking ticket. Citing Richelieu's influence on the consolidation of France as a global power in the 17th century ("I sure did that thing"), the counsel asks that his expertise be taken into account in the sentencing of the defendant, Harry Larch. Perhaps predictably, this "expert witness" is later revealed by an inspector to be a professional Cardinal Richelieu impersonator and not the real Cardinal Richelieu as promised. (A key piece of evidence pointed out by the constable was that the real Richelieu had been dead for several hundred years.)

Religious inquisitors (Cardinals Ximenez, Biggles, and Fang) appear again as part of the legendary and much feared Spanish Inquisition sketch in episode 15. The legendarily fanatical Catholic zealots burst into the middle of another skit, where a befuddled character proclaims that, while under questioning, he hadn't expected "a sort of Spanish inquisition!" Whereas their abrupt entry may be read as a meta-commentary on the overuse of linguistic clichés, or (conversely) on the inherent power of language (as evidenced by illicit summoning rituals), the unexpected arrival of the Spanish Inquisition can also be read as a commentary on the potentially abusive power of religious authority.

The original Spanish Inquisition was one of the most horrific misuses of power in Church history. As Palin, in the role of Cardinal Ximenez points out in the skit, "Fear is one of our key weapons." As many commentators on the Spanish Inquisition have shown, this statement was entirely true. Toby Green, in his book *Inquisition: The Reign of Fear*, notes that "it was the relentless injustice of the system that created fear among prisoners" during the Inquisition."[15] Any potential heretic could be arrested at any time, for any or no reason, because of even the most unlikely accusation, then locked away as long as the Inquisition thought appropriate and then most likely tortured and eventually executed in public as a lesson for others not to stray into heresy. Luckily for old Lady Mountback in the Python skit, this incarnation of the Spanish Inquisition is too embarrassed after forgetting their "lines" to actually torture her, and aside from putting her in a rather comfy chair and setting a dish rack on her chest, they are powerless to hurt her—their power, centuries removed from their "natural" time period, lacks any real meaning. Without the context of their time period to create fear, the inquisitors are not representative of an overtly violent interpretation of God's will; they are merely a reminder of how laughable it is to torture in the name of God.

A similarly laughable—and in some ways similarly impotent—religious figure to appear in *Monty Python's Flying Circus* is the Reverend Ronald Simms, the Dirty Vicar of St. Michael's (Jones) who simply cannot control his sexual urges despite his own best efforts at making a proper first impression on his parishioners (episode 39). Other notable religious figures include the "dead bishop on the landing," who mysteriously turns up in the "Salvation Fuzz" sketch (episode 29); through the power of prayer (and Gilliam's animation) the Church Police call upon the "hand of God" to come down and point out the culprit. Other appearances by clergy include the noir genre parody, "The Bishop" (episode 17) wherein a rough and tumble (but sadly unnamed) bishop repeatedly arrives too late to stop assassination attempts on church officials. In these sketches, historical religious authority figures are made laughably impotent, while fictional religious authority figures are so radically displaced contextually that they are made comic (*de facto* wizards and detectives in church clothing). Silly stuff, really.

All of these examples focus on God's mortal representatives, of course, and not on God Himself. The Pythons' most direct investigation of God occurs in "Wrestling Epilogue: A Question of Belief" (episode 2). The classic sketch recalls the (now late and lamented) intellectual debate shows of the 1960s and 1970s; Dick Cavett comes to mind, as does William F. Buckley's *Firing Line*. A pompous and overserious introduction from the talk-show host (Cleese) opens the sketch, chiefly recalling the scholastic vitae of participants:

> Good evening, and welcome once again to the Epilogue. On the programme this evening we have Monsignor Edward Gay, visiting Pastoral Emissary of the Somerset Theological College and author of a number

of books about belief, the most recent of which is the best seller "My God." And opposite him we have Dr. Tom Jack: humanist, broadcaster, lecturer, and author of the book "Hello Sailor."

So far, this is a standard—albeit somewhat silly—introduction to a talk show where presumably intellectual issues are to be vocally debated via cagy logic, emotional appeal, and rhetorical flourish. However, Idle abruptly upsets viewer expectations, saying:

> Tonight, instead of discussing the existence or non-existence of God, they have decided to fight for it. The existence, or non-existence, to be determined by two falls, two submissions, or a knockout.

At this point in the sketch, the debaters move to a literal wrestling ring, where the scholars are revealed to be professional wrestlers who circle each other and physically engage in some form of Greco-Roman/professional wrestling. The stakes, of course, are a tad higher than a mundane title or championship belt: God is on the line.

During the bout, the commentator follows the traditional clichés and cadence of sportscasting, announcing to the audience that, "Dr. Jack's got a flying mare there. A flying mare there, and this is going to be a full body slam. A full body slam, and he's laying it in there, and he's standing back. Well . . . there we are leaving the Epilogue for the moment, we'll be bringing you the result of this discussion later on in the programme." Thankfully, by the end of this second episode of *Monty Python's Flying Circus*, viewers learn (spoiler alert!) that the good Lord has been proven to be a "real" deity, the decision coming via "two falls to a submission."[16] Python often wrestled with important issues on their program, but it was rare when the existential stakes were this high.

Although the "Wrestling Epilogue" may be a silly sketch, and at first blush hardly offers a ringing endorsement of God's eternal existence, it is a far cry from the comic dismissal of God by Python-friend and sometime contributor Douglas Adams. In Adams's (increasingly ill-named) *Hitchhiker's Trilogy*, God Himself logically proves His own nonexistence, an unintended result of His Own creation of the "mind-bogglingly useful" babel fish. The argument—as it appears in *The Hitchhiker's Guide to the Galaxy* (1979)—is pointed:

> "I refuse to prove that I exist," says God, "for proof denies faith, and without faith I am nothing."

"But," says Man, "the Babel fish is a dead giveaway, isn't it? It could not have evolved by chance. It proves that You exist, and so therefore, by Your own arguments, You don't. QED"

"Oh dear," says God, "I hadn't thought of that," and promptly vanishes in a puff of logic.[17]

By comparison, the Pythons—far from denying God's existence or shouting proatheism slogans—grant God their stamp of approval in the "Wrestling Epilogue." The methods by which humans come to determine God's existence (Greco-Roman wrestling being but one example), on the other hand, are called into question as a means of intellectual debate. Is it any sillier, the Pythons seem to ask, for humans to verbally debate the existence of an all-powerful, all-knowing, ineffable God than it is for His creatures to physically debate His existence in the squared circle? This was, of course, long before the public learned that most of wrestling was fixed, so make of that what you will.

Monty Python and the Holy Grail

If the "Wrestling Epilogue" (1969) attempted to justify God's existence—via a reversal of the old medieval "trial-by-combat" motif (wherein God enacts justice in the mundane world by providentially ensuring that only the righteous remain victorious in battle)—then *Monty Python and the Holy Grail* (1975) dispenses any lingering doubt among their viewers; in this twisted take on Arthurian legend, God exists: no ifs, ands, or buts. And no groveling! (He hates that.)

Oral references to God (fewer blasphemes than you'd think), the Bible (via the obscure *Book of Armaments*), and religious figures (chanting penitent monks who repeatedly ask Jesus to "give us rest," while ceaselessly smacking themselves in the head with wooden planks) litter the landscape of *Holy Grail* and show that, although the film has no beef with God directly, there is still plenty of bloody criticism available for silly religious practices, questionable Establishment icons, and dubious claims of authority. It is also a fairly accurate portrayal of the central role of religion in medieval public life. To *not* evoke religious belief would have spoiled the mood of the film.

One way of invoking the ubiquitous belief of the time is to invoke the god of the time, repeatedly.[18] King Arthur (Chapman), for example, insistently invokes the Lord's name throughout the film. These invocations are generally intended as sufficient justification for Arthur's divinely sanctioned actions, and are just as generally ignored by anyone with "an outrageous French accent." As a result, the Pythons insistently remind viewers of the limits of secondhand authority. Arthur may be "charged by God with a sacred quest," but his own authority is questioned and undermined at every turn, most famously by the "Constitutional Peasants" of scene 4 ("How'd you get to be king, eh?"). And, just as many kingly figures (middle-management types) are wont to do when confronted with peasants (minimum-wage earners) who refuse to recognize their own overblown sense of authority, Arthur is reduced to shouting impotently before walking off in a huff to the next castle (cubicle). Arthur's overreliance upon a fallacious *argumentum ab auctoritate*—his rhetorical "argument from authority"—reveals his own tenuous authority within the film and the tenuous authority of all who argue for authority via authority.

As with Arthur's vocal appeal to authority, textual appeal to authority—even a text as revered as *The Book of Armaments*—is likewise problematized, at least generically, in the film. Like the Bible (and many other oral-literate repositories of authority), *The Book of Armaments* is replete with authoritative wisdom, but not everything recorded, the Pythons seem to say, is worth reading/revering.

Outside the Cave of Caerbannog (in scenes 21–22), Arthur is presented with a decidedly deadly *globus cruciger*, a golden bejeweled orb surmounted by a cross—essentially a ringer for the Sovereign's Cross. Part of the British Crown Jewels and among the most recognizable icons of the British Monarch, the Sovereign's Cross denotes the British Monarch's authority as Defender of the Faith: Nothing could be more symbolically apt, as monarchs since Charles II have held the orb—and thus symbolically the entire Christian world—in the palm of their hand. A more obviously violent version of this long-revered Establishment icon, the Holy Hand Grenade of Antioch, will enable Arthur might smite his deadly foe, the "cute little bunny," which has just decimated his most puissant knights. But before he lobbeth the grenade, the gathered friars (in particular Palin) offer Arthur instruction on the use of the divine device, via a reading from *The Book of Armaments* (in language and cadence recalling readings from the King James Bible):

> And Saint Attila raised the hand grenade up on high, saying, "O Lord, bless this Thy hand grenade that with it Thou mayest blow Thine enemies to tiny bits, in Thy mercy." And the Lord did grin and the people did feast upon the lambs and sloths and carp and anchovies and orangutans and breakfast cereals and fruit bats and large chu . . .

Brother Maynard (Idle) then urges Brother Maynard's Brother (Palin) to "skip on a bit, Brother." Even though in the end *The Book of Armaments* and the Holy Hand Grenade prove quite effective (despite Arthur's numerological handicap), the presentation of these two symbols of divine authority as only selectively useful or inherently violent casts some doubt upon their assumed grace. Literary authority—like any other earthly authority—is thus questioned by the Pythons. Heck, even God admits that the "miserable Psalms [are] so depressing."

Yet if Python presents all mortal authority—literary, iconic, or human— as inherently flawed, God is presented with a bit more sympathy. Entering the film in scene 7, God—here depicted in all His two-dimensional glory by the talented but deranged Terry Gilliam and voiced with impatient gravitas by the talented but (then-)detoxing Graham Chapman—graces Arthur with a "good idea" (of course): to seek the Holy Grail and thus present his knights as "an example in these dark times." As in the medieval tradition (from Chrétien de Troyes onward), the Lord's sacred quest is a good idea . . . it's just the human execution of the quest that is faulty. In *Monty Python and the Holy Grail*, the various knights fare variously in their quests for the grail: Sir Lancelot (The Brave) violently attempts to rescue an imprisoned maid from Swamp Castle, only to find he has been "catfished";[19] Sir Galahad (The Pure) nearly suffers untold pleasures at the hands (and lips and . . . erm . . . never mind) of the lonely maidens of Castle Anthrax before being "rescued" by his (traditionally) adulterous dad; and, of course, Sir Robin (The-Not-Quite-So-Brave-As-Sir-Lancelot) scarpers at the first three-headed sign of trouble. Again, it is not God that the Pythons lampoon in these scenes, but as seen previously in the television series, God's faulty servants (and in this case, the medieval tropes they represent).

God exists in *Monty Python and the Holy Grail*: of that there can be no doubt. His presence permeates the reel medieval landscape, just as it would have in the real European Middle Ages. *Monty Python and the Holy Grail* is, comedy aside, a lovingly rendered depiction of Medieval Europe—warts, filth, and all. God's existence could no more be denied within that cinéma vérité than could the existence of the legendary King Arthur himself, or that of the most holy and eponymous of grails. The fact that Terry Gilliam chose to use the visage of "the greatest cricketer of all time"—W. G. Grace (1848–1915)—as the template for his glaring, wildly bearded, Old Testament God in Heaven, may either be a tremendous insight into Python's uniquely British attitude, a coy play on William Gilbert's surname and God's gift of salvation, or a convenient clipping of a fellah with a big ol' bushy beard.[20] Like God, the workings of Python—and the workings of the self-appointed "St. Paul that brought the Christianity of Monty to America"—remain in many ways ineffable.[21]

Life of Brian

When *Monty Python's Life of Brian* was released in 1979, the troupe was almost immediately attacked as being willfully offensive (at least) and downright sacrilegious (at best/worst). The film was decried by enthusiastic critics (many of whom had not actually seen the film) as a deliberate and tasteless attack on Christianity. Yet, to more reflective viewers, it seems as though the main point of the film was actually not to be impious at all. In fact, as is well documented in accounts of the making of the film,[22] Python never directly attacks or even criticizes the teachings of Jesus Christ in particular; nor do they mock *his* divinity. Instead, as usual, the Pythons question the tendency of organized religion to preach mindless obedience rather than free thinking: the issue at stake is authority, not divinity.

While preparing the film, the Oxbridge comedians decided to deflect some obvious sources of criticism by extensively rereading the Gospels and rediscovered their laudable and humanistic message. Although Idle has—the scamp!—often delighted in recounting his initial titular inspiration for the film ("Jesus Christ: Lust for Glory!"), upon rereading the Gospels, the Pythons discarded the idea of satirizing Jesus and instead chose to attack those who took to religion for the sake of zealous orthodoxy rather than to actually follow what Jesus had preached in the gospels. Idle once summarized *Life of Brian* as "an attack on churches and pontificators and self-righteous assholes that claim to speak for God, of whom there are still too many on the planet."[23] The Pythons wanted to understand *not* why so many people put their spiritual faith in God, but rather why so many followed mundane religious authority without question.

Python had chosen a deliberately provocative topic, to be sure, but they meant to satirize blind obedience to authority rather than piety. *Life of Brian* was emphatically *not* about Jesus; the Pythons made it clear again and again in the film that although the movie was taking place at the time of Jesus, Brian was not meant to be a "stand-in" for Jesus. In fact, Jesus cameos as a background character early in the film (scene 2), thus bypassing any possible confusion or conflation of the two characters. Brian cannot, in fact, be Jesus, as he in fact attends a sermon given by Jesus. He is not, emphatically, a nebbishy Clark Kent to the divine Superman. Furthermore, the comedy of the "Sermon on the Mount" scene derives not from the words Jesus utters, but from the misunderstanding of his words among the masses. (To be fair, the crowd *was* rather large . . . like Brian's nose.)

Nevertheless, the film caused predictable controversy. Under the almost too predictable storm of outrage that followed the release of *Life of Brian*, many who never saw the film people did not realize how much time Python spent in constructing the film in order to *avoid* antagonizing the faithful. (Admittedly, there was probably no way to handle the topic that would not have upset some people.) Python tried, perhaps in vain, to parody blind obedience to religious dogma, not the many positive benefits of a belief system. At the height of the controversy, Palin jotted down in his diary that it was frustrating that some people didn't "get" *Life of Brian*, noting that the main theme of the film was "power—its use and abuse by an establishment."[24] Sadly, many religious leaders took the film to be an attack against religion and belief, rather than a corrective against needless orthodoxy.

There is always more to a Python film than meets the eye, and in retrospect, it is clear that *Life of Brian* has many disparate points to make. Some are clearer than others. The Roman Occupation comes across as a running gag about stern British authority figures (more like schoolmasters than occupiers); the schisms among the squabbling Judaic revolutionary groups all come across as patently silly, self-defeatist, and unlikely to make any real changes if they ever did come into power. The very idea that one organization is better than all others reveals not a revolutionary spirit, but rather a tendency toward authoritarianism—anathema to the Pythons, at least in theory.

Palin later reflected back on the making of *Life of Brian* and noted that what they were trying to do in the film was to emphasize a "Python ideology," where the group was "really resisting people telling you how to behave and how not to behave. It was the freedom of the individual, a very 60s thing, the independence which was part of the way Python had been formed, the way Python had gone on, and the way Python had sort of arrogantly assumed that whatever we did was right and whatever other people did was wrong."[25] The Pythons were keenly aware of how far they had gone in treading unprecedented comedic ground. As a result, even the Pythons could come across as self-assured to the point of arrogance, which may well have cost them much of their momentum as filmmakers and most likely some of their hard earned global reputation as innovative and daring comedians. The Pythons had grown up in a post-war Great Britain as the British Empire was finally crumbling; all the world watched as they lost control of more and more of their former colonies. Palin noted that an unstated theme of *Brian* was "the whole British imperialism which was something we were all brought up on."[26] Whenever Python challenged the hegemony, whether making fun of the monarchy or the Church of

England, they felt resistance because, as Palin put it, "People in power don't like comedy because it's essentially subversive."[27] Perhaps the real objections to *Life of Brian* were not just its perceived attacks on Christianity, but also how they challenged the way in which some human beings had, throughout history, used organized religion as a convenient cover for gaining temporal power.

The only American member of Python, Terry Gilliam, thought that Americans would see the film differently than the English audience, stating that during "*Life of Brian*, in a strange way we were being very cautious about not being blasphemous, by being totally blasphemous but about another guy. My mother, an avid church-goer, saw it but she didn't have a problem because it wasn't about Jesus."[28] Even though Gilliam's mother's critique did little to mollify persistent criticism, it may also have been the fact that many were far too outraged to actually *see* the film and make a thoughtful critique based on the film's merits. Cleese summed up the Pythons' quandary with *Life of Brian* by pointing out that "Quite genuinely I don't know how you could try to be funny about Jesus' life, there would be no point in it. What is absurd is not the teachings of the founders of religion, it's what followers subsequently make of it. And I was always astonished that people didn't get."[29] And Cleese was right: The subject matter alone was enough to cause suspicion (rightfully in some cases) that Python made a career out of exposing all forms of organized authority as illegitimate and silly. The Pythons (and many of their fans) continue to defend the film to this day, with Cleese remarking that on *Life of Brian*, "We were making some very good jokes about some very important things";[30] unfortunately, their well-intended and important humor did not readily come across to the general public. The critiques did one important thing though; they sharpened the Pythons' already formidable debate skills.

As the BBC gives more time to serious debate than most of the rest of the world, it was only a matter of time before the members of Python were invited to debate the merits of *Life of Brian* on national television. Palin and Cleese were invited to participate in a televised debate with long-time writer and British public intellectual Malcolm Muggeridge as well as the Bishop of Southwark. The producer had assured them that the tone would be civil, and after meeting the Bishop backstage, Cleese and Palin thought that the debate would not be rancorous but instead a thoughtful exchange of ideas. However, when it came to airtime, things were quite different than expected. Cleese and Palin were both quickly attacked by both the Bishop and Muggeridge. (The latter had arrived late to the show and also had not found the time in his busy schedule to actually view the film he condemned.)

Muggeridge had little patience for Cleese and Palin's defense of the film and was dismissive of the Pythons' point of view, which led to a heated and memorable exchange: "When he [Muggeridge] said that Christianity had been responsible for more good in the world than any other force in history, John said, 'What about the Spanish Inquisition?'"[31] Unfortunately, like a pantomime Queen Victoria, Muggeridge and the Bishop were "not amused." Although the Pythons were never going to win over many critics with *Life of Brian*, they made a valuable and hilarious contribution to the debate over the position of organized religion in civic society. The stakes could scarce be higher . . . or could they?

The Meaning of Life

Monty Python's The Meaning of Life (1983) opens with a school of existentially minded fish (metaphor!) looking upon the death of their fellow fish, Howard. A musical number then helpfully outlines the film's *raison d'etre*: Monty Python is going to finally "sort it all out" for their viewers and parse the "meaning of life." Now, as philosophers throughout the ages have argued, "the meaning of life" is itself a riddle wrapped in an enigma, a question that raises a series of subquestions, including "Is God really real?" and (assuming the previous question holds positive) whether humans are "just one of God's little jokes." Of course, this being a Monty Python joint, the answers are ambiguous (if not mutually contradictory) and the overall experience rather surreal. Come to think of it, the film is very much like life. Makes you think, doesn't it?

On the one hand, the film's organization seems grounded in conventional logic: Chapters progress with chronological certitude from "The Miracle of Birth" to "Growth and Learning," "Middle Age," "The Autumn Years," and finally "Death." On the other hand, additional chapters are peppered throughout—including "Fighting Each Other," "Find the Fish," "Live Organ Transplants," and "The Meaning of Life"—which remind viewers of Python's surrealistic tendencies and, perhaps, the unpredictability of life itself. In the end, the Pythons do not (spoiler alert!) reveal whether God is "really real," whether humans are just one of (a potentially real) God's "little jokes," or whether there is, in fact, any meaning at all to life. As Palin's pepperpot film critic summates metatheatrically at the end of the film: "Where's the fun in pictures?"

The Pythons' final film is, like most early *Monty Python's Flying Circus* episodes, a series of loosely connected sketches. All at least tangentially contribute to an understanding of life. Somehow. Metaphor is often involved. A cartoon stork (LIFE) appears to drop a baby down a chimney.

Martin Luther (RELIGION) appears in a deleted scene. Death (DEATH) appears alongside the salmon mousse. But God (GOD) never appears, at least not directly (a baby Jesus is presumably in the manger scene near the end of the film, but his role is so limited he didn't even need a SAG card).[32] It's almost as if the Pythons chose to excise God from His creation, from the meaning of life, rather than incite that particular controversy again. However, as usual, the Pythons are not shy about lampooning the authority of religion. As a most fertile Yorkshire Christian (Palin) notes to his many, many destitute children (whom he must now sell "for scientific experiment"):

> Blame the Catholic Church for not letting me wear one of those little rubber things. Oh, they've done some wonderful things in their time: they preserved the might and majesty, even the mystery of the Church of Rome, the sanctity of the sacrament and the indivisible oneness of the Trinity, but if they'd let me wear one of the little rubber things on the end of my cock we wouldn't be in the mess we are now.

Following this overt critique of that Catholic Church's views on birth control, the children (as well as nearby Cardinals, nuns, priests, mourners, jugglers, and so forth) launch into the highly controversial "Every Sperm Is Sacred" musical number. The carrying on of the neighborhood Christians escalates into the streets and is subsequently noticed by a prim-and-proper Protestant couple (Chapman and Idle) taking tea.

As the "fiercely proudly" Protestant husband, Mr. Blackitt, opines: "When Martin Luther nailed his protest up to the church door in 1517, he may not have realized the full significance of what he was doing"; this is, historically speaking, very likely true. Luther never intended to start a Reformation; nor did he, even in the Pythonverse, intend to start the prophylactic industry. Yet as far as Chapman's rant is concerned, wearing condoms (or French Ticklers, Black Mambos, and Crocodile Ribs) is "what being a Protestant's all about." Typical of their "extreme limit" humor, Python reduces the most significant religious event of the 16th century to a dick joke. But they leave God out of it.

Conclusion

At the end of the day, after all the controversy and debate, the question remains: Why did the Pythons take the piss out of organized religion with such gusto? The best way, we feel, of justifying their comedic targets is to note how consistent they were in their overall critique. Any establishment was ripe for satire, whether it was the monarchy, the BBC, or even the Lord. Python was not impiously attacking belief for the sake of controversy, but blind obedience and conformity.

In the critical collection *Monty Python and Philosophy*, Stephen Faison argues that, "By lampooning reactions to God's omnipresence in our lives, the Pythons compel us to examine this [doctrinally based] relationship."[33] The Pythons may satirize, ridicule, and lampoon religious leaders, religious organizations, and religious icons, but they do so from an assumption of "God's omnipresence in our lives." This is not to say that Monty Python believed in God, but they understood that the world—flawed, funny old place that it is—was inhabited by folks who did.

God help us all.

Notes

1. Truth be told, any Gumby's answer to any question will more likely include the phrases "urm," "gorn," and "who?"

2. Although that last bit turned out to be a bit of a three-way dodge, eh?

3. Naturally, once someone invented the internets, they invaded that too. Probably the webbies as well.

4. Granted, the representation of the last third of the Trinity is a bit of a cheat, but then the Holy Spirit is traditionally the least photogenic member of the Godhead.

5. We ignore, for now, their various concert films and *And Now for Something Completely Different*, which remade several previous sketches for a film release.

6. Richard Topping, *Monty Python: A Celebration* (London: Virgin Books, 1999), 13.

7. Brian Cogan and Jeff Massey, *Everything I Ever Needed to Know About _____* I Learned from Monty Python* (New York: Thomas Dunne, 2014). It makes an excellent Christmas, Ramadan, or Hanukah gift.

8. Although one could certainly catalogue it. See Darl Larsen, *Monty Python's Flying Circus: An Utterly Complete, Thoroughly Unillustrated, Absolutely Unauthorized Guide to Possibly All the References, from Arthur "Two Sheds" Jackson to Zambesi* (Lanham, MD: Scarecrow Press, 2008) for a fine compendium of "all the references."

9. Bob McCabe, ed., *The Pythons Autobiography by The Pythons* (New York: St. Martin's Press, 2003), 350.

10. Jones's scholarly efforts have attracted critical attention for some time, culminating in the recent academic collection, *The Medieval Python: The Purposive and Provocative Work of Terry Jones*, ed. R. F. Yeager and Toshiyuki Takayima (New York: Palgrave Macmillan, 2012).

11. Although he did come back, briefly, for the Python reunion in Aspen. Sorta.

12. David Morgan, *Monty Python Speaks!: The Complete Oral History of Monty Python, as Told by the Founding Members and a Few of their Many Friends and Collaborators* (New York: Harper, 2005), 71–72.

13. All citations from *Flying Circus* episodes are drawn from Graham Chapman, Eric Idle, Terry Gilliam, John Cleese, Terry Jones, and Michael Palin, *The Complete Monty Python's Flying Circus: All the Words*, vols. 1 and 2 (New York: Pantheon, 1989).

14. Shameless plug #2: see Cogan and Massey, *Everything I Ever Needed To Know*, 76–18, 272–75.

15. Toby Green, *Inquisition: The Reign of Fear* (New York: St. Martin's Press, 2007), 82.

16. It is perhaps worth noting that, while this episode aired second, it was the first one filmed by the Pythons. They established—very early on—the existence of God in the Pythonverse.

17. Douglas Adams, *The Hitchhiker's Guide to the Galaxy* (New York: Pocket Books, 1979), 59–61. See also Michèle Friend. "God . . . Promptly Vanishes in a Puff of Logic," in *Philosophy and the Hitchhiker's Guide*, ed. Nicholas Joll (New York: Palgrave Macmillan, 2012), 185–212.

18. Although historically, that would have been a no-no.

19. According to the MTV promotional website for the TV show of the same name, "to catfish" is "to pretend to be someone you're not online by posting false information, such as someone else's pictures, on social media sites usually with the intention of getting someone to fall in love with you." MTV, "About Catfish: The TV Show," *Catfish: The TV Show*, March 17, 2014, http://www.mtv.com/shows/catfish/. While Prince Herbert may not have intentionally mislead Sir Lancelot, the end result is similar (especially if one takes *Spamalot* into consideration—but that's another story). As with the mash-up phenomenon, Monty Python predicted the internets yet again.

20. John Cleese, Terry Gilliam, Eric Idle, Terry Jones, and Michael Palin, "Commentaries," Disc 2, *Monty Python and the Holy Grail*, directed by Terry Gilliam and Terry Jones (Culver City, CA: Columbia TriStar Home Entertainment, 2001), special ed. DVD.

21. Steve Marsh, "The Vulture Transcript: Terry Gilliam Gets Real About the Making of *Monty Python and the Holy Grail*," *The Vulture*, April 4, 2012, accessed March 17, 2014, http://www.vulture.com/2012/04/terry-gilliam-monty-python-and-the-holy-grail-interview.html.

22. See, for example, Kim "Howard" Johnson, *Monty Python's Tunisian Holiday* (New York: Thomas Dunne, 2008).

23. Topping, *Monty Python: A Celebration*, 226.

24. Michael Palin, *Halfway to Hollywood: Diaries 1980–1988* (New York: Thomas Dunne, 2009), 594.

25. McCabe, *The Pythons*, 306.

26. Morgan, *Monty Python Speaks!*, 226.

27. Ibid., 237.

28. McCabe, *The Pythons*, 279.

29. Ibid., 280.

30. Ibid., 307.

31. Ibid., 301.

32. This was not the first time that God did not make the final cut in a Python film. According to DVD legend, one lost idea for *Holy Grail* was that Brian would escape from the cross and run to a getaway car where "God, visibly nervous" waited for him.

33. Stephen Faison, "God Forgive Us," in *Monty Python and Philosophy: Nudge Nudge, Think Think!*, ed. Gary L. Hardcastle and George A. Reisch (Chicago: Open Court, 2006), 126–27.

God and Politics and Commerce

CHAPTER FIVE

God in the Well of the Senate

Jeremy G. Mallory

Margaret Bayard Smith thought "the gay community who thronged the H[ouse] of R[epresentatives] looked very little like a religious assembly," according to her letters documenting life in Washington at the beginning of the 20th century.[1] Even though "[t]he marches [the Marine Band] played were good and inspiring," "their attempts to accompany the psalm-singing of the congregation" were ineffective, and "after a while, the practice was discontinued—it was *too* ridiculous."[2] Rather than a sober religious observance, the services seemed more like an occasion for the "youth, beauty, and fashion of the city" to mingle. "[S]miles, nods, whispers, nay sometimes tittering marked their recognition of each other, and beguiled the tedium of the service."[3]

To a contemporary American, the possibility of a religious service being held in the seat of government by an ordained minister on the public payroll evokes cognitive dissonance. Nevertheless, the congressional chaplains have been an entrenched part of the federal government since before the Revolution. The relative quiescence of the congressional chaplains contrasts, however, with the troubled, litigious history of state, county, municipal, and other local chaplains, culminating in *Town of Greece v. Galloway* heard by the Supreme Court in November 2013.

What accounts for the differences between the two types of chaplain is also the key to understanding what role this bizarre office has played in American culture: congressional chaplains tend to face "inward," focusing on their obligations to the legislative body; chaplains at other levels of government tend to face "outward," representing their faith to the public through prayer at public occasions. I suggest that the nonpublic nature of congressional chaplains makes them authoritative figures in popular culture.

The inward-facing nature of congressional chaplains links them to an idealized America, a dreamlike notion of the nation that permeates our shared culture.[4] Concretely, congressional chaplains allow us to believe that something slightly more noble than venality (might) guide (some) decisions in Congress. Constructively, such a hope illuminates a conception of legislative ethics that goes beyond mere non-maleficence, embodying the ideal "public office is a public trust."[5]

What Are These Chaplains and How Can They Be Legal?

Concisely put, chaplains are people—almost always ordained clergy—who pray in front of legislative bodies, usually for the legislators in their public capacities. Some are paid from the public fisc. Although they seem like obvious violations of the Establishment Clause of the First Amendment, the issue was not litigated to the Supreme Court until 1983, when it held that congressional chaplains are constitutional,[6] more or less as a bald-faced exception to the Establishment Clause.[7]

Legislative chaplains fall into two broad categories according to how they are appointed, which happens to coincide with the level of government: the federal Congress employs "situated" (appointed) chaplains; other levels of government have "rotating" chaplains who are selected to give individual invocations.[8]

Situated chaplains appear, from the outside, more like a traditional pastoral chaplain. The congressional chaplains are appointed under each chamber's power to select its own officers.[9] A chaplain is thus "an officer of the house which chooses him and nothing more."[10] Historically, chaplains served for a year or two then another was selected, generally as a "spoil" handed out by the majority party. Over time, they came to hold office for longer periods. The first sitting chaplain "lost" an election in 1947, when Frederick Brown Harris was replaced by Peter Marshall.[11] From that point, chaplains were generally reappointed as a courtesy until they decided to retire. These chaplains regard the whole legislative body as their congregation, often extending that care to family and staff as well.[12]

Rotating chaplains, by contrast, are appointed by a variety of means. In *Simpson v. Chesterfield County*, a case involving a Wiccan priestess who applied to deliver an invocation, the chaplain was selected by a "random" selection from a phone book plus a list of volunteers.[13] In the case of *Hinrichs v. Speaker of the House*, which evaluated the Indiana General Assembly's chaplaincy practices, chaplains were selected by the Speaker of the House with recommendations from individual legislators.[14]

Rotating chaplains have been the focus of controversy. In *Hinrichs*, a pastor caused several legislators to walk out in protest after leading a revival-style round of "Just a Little Talk with Jesus."[15] After applying to pray in front of the Chesterfield (Virginia) County Board of Supervisors, the Wiccan priestess's parrot was beheaded and stuffed into her mailbox with a note saying "You're Next!"[16] Her application was denied after she was derided as "a good witch like Glenda" whose faith was "a mockery."[17] Although these offices have also long existed, they have spawned many more lawsuits than the situated congressional chaplains.

For the time being,[18] one of the few clear legal points about legislative chaplains is that they are constitutional.[19] Federal appeals courts show no record of litigation over the question until *Marsh v. Chambers* reached the Supreme Court in 1983. To the extent any clear holding arises from *Marsh*, it is simply that congressional chaplaincies are constitutional.[20] Despite the fact that "perhaps no other Establishment Clause topic has seen as much litigation" over the last decade,[21] legislative chaplaincies are regarded as a "sideshow."[22] At the end of his class on the First Amendment, one law professor asks his class to pick out one decision that they feel was in error and propose either a judicial or constitutional fix; each year, *Marsh* has beat out even more controversial decisions such as *Citizens United*.[23]

At the same time, legislative chaplaincies are both reviled and utterly uncontroversial. On the one hand, congressional chaplains have been an integral part of the legislative body itself and popular exponents of ways to work out the duality of living faith in a political world. On the other hand, as Justice Brennan put it, they are a violation of the Establishment Clause, obvious to "any group of law students."[24] Even though they have existed since before the Revolution, only one popular movement arose (in the early 1850s) to have the offices banned, and it was turned back by Congress in ringing terms: "If there be a God who hears prayer—as we believe there is—we submit, that there never was a deliberative body that so eminently needed the fervent prayers of righteous men as the Congress of the United States."[25]

Chaplains in Popular Culture

Although situated chaplains have been more uncontroversial, they have also been far better known than more local chaplains. Although the congressional chaplains are obscure, occupants of the office have held fame beyond their individual chambers. Over time this entry into popular culture has been deepened. The rotating chaplains at other levels of government, by contrast, have never gained traction in culture (outside of court cases).

The Treasonous First Chaplain: Jacob Duché

The first chaplain to the Continental Congress and the Constitutional Convention, Jacob Duché, started the office off with a polarizing bang. He was known for penning "priggish and affected"[26] poetry, including a paean to "George the Good."[27] Nevertheless, in 1774 the Continental Congress appointed him to deliver an opening prayer each day.[28] As an Anglican priest, his appointment held a particular potency as a symbol.[29] As rumors of a British bombardment of Boston were arriving in Philadelphia, Duché delivered the appointed psalm[30] and launched into an extemporaneous prayer that deeply moved the assembly[31] and became the basis for one of the stained-glass panels in the Liberty Window of Christ Church Cathedral in Philadelphia.

Nevertheless, the Declaration of Independence was too much for Duché. Not long after assuming his duties as chaplain to a now-explicitly-independent Congress in July of 1776, he resigned his post in October.[32] In September 1777, after the British took Philadelphia, Duché reinstated the prayers for the king, which had been omitted since the Revolution began.[33] To seal his change of heart, he wrote to General George Washington, pleading with him to "represent to Congress the indispensable Necessity of rescinding the hasty and ill-advised declaration of Independency."[34] The first congressional chaplain lambasted Congress as "bankrupts, attorneys, and men of desperate fortunes."[35] In the most vivid terms he exhorted Washington to surrender.[36] Washington turned the letter over to Congress, bringing Duché's career to "a disastrous end."[37] John Adams, who had earlier praised Duché highly for his homiletics, wrote to Abigail: "Mr. Duché, I am sorry to inform you, has turned out an apostate and traitor. Poor man! I pity his weakness and detest his wickedness."[38]

The Catholic Chaplain: Charles Constantine Pise

In 1832, during a period when anti-Catholic sentiment in the United States was palpable, Sen. Henry Clay nominated a Jesuit priest, Charles Constantine Pise, to be the Senate Chaplain.[39] Pise had only been ordained in 1825[40] but was already making a name for himself in literary circles, with an unsuccessful history of the Roman Catholic Church and a more successful foray into fiction.[41] He was also active in countering the anti-Catholic screeds popular at the time.[42] After defeating strong opposition to his appointment as Senate Chaplain, he delivered an *apologium* in a speech before the Maryland House of Delegates:

I acknowledge no allegiance to [the pope's] temporal power; I am not subject to his dominions; I have sworn no fealty to his throne; but I am, as all American Catholics glory to be, independent to all foreign temporal authority, devoted to freedom, to unqualified toleration, to republican institutions.[43]

After he left the chaplaincy in 1833, he became "an acknowledged controversialist,"[44] defending the Roman Catholic Church against charges of anti-Americanism, including a patriotic poem called "The American Flag," which gained some repute.[45] Despite the rising tide of anti-Catholicism of the time, a Catholic priest (Jesuit, no less) who was already known for defending Catholic interests became the Senate Chaplain and continued articulately advocating for his faith in literary salons of the day.

The Celebrity Chaplain: Peter Marshall

Although Peter Marshall gained office through an unprecedented ousting of the prior chaplain and held it for only two years, his tenure marked a dramatic change. Over those two years, "Peter Marshall had become more than a leader in his denomination; he was a recognized spiritual leader for all America."[46] Even the *Washington Post* commented on the change in tone after the Presbyterian minister took office: "Till Dr. Marshall came to the Senate 2 years ago, the Senators had heard a more or less perfunctory sort of 'grace' before they began their deliberations. The Presbyterian minister opened the ears of the bowed Senators to his words of prayer, and he put those words alongside their subsequent speeches."[47] Marshall identified himself as "the conscience of the Senate," stating that "[t]he Senators may not want me long for their chaplain, but I must speak out."[48]

Marshall died suddenly in office in 1949. His wife Catherine immediately published a collection of his sermons (*Mr. Jones, Meet the Master*), then wrote a book based on his life that became a commercially successful movie (*A Man Called Peter*).[49] Many people first became acquainted with the office of the chaplaincy through these books and the movie—legislative chaplains entered into popular culture in a decisive manner.[50]

Contemporary Chaplains: Lloyd John Ogilvie and Barry C. Black

When Lloyd John Ogilvie was selected as the Senate Chaplain in 1995, the Capitol Hill publication *Roll Call* trumpeted, "New Senate Chaplain: Direct from Hollywood."[51] By this time, the Senate was vastly more diverse than it had been for many decades: "Thirteen denominations of Christianity are represented among the senators, and Ogilvie trie[d] to craft a prayer that isolate[d] none of them" as well as giving a prayer reflective of the religious themes behind the Jewish High Holy Days.[52] In 1995, he held the first Passover Seder in the Capitol.[53] Ogilvie was also charged with maintaining *gravitas* and decorum through difficult national events such as the impeachment trial of President Bill Clinton[54] and the attacks on the World Trade Center in 2001.

Barry Black, the first Seventh-day Adventist appointed as Senate Chaplain, gained a reputation during the government shutdown of 2013. His invocations took Congress to task for permitting the shutdown to occur, imploring God to "[f]orgive them for the blunders they have committed."[55] His prayers were even parodied on *Saturday Night Live* by comedian Kenan Thompson, paraphrased as "bless these braying jackasses."[56]

The Chaplain's Two Faces

Congressional chaplains have firmly entered popular culture but seem antithetical to popular conceptions of the separation of church and state. Even though they clearly appear to violate the Establishment Clause, they are a constitutional exception. How can we understand these two faces of the office and how it has persisted despite these deep conflicts?

The key piece of evidence lies in comparing the amount of controversy over the different types of chaplain: Despite the flurry of litigation regarding the rotating chaplains found in state, county, and municipal legislative bodies,[57] *no litigation whatsoever* regarding the chaplains in Congress has reached an appeals court since 1987.[58] One method of practicing the office has resulted in interminable conflict, and the other has been ratified by the Supreme Court as constitutional, entered the popular imagination, and has become essentially uncontroversial.

Perhaps the reason situated chaplains have become so widely accepted is their inward focus. As the evolution of the office shows, they remain focused on pastoral care to a diverse congregation.[59] Even as Black said what was on many people's minds during the government shutdown, he declined subsequent interviews and faded back into his role.[60] These chaplains have become known for reaching across denominational lines without being self-consciously ecumenical.[61] Even *Marsh* pointed out that the chaplain in question modified his prayers after a conversation with several Jewish legislators.[62]

However, rotating chaplains, such as those in state legislature, are outward-facing. Although they speak from the same well, they tend to orient more toward the gallery than to the legislature. In these cases, the chaplain acts more "as a member[], leader[], or spokesperson[] of particular religions,"[63] rather than "an officer of the house which chooses him and nothing more."[64] These rotational practices have invoked difficult questions of how chaplains are selected as well as the prayers they deliver.[65]

The different methods of selection (situated/appointed versus rotating/volunteer) have given rise to different ways of practicing the office (inward- vs. outward-facing). One of those practices has followed a tranquil trajectory into the popular imagination, while the other has spiraled into hard-fought litigation over the Establishment Clause, one of the thorniest swamps the First Amendment has to offer.

Inward Focus: Cleaning Up the Swamp

The inward-facing nature of congressional chaplains allows us to believe that something slightly more noble than venality (might) guide (some) decisions in Congress. Jedediah Purdy flatly asserted that "[b]etterment remains the great possibility of public life."[66] This assertion coincides with an aspirational view of national life that allows that "people can be improved, but not beyond the need for one another and for common institutions that fix out best commitments and constrain and redirect our worst impulses."[67] Such an optimistic view of politics contrasts starkly with Machiavellian or realist views of political life that echo Hobbes's description of it as "solitary, poore, nasty, brutish, and short."[68] Peter Marshall's self-identification as "the conscience of the Senate"[69] speaks volumes in this regard: The chaplain can be an exponent of "the better angels of our nature,"[70] in the hope that those win out in the end.

Such an understanding of the aspirational possibilities of situated chaplains invokes a shared sense of morality and ethics that seems foreign to how we think about Congress. Purdy discusses three sets of "commons" we share: "the natural world on which we all depend"; "the political and civic institutions that create and enforce laws, shape economies, and maintain communities"; and the "moral ecology" of "cultural practices and individual dispositions."[71] Even though we understand the need to clean up the natural ecology (environmental stewardship) and social commons (political and economic corruption), we often forget about our connection to the moral ecology: "Unless we are especially attentive, we tend to notice the moral ecology only when it fails. Commonplace goodness does not move us much, until we have been squarely confronted with commonplace badness."[72]

The history of congressional ethics rules shows that it is both a political and a moral ecology.[73] For the first 150 years of its existence, Congress (and especially the Senate) relied primarily on an ethics of virtue and dignity to enforce its integrity—but only when public scandal threatened.[74] As scandals erupted and multiplied, an official code of ethics did not take hold until 1964.[75] Rather than solving the problem, the code presented a roadmap to circumvention and trivialization to the point of the "Toothpick Rule," limiting legislators to foods that can be eaten with fingers or toothpicks.[76] Congress has increasingly subsisted on both formal ethics rules and informal norms.[77]

Whereas much commentary has been directed at written rules governing the political ecology, little has been said about the informal norms of Congress's moral ecology other than that they have been decaying over the course of decades. The Hastings Center concluded, "[l]egislators must now largely rely on the resources of their own moral imaginations—their own personal commitment to ethical standards and their own intellectual capacities for critical judgment, discernment, and reflection—to fill the vacuum left by the breakdown of informal norms."[78] As one commentator observed, "[c]ritics may suggest that we cannot rely on individual good will. In the final analysis, we may have no choice."[79]

It is precisely at this juncture that the chaplain's leverage becomes apparent: The chaplain uniquely can speak to the good will that guides legislators above and beyond the base sense of not violating rules. "Public office is a public trust,"[80] but the admonition is hardly self-unpacking. A good beyond the mere observance of rules animates what it means to truly govern well, and the chaplain's role in speaking toward that good can bring it closer: "articulation can bring us closer to the good as a moral source, can give it power."[81]

The situated congressional chaplain acts as a steward for Congress's polluted moral ecology, recovering the possibility of something beautiful in what otherwise seems to be pervasive mire. Because situated chaplains have maintained this inward focus on the legislature itself, they have avoided the controversy that has attended rotating volunteer chaplains. This orientation has allowed them to cultivate ongoing pastoral relationships across denominational lines, creating a popular image as a respected advisor[82] who can bring valuable sanity to a sometimes off-kilter sausage factory. The office has persisted through moments sublime, humorous, regrettable, and unexpected. At the same time, it is a violation of the Establishment Clause obvious to "any group of law students"[83] but also "so venerable and so lovely, so respectable and respected."[84] Perhaps the key reason for its persistence in the face of litigation, opposition, and the separation of church and state is the simple fact that it reminds us of an ideal that is otherwise unavailable.

Notes

1. Robert C. Byrd, "Senate Chaplain," in *The Senate, 1789–1989: Addresses on the History of the United States Senate*, vol. 2 (Washington: Government Printing Office, 1991), 300, quoting Margaret Bayard Smith, *The First Forty Years of Washington Society*, ed. Gaillard Hunt (New York: Frederick Ungar, 1965; reprint of 1906 edition), 13–14. Obviously, the meaning of the phrase "gay community" also differs from contemporary idiom.

2. Ibid.

3. Ibid.

4. Popular versions of this vision differ across the political spectrum, from Ronald Reagan's (Peggy Noonan's) "Morning in America" vision of a city on a hill to Camelot to Aaron Sorkin's "America is advanced citizenship" speeches in *The American President* and *West Wing*. The ongoing power of this imaginarium is felt in Maureen Dowd's account of Sorkin's account of a meeting between Barack Obama and Jed Bartlet. See Maureen Dowd, "Two Presidents, Smoking and Scheming," *New York Times*, October 6, 2012, accessed April 17, 2014, http://www.nytimes.com/2012/10/07/opinion/sunday/dowd-two-presidents-smoking-and-scheming.html.

Notably, these aspirational visions in culture seem to involve the Executive Branch much more often than the Legislative Branch. By analogy, perhaps chaplains do for Congress what Noonan and Sorkin do for the White House.

5. Select Committee on Ethics, *Senate Ethics Manual*, Appendix E, 436, quoting *Code of Ethics for Government Service*, H. Con. Res. 175, 85th Cong., 2d Sess., July 1, 1958.

6. *Marsh v. Chambers*, 463 U.S. 783, 792 (1983).

7. *Marsh*, 463 U.S. at 796 (Brennan, J., dissenting).

8. Although one judge has acknowledged the distinction, *Snyder v. Murray City Corp.*, 159 F.3d 1227, 1238 (10th Cir. 1998) (Lucero, J., concurring), courts have not placed any legal significance on the difference. I have argued elsewhere that this is a short-sighted approach that misunderstands the different pastoral nature of the two types of chaplain. See generally Jeremy G. Mallory, *"Well, But That System Has Failed Entirely": Using Theological and Philosophical Methods to Resolve Jurisprudential Confusion Over Legislative Prayer*, 33 Whittier L. Rev. 377 (2012); and Mallory, Comment: *"An Officer of the House Which Chooses Him, and Nothing More": How Should* Marsh v. Chambers *Apply to Rotating Chaplains?*, 73 U. Chi. L. Rev. 1421 (2006).

9. U.S. Constitution, art. I §§2 (House), 3 (Senate). The committee charged with determining the rules of the Senate was also directed "to take into consideration the manner of electing chaplains." Senate, *Annals of Congress*, 1st Cong., 1st Sess., 18. From inception, congressional chaplains were regarded as an integral part of the institution.

10. Senate Committee on the Judiciary, *To Abolish the Office of Chaplain in Both Houses of Congress and in Army and Navy*, 32nd Cong., 2d Sess., 1853, S. Rept. 376, 2.

11. Richard Baker, "The Senate Elects a Chaplain," *Senate Historical Minute*, October 10, 1999, http://www.senate.gov/artandhistory/history/minute/The_Senate_Elects_A_Chaplain.htm. After Marshall's tenure, Brown was reappointed.

12. See Congressional Globe, 36th Cong., 1st Sess., 1859, 98 (Sen. Henry Wilson, calling for "a Chaplain who would become acquainted with us, and who would know the interests and wants of the body"); Karen Feaver, "The Soul of the Senate," *Christianity Today* 39, no. 1 (January 9, 1995): 29; Byrd, *The Senate,* 302. Sen. Wilson's plea came at the conclusion of a short period when the Senate adopted a rotating model of chaplaincy. The Senate invited local clergy to pray for two years, but returned to a situated chaplaincy soon after Wilson's speech. The House tried a similar rotation and abandoned it after six years with the terse commentary of Rep. Thomas Florence: "Well, but that system has failed entirely." Congressional Globe, 36th Cong., 1st Sess., 1860, 994.

13. *Simpson v. Chesterfield County Bd. of Superv'rs,* 404 F.3d 276, 279 (4th Cir. 2005).

14. *Hinrichs v. Speaker of the House of Representatives,* 506 F.3d 584, 598 (7th Cir. 2007).

15. *Hinrichs,* 506 F.3d at 604.

16. Christopher C. Lund, *Legislative Prayer and the Secret Costs of Religious Endorsements,* 94 Minn. L. Rev. 972, 975 n.14 (2010).

17. *Simpson,* 404 F.3d at 285 n.4.

18. As of the writing of this chapter, the Supreme Court has not yet ruled in *Town of Greece v. Galloway,* which could, in theory, find chaplains unconstitutional.

19. *Marsh,* 463 U.S. at 795.

20. Later litigation has created a mare's nest of misunderstanding about *Marsh's* scope. See Mallory, 33 Whittier L. Rev. at 387–91. Although it ostensibly only addressed the chaplaincy of a single state (Nebraska), it has been taken to apply to any sort of legislative chaplaincy, ibid., and has even been cited for other First Amendment questions far afield, Mallory, U. Chi. L. Rev. at 1431, n.63. Whatever else *Marsh* stands for, it assuredly stands for the proposition that congressional chaplaincies are constitutional, an exception to the Establishment Clause, *Marsh,* 463 U.S. at 796 (Brennan, J., dissenting).

21. Christopher C. Lund, *Legislative Prayer and the Secret Costs of Religious Endorsements,* 94 Minn. L. Rev. 972, 976 (2010).

22. Richard C. Schragger, *The Role of the Local in the Doctrine and Discourse of Religious Liberty,* 117 Harv. L. Rev. 1810, 1881 (2004).

23. Jonathan H. Adler, "Which First Amendment Decision Would You Overturn?," *The Volokh Conspiracy,* January 4, 2014, http://www.volokh.com/2014/01/04/first-amendment-decision-overturn/.

24. *Marsh,* 463 U.S. at 800.

25. House Committee on the Judiciary, *Chaplains in Congress, and in the Army, and Navy,* 33d Cong., 1st Sess., 1854, H. Rept. 124, 6. The issue was never dignified with a vote: each house of Congress submitted the petitions for abolition

of the office to their respective Judiciary Committees, each of which delivered a strident defense of the office.

26. George E. Hastings, "Jacob Duché, First Chaplain of Congress," *South Atlantic Quarterly* 31 (October 1932): 390.

27. Jacob Duché and Francis Hopkinson, *An Exercise on the Accession of His Present Gracious Majesty, George III* (Philadelphia: W. Dunlap, 1762), cited in Hastings, "Jacob Duché," 390.

28. John Adams to Abigail Adams, Philadelphia, PA, September 16, 1774, in *The Letters of John and Abigail Adams*, ed. Frank Shuffelton (New York: Penguin Books, 2004), 35.

29. Martin Medhurst, "From Duché to Provoost: The Birth of Inaugural Prayer," *Journal of Church and State* 24 (Autumn 1982): 576.

30. Psalm 35 ("Plead thou my cause, O Lord, with them that strive against me: and fight thou against them that fight against me.")

31. John Adams to Abigail Adams, in Shuffleton, *Letters*, 35.

32. Hastings, "Jacob Duché," 394.

33. Ibid., 395.

34. Ibid., 396; Elizabeth Phillips Graver, "The Turncoat Chaplain," Bicentennial Document, from the files of the United States Senate Historical Office, 34.

35. Jacob Duché to George Washington, Philadelphia, PA, October 8, 1777, in *The Washington-Duché Letters*, ed. Worthington Chauncey Ford (Brooklyn, NY: privately printed, 1890), 11.

36. Duché to Washington, in Ford, Letters, 20–21.

37. Graver, "Turncoat Chaplain," 35.

38. John Adams to Abigail Adams, Yorktown, PA, October 25, 1777, in Shuffelton, 320.

39. Senate Journal, 22d Cong., 2d Sess., Dec. 11, 1832, 25; Register of Congressional Debates, 22d Cong., 2d Sess., Dec. 11, 1832, 5–6; M. Eulalia Teresa Moffatt, "Charles Constantine Pise (1801–1866)," *Historical Records and Studies*, vol. 20, ed. Thomas F. Meehan (New York: U.S. Catholic Historical Society, 1931), 79.

40. Charles Whittier, "The Only Roman Catholic Chaplain of the United States Senate," Congressional Research Service Report, in the files of the United States Senate Historical Office, March 27, 1986, 1; Moffatt, "Pise," 70–71.

41. Moffatt, "Pise," 74. Moffatt notes that Pise "gained for himself the honor of being the founder of Catholic fiction in this country" with his publication of *Father Rowland: A North American Tale*. Ibid.

42. Ibid., 78.

43. Ibid., 80–81.

44. Ibid., 81.

45. Ibid., 90–91.

46. Mary Elizabeth Goin, "Catherine Marshall: Three Decades of Popular Religion," *Journal of Presbyterian History* 56, no. 3 (Fall 1978): 221.

47. "Dr. Marshall," *Washington Times Herald*, January 26, 1949.

48. Tris Coffin, "The Daybook," *Washington Times Herald*, January 28, 1949.

49. Goin, "Catherine Marshall," 219; Peter Marshall, *Mr. Jones, Meet the Master: Sermons and Prayers* (New York: Revell, 1949); Catherine Marshall, *A Man Called Peter: the Story of Peter Marshall* (New York: McGraw-Hill, 1951).

50. Goin, "Catherine Marshall," 219.

51. Alice A. Love, "New Senate Chaplain: Direct from Hollywood," *Roll Call*, January 23, 1995.

52. Jonathan E. Fasman, "Hill Profile: Dr. Lloyd John Ogilvie," *The Hill*, November 19, 1997.

53. Ibid.

54. Ogilvie's prayers were bound into a commemorative pamphlet. Lloyd John Ogilvie, *Opening Prayers: Impeachment Trial of the President of the United States, January 7–February 12, 1999* (U.S. Senate, 1999).

55. Hamil R. Harris, "Senate Chaplain's Popularity Up After Fire-and-Brimstone Prayers Amid Shutdown," *Washington Post*, November 1, 2013, http://www.washingtonpost.com/local/senate-chaplains-popularity-up-after-fire-and-brimstone-prayers-amid-shutdown/2013/11/01/ad1c3940-3c23-11e3-b7ba-503fb5822c3e_story.html.

56. Ibid.

57. Professor Chris Lund has noted that it is one of the most litigated of all Establishment Clause questions, which is notable given that this category includes school prayer, Ten Commandments monuments, and crèches in town squares. See Lund, 94 Minn. L. Rev. at 972, 976.

58. *Kurtz v. Baker*, 829 F.2d 1133 (D.C. Cir. 1987).

59. Feaver, "Soul of the Senate," 29.

60. Harris, "Senate Chaplain's Popularity Up."

61. This capacity was poignantly noted by Sen. Joseph Lieberman, a Conservative Jewish senator, upon the retirement of Richard Halverson, a Presbyterian. Joseph Lieberman, 104th Cong., 1st Sess., *Congressional Record* 141 (March 10, 1995): S 3763.

62. *Marsh*, 463 U.S. at 793 n.14. Although Robert Palmer, the chaplain in question in *Marsh*, was employed by a state legislature, he was a situated chaplain exactly like the congressional chaplains. This incongruity is part of the reason Judge Lucero questioned whether *Marsh* could even apply to the rotating volunteer chaplaincies found elsewhere. *Snyder*, 159 F.3d at 1237–39 (Lucero, J., concurring) (emphasizing the difference between rotating and situated chaplaincies).

63. *Snyder*, 159 F.3d at 1238 (Lucero, J., concurring).

64. Committee on the Judiciary, S. Rep. No. 376, 32d Cong., 2d Sess. 2 (1853).

65. Mallory, 73 U. Chi. L. Rev. at 1440–43.

66. Jedediah Purdy, *For Common Things: Irony, Trust, and Commitment in America Today* (New York: Knopf, 1999), 207.

67. Ibid., 128.

68. Thomas Hobbes, *Leviathan* (Oxford: Oxford University Press, 1909), 99.

69. Coffin, "The Daybook."

70. Abraham Lincoln, First Inaugural Address (March 4, 1861).

71. Purdy, *For Common Things*, 98, 100, 101.

72. Ibid., 99–100.

73. See generally Jeremy G. Mallory, "If There Be a God Who Hears Prayer: An Ethical Account of the United States Senate Chaplain" (Ph.D. diss., University of Chicago Divinity School, 2004), 203–30.

74. Ibid., 203.

75. Ibid.

76. Zachary Roth, "The Toothpick Role," *Washington Monthly*, February 28, 2007, http://www.washingtonmonthly.com/scoop/issues/070228scoop.html.

77. Hastings Center, *The Ethics of Legislative Life* (Hastings-on-Hudson, NY: Institute of Society, Ethics, and Life Sciences, 1985), 19.

78. Ibid., 24.

79. John D. Saxon, "The Scope of Legislative Ethics," *Representation and Responsibility: Exploring Legislative Ethics*, ed. Bruce Jennings and Daniel Callahan (New York: Plenum, 1985), 218.

80. Select Committee on Ethics, *Senate Ethics Manual*, Appendix E, 436, quoting *Code of Ethics for Government Service*, H. Con. Res. 175, 85th Cong., 2d Sess., July 1, 1958.

81. Charles Taylor, *Sources of the Self: The Making of the Modern Identity* (Cambridge, MA: Harvard University Press, 1989), 92.

82. With the notable exception of Jacob Duché, who is remembered both for his pious role in originating the office and his ignominious end.

83. *Marsh*, 463 U.S. at 800.

84. Senate Committee on the Judiciary, *To Abolish the Office of Chaplain in Both Houses of Congress and in Army and Navy*, 32d Cong., 2d Sess., 1853, S. Rept. 376, 4.

CHAPTER SIX

The Evangelist and the Venture Capitalist: A Parable for the 21st Century

Robert Brancatelli

Even though the Christian church teaches that the message of the Gospels is unchanging in its call for repentance and a radical turning toward God through Jesus Christ, the context in which that message is proclaimed has changed dramatically over the centuries. An ongoing task of religious educators, theologians, academics, and ministers has been to recontextualize the Gospels in the images, metaphors, and narrative of the contemporary era. This is not an easy task, since the cultural, historical, and sociopolitical ethos of first-century Palestine cannot be readily ignored. Nor should it be. But while recontextualization has yielded fresh insights and understanding into the meaning of the Good News for today's Christians, it often fails to convey a fundamental aspect of that message. Originally, the radical turning toward God was best expressed through parables. Parables such as the Mustard Seed (Mark 4:30–34), the Prodigal Son (Luke 15:11–32), and the Multiplication of Loaves (John 6:1–15) contain a counterintuitive logic that demands openness on the part of the listener. Others such as the Workers in the Vineyard (Matthew 20:1–16), the Talents (Matthew 25:14–30), and the Rich Young Man (Mark 10:17–31) deliberately involve work and money. The setting of these parables—vineyards, pastures, markets—show people engaged in the exchange of goods and services for profit and livelihood.

In order to have an impact equal to that of their first-century counterparts, parables for the 21st century can no longer include scenes of agriculture and livestock, but, like the Gospel parables, should include people at work and earning a living. Today, most people earn a living in the business world, which also provides an identity for many, especially if their work is seen as a vocation. Naturally, the business world is vastly more complicated than it was 20 centuries ago. Therefore, parables need to keep pace with this changed environment while still retaining their power to surprise, turn reality on its head, and make demands on the listener that lead to repentance and a radical turning toward God. Today, the turn toward God may not be expressed as such, and there may be less of an institutionalized understanding of church, sacrament, and the transcendent, but this begs the question about both the relevancy and efficacy of the traditional ways in which revelation is experienced. In other words, questions of ultimate meaning are just as likely to be dealt with on the floor of the stock exchange or office than the church sanctuary.

This chapter will offer a parable for this new environment and explore ways in which the parable reflects a different way of understanding discipleship and church. The parable and its analysis are intended to be creative and speculative rather than fully systematic. The chapter will also consider whether business, rather than doctrine and theology, provides the best forum for questions of ultimate meaning.

The Parable of the Evangelist and the Venture Capitalist

In creating a parable for today, several questions must be addressed, including the purpose of the parable, the specific message it intends to convey, the setting, characters, tone, and voice, as well as larger issues such as the way in which God is revealed and the nature of that revelation. For instance, does the parable challenge the listener to a new way of life, to repentance of sin or wrongdoing, renunciation of possessions, a deeper commitment to existing relationships, or a specific expression of discipleship? And what, exactly, constitutes discipleship today? What kind of God or image of God is portrayed in the parable?

The following parable consists of two people: a venture capitalist (or someone who has money to invest in a new idea) and a young man (an "evangelist," with such an idea for a business enterprise). The young man is not so much interested in making money, although he recognizes that he needs enough to meet the basic necessities of life and keep working. What motivates him is something more. In a spiritual context, one might call it *magis*, or the desire to become more authentically human. He pitches his concept to the venture capitalist after having arranged the meeting.

Once there was a young man who attended a business conference in the city. Wearing blue jeans and a blazer, he walked into the meeting room, introduced himself politely to the venture capitalist, and sat down. He had a disheveled look, although not unkempt, with bright eyes and an eager smile. It was obvious that he hadn't slept in a while. He carried an expensive portfolio from which papers and an umbrella handle stuck out.

"Is it raining?" the venture capitalist asked, not having been outside the hotel all morning.

"No, it's a sunny day," the young man said.

"But you're expecting rain?"

"No, why?"

The older man looked at him. "No reason. So, tell me, what did you want to see me about?"

"Games," the young man said.

"All right, I'm listening."

"I want to build a game layer over the world."[1]

"A what?"

"A game layer. Specifically, a platform for games of all kinds on smartphones, iPads, personal computers, laptops, tablets, you name it."

"Why?"

"It's where we're all headed."

"Who's headed?"

"Society."

The venture capitalist wasn't sure what to make of this, but before he could react, the young man went on.

"See, the last 10 years were about social media, but the next 10 will be about games. You already see it with Facebook and Candy Crush's $7 billion valuation. That's why I want to build a platform based on game theory that will allow people to make a game out of everything they do."

"A game out of everything?"

"Well, life's a game, right? I mean, everything we do has give-and-take or risk and reward built in: business loans, credit cards, mortgages, college education, even marriage. They all have varying levels of risk, and what lures people in is the payoff."

"Isn't that a cynical way to look at things?"

"Only if you think the game is rigged and you have no control over your odds of winning, which is why I've developed a way for people to create games based on a set of dynamics."

"Which dynamics?"

"It's all here in my business plan. I call my new company Gamella."

The young man took a business plan from his portfolio and handed it over. Then he opened the umbrella and held it over his head.

"If we build an umbrella of game dynamics over the entire world," he said, "people will be more connected than ever before, not only to their friends and family but to strangers and even their enemies. Eventually, their behavior will change as a result of teaming up or competing with people from around the globe."

"That's all very nice, but how does Gamella make money?"

"The umbrella belongs to us. Think of it as the operating system that everyone will use to create their games in whatever application or format they desire. We'll be like Microsoft at the beginning of the personal computer craze. I've calculated that with an initial investment of $750,000, this will grow into a one $1 billion-a-year business."

"What's the downside?"

"That somebody else will beat us to it. The umbrella is going to be deployed, I have no doubt about it. It's just a question of who will do it and when. But I'll tell you this: Gamella will be revolutionary. It won't just be more of the same in a cloud-based platform. It will literally change the way people think and act. There'll be no frontiers anymore, and players will identify with characters or locations in their game. Gamella will give them a new way of being."

The venture capitalist looked at the young man, umbrella opened above his head, then down at the business plan, fairly certain that he was crazy. Still, his resume was impressive and he seemed to have the kind of initiative and drive the investor was looking for. He also liked the fact that the plan involved new technology.

"There's one other thing," the young man said.

"What's that?"

"It's not that I'm against making money, you understand. I like nice mountain bikes and snowboards and all that, but the business itself doesn't interest me."

"It doesn't?"

"No, I already have most of the things I need."

"So what do you want?"

"What money can't buy."

"Like?"

"I want to build a game umbrella over the world."

"I see."

"So, are you in or out?"

The parable ends, as many do, with a twist or question that challenges not just the venture capitalist but the reader to make a decision. The decision concerns more than just a game platform, and this is perhaps one of the greatest characteristics of parables, which point to something beyond themselves in a semiotic way. Here, two worlds come into contact, an old and new, requiring new thinking and insights, similar to Jesus's encounter with Nicodemus concerning the need to be born again (John 3:1–15).

The Meaning of the Parable

Perhaps the first thing to note about the parable is that it is not overtly religious or even spiritual, although the basic struggle the young man experiences is common among entrepreneurs; that is, the difference between the *desire* to make a dream come true and the *need* for money to make it come true. This represents a spiritual struggle of being and doing and the need to align both dimensions of life to achieve ontological wholeness. There is also misalignment between the two men, not all of it generational or due to socioeconomic background or educational level. In a word, they see things differently. This reflects another characteristic of parables in their depiction of two often-competing visions or interests. The clash that occurs between them can be jarring as in the Good Samaritan (Luke 10:25–37), challenging as in the Sower (Mark 4:1–8), or condemning as in the Rich Man and Lazarus (Luke 16:19–31). Here, there are clearly two ways of looking at innovation and entrepreneurship: one emphasizing profit, the other societal transformation. Putting the merits of a game umbrella aside, the fact that the two men are suspicious of each other tends to support the young man's claim that the concept is "revolutionary." It doesn't resemble anything in the older man's experience, and he even lacks a language for the idea. He does recognize the potential for profit, however, which compels him to converse with the young man and face the final question of whether he is "in or out."

What are the purpose and message of the parable? The purpose is to show that revelation occurs today in an ongoing way in the same kinds of settings that it did during the time of Jesus's ministry and the early church; that is, the equivalent of vineyards, pastures, and markets. In this instance, the backdrop is a hotel during a business conference of investors and entrepreneurs. This point is crucial to understand the parable, since entrepreneurs like the young man often associate with like-minded peers for support and to exchange ideas. They are motivated by their vision to do something extraordinary, even revolutionary, with profit being a welcome byproduct. This is evident in countless case studies, not the least of which is the recent rejection of a $3 billion cash offer by Facebook for a start-up company called "Snapchat."[2] Although the young founders were reported to be holding out for an even bigger offer, they were motivated to start the business because of a trend they perceived in social media, with younger customers no longer being interested in sharing details of their personal lives in a public forum. (Snapchat provides text messages that disappear after viewing.) The service "offers a reprieve from worrying about awkward or unflattering photos turning up unexpectedly."[3] Perhaps unwittingly, it also contributes to a counter-Information Age phenomenon that might best be called "impermanence," or the rejection of permanent records of data for every individual. The implications, of course, are enormous, especially given the current environment of privacy issues and NSA revelations. It is no wonder, therefore, that entrepreneurs like the Snapchat founders and the young man in the parable often refer to themselves as "evangelists." They are evangelists not just for a particular idea, invention, or brand, but a way of life.

The message of the parable needs further analysis, since it involves more than organizing gamers and systematizing their games into a universal platform. The young man clearly states that his vision is to use the platform and new company not merely to make money but to redefine the way people think about themselves and their relationships. Without putting too fine a point on it, in a theological context this would be building the kingdom of God so that the old understandings and boundaries fall away to make room for something new (Isaiah 43:18–21). Absent theological language, the young man articulates a vision of the future in which virtue, integrity, and equality reign and an environment exists in which human beings learn to live in harmony with each other and the planet.

It is interesting to note that the role of Jesus in this parable is ambiguous, if it exists at all. Another way of putting the question is to ask, is the young man's vision attainable without the person of Christ? The immediate answer would be yes, but a more thoughtful approach would consider the point of any parable. With few exceptions—the Great Feast (Luke 14:15–24); the Tenant Farmers (Mark 12:1–12)—Jesus is not included or alluded to in the Gospel parables, even though he is the one recounting them. The parables are generally concerned with repentance of sin and deepening one's relationship with the Father. Some, like the Unforgiving Servant (Matthew 18:21–35) do so around the theme of debt and money. Jesus does not have any principal role to play except as the teacher who uses parables to instruct. The same understanding could be applied here, which points to another characteristic of parables: They rise above theological truth claims to speak about human experience in a new way. That way might include a broader understanding of salvation and grace and a creation spirituality that is less anthropocentric.

The setting, characters, tone, and voice of the parable all come together to deal with questions of ultimate meaning. The evangelist and the venture capitalist may be misaligned, as stated earlier, but they are searching for ways to work together to give birth to a new entity, one that the evangelist hopes will respond to changes that are already taking place in society. The venture capitalist hopes to make money from the project, but he is not heartless. One might imagine his answer to the final question as being yes, but with reservations. Experience tells him that bright ideas are a dime a dozen and that everything depends on execution. At least in this regard he would not be without sympathizers in the church: those involved in faith formation, education, and the development of moral and religious insight among the faithful.[4] But he is not just judging the business plan and proposal. He is also judging the young man sitting in front of him holding an umbrella over his head. He wants to take the leap of faith required to support a project like this but he has other commitments and a reputation to safeguard. There are responsibilities to attend to before he can become a "follower" of the evangelist (Luke 9:57–62).

The Business of Ultimate Meaning and Discipleship

A distinction should be drawn between entrepreneurship and the accumulation of capital for no other purpose than to get rich. Most entrepreneurs are not in it for the money, as can be seen with the young man in the parable. They have a vision for changing the status quo with a creative, innovative idea often designed to make life easier, more enjoyable, and meaningful for people. They expend nearly all of their time thinking of, talking about, working on, and selling their ideas to others, including colleagues and coworkers in addition to potential investors. The fact that their ideas may not explicitly involve themes like creation, sin, death, salvation, and grace does not mean that they do not in some way deal with the lived reality of those themes. For instance, the young man's vision for Gamella includes a very practical solution to the problem of isolation and mistrust among people that, one might argue in a theological sense, is the result of original sin. In addition, the Gospels are quite explicit about the evils of greed and covetousness (Philippians 2:12–18, James 4:2–5:6), and there are few in the world of startups and entrepreneurship who would take issue with this, despite the oft-cited havoc wreaked by "unfettered capitalism." Entrepreneurs, as evangelists, are concerned about turning their dreams into reality. Social entrepreneurs are concerned about curing social ills like poverty, hunger, overpopulation, and scant water resources with innovative ideas involving all stakeholders.

This distinction is important for another reason, because even though accumulating wealth for its own sake is condemned in the Gospels and shown to be the antithesis of the Kingdom of God (the Rich Man and Lazarus [Luke 16:19–31]), *zeal* for establishing the Kingdom is praised as an essential trait of discipleship (Matthew 10:37–39, Mark 8:34–38, Luke 9:62). What, specifically, is this zeal for? It is directed toward a new vision of reality that turns the current order upside down and establishes heaven on earth. This vision is outlined in the Lucan Beatitudes (Luke 6:20–26), which set up the parameters for a new world: the poor, the hungry, and those who suffer will be delivered from their misery, but the rich, who have already received their reward (v. 24), will receive nothing more. Such a world and reality are what motivate entrepreneurs to pursue their dreams so that there is more connectivity, transparency, relationship-building, and sharing of lives across the boundaries of time and space. Of course, technology has limits and negative effects, and perhaps the young man's hopes for a game layer will not bear fruit but the zeal with which he works and shares his vision is inspiring. It is similar to the zeal for the Kingdom without the theological language and categories of inherited truth claims. Neither is it overtly Christian, but it may challenge the church to define more clearly what "Christian" means in a global context given that its mandate is to baptize *panta ta ethnē* (Matthew 28:19, "all the nations").

There are implications for understanding both entrepreneurship and discipleship. If the young man is truly an evangelist and the message he proclaims includes to some degree the mission but not the person of Christ, what significance does this have for the premise that entrepreneurship is a contemporary form of divine revelation? And is it enough to express zeal for Kingdom principles without having an explicit commitment to Christ? It would seem that not everyone who does the will of the Father is a disciple, no matter their zeal: "Many will say to me on that day, 'Lord, Lord, did we not prophesy in your name? Did we not drive out demons in your name? Did we not do mighty deeds in your name?' Then I will declare to them solemnly, 'I never knew you. Depart from me, you evildoers'" (Matthew 7:22–23). Even those Gospel passages that depict other prophets driving out demons and doing good works, do so either because they are disciples (Matthew 10:42b), or in Jesus's name (Mark 9:39b).

It is possible to come to terms with these issues by positing a twofold understanding of revelation, one that involves a general revelation of transcendence that is also imminent and immediate (an Augustinian understanding), and the other specifically Christian. Divine revelation in an entrepreneurial sense would move the individual and business community to take responsibility for themselves and others, engage in social cooperation as a constitutive part of doing business, and assume a "voluntary spirit."[5] Doing these in the name of Christ or because of an explicit commitment to Christian discipleship would make the response overtly Christian. What makes divine revelation one form or the other is not dependent upon human action, but certainly the ways in which people respond to God's grace are culturally and religiously mediated.

There is yet another way in which entrepreneurship can be seen as a mode of divine revelation, and that is through immediacy. Part of this is the result of the Information Age and the central role played by technology. Communication that is instantaneous, short lived, and of limited capacity is the hallmark of what is considered modern and cutting edge. Organizations invest large sums of money in cutting-edge systems and technology, partly to cut costs and increase revenue, partly to ensure that they continue to thrive in the marketplace by meeting people's needs. For all of the drawbacks that are evident with technology: its reduction of experience to shallow bytes of information, the constant churning of data, the disruption of personal spirituality, and the invasion of privacy—to name a few—it has the advantage of being flexible and light enough to reflect human experience and to give nearly everyone a platform from which to enter the public forum. In this sense, it represents a defining characteristic of modern history, business included: democracy. There is a sense of liberty and an opportunity for people with few resources to come together to solve problems rather than rely on other agencies, the government included, to solve them for them.

As is evident in the parable, vision, drive, risk, and the suspension of disbelief are all part of the entrepreneurial spirit. The evangelist who sets out to turn an idea into reality must have the kind of faith that moves mountains. Otherwise, the project can get weighed down with the minutiae of financial statements, Excel spreadsheets, government regulations, earnings reports, and even the business plan. Even more challenging is working with others not just to execute the vision but to make sure that everyone understands and agrees to it. It is not necessary that everyone on the team be in lock step with the evangelist, but it is vital that they share his or her passion in some way and then make that passion their own.

The actual young man who is the inspiration for this article's parable has been described as regarding anything that distracts from his work as "evil" and anything that enhances it and his vision as "awesome."[6] Perhaps awesome has become the new "amen." However, this kind of fervor, which many see as necessary for success, is also detrimental if done to excess. This may seem like a contradiction, but it has been noted that entrepreneurs who are so fixated on their idea or business may suffer from "hypomanic episodes," which could explain the young man holding the umbrella over his head.[7] It certainly explains his devotion to the cause.

Finally, much has been written about St. Paul's personality and his drive for spreading the Good News to the gentiles. The vision he received and responded to with such zeal permitted him to be called an apostle not unlike the youthful evangelist in the parable here (1 Corinthians 15:8–10, Galatians 1:15–16). Even though he may have suffered from hypomanic episodes as well, it is evident that he had a clear, focused vision and plan for implementing it. In fact, he states in Acts 20:

> But now, compelled by the Spirit, I am going to Jerusalem. What will happen to me there I do not know, except that in one city after another the holy Spirit has been warning me that imprisonment and hardships await me. Yet I consider life of no importance to me, if only I may finish my course and the ministry that I received from the Lord Jesus, to bear witness to the gospel of God's grace. (vv. 22–24)

Although, Gamella is not concerned with the "gospel of God's grace," the young evangelist hopes to solve a very real problem in a world growing smaller and more restive by technology. That he wants to use technology to help solve the problem created by technology is a testament to his creativity and resolve to cross boundaries. How much of that is due to his hypomania? It may not be a relevant question, just as it may not be with St. Paul. They both exhibit a form of what the author has called elsewhere "entrepreneurial discipleship."[8]

Conclusion

This chapter has been concerned with looking at entrepreneurship as a mode of divine revelation and the settings within which entrepreneurship and business take place as the new backdrop for parables about God. For the most part, people no longer understand, let alone exist in, pastoral settings. If parables are to retain their creative power, they must assume the ethos of the 21st century, which differs markedly in form and content from that of the Gospel parables. This ethos is increasingly concerned with markets and the exchange of goods and service on a global basis. Even so, the focus of this chapter has been limited. There are much larger issues than the ones addressed here that should be considered going forward. For instance, work and the workplace as the locus of vocation have already been explored to a fair extent, and stories within a business setting that have spiritual growth and formation as their themes already exist.[9] These themes need further attention and development. There also needs to be further thought given to the issue of technology and the current trend, among technology companies at least, to create open communities of workers by tearing down walls and partitions. Yahoo! is one example of this, but a similar effort occurred in West Germany during the 1950s and proved less than effective.[10]

A modern-day parable concerning entrepreneurship also leads to broader issues regarding the nature of capitalism, a theology of work, the relationship of capital to labor, a spirituality of entrepreneurship, and, finally, a consideration of alternative economic systems more capable of bringing about the young evangelist's vision than the present-day system, which some have accused of being nothing more than "crony capitalism."[11] The greatest issue, however, and one with which this chapter began, is the nature of revelation and how God may be revealed to people today. Is it by attempting to recontextualize the founding images and stories of salvation history, or discovering the essence of revelation in the here and now? This is a sweeping question, one that speaks to the nature of translation and how age-old experiences can come alive again in a world that has experienced calamity and misery throughout the 20th century. The old answers no longer ring true for many people searching for the truth. If, in fact, people are relying more on culture than doctrine to feed their religious imagination, the fault may not be with them but with those who insist on forming them with stories about virgins and oil lamps, even if those stories are sent via Twitter.

Notes

1. The inspiration for the parable and "game layer" comes from David Segal, "Just Manic Enough: Seeking Perfect Entrepreneurs," *New York Times*, September 18, 2010, accessed March 3, 2014, http://www.nytimes.com/2010/09/19/business/19entre.html?pagewanted=all&_r=0.

2. Jenna Wortham, "Rejecting Billions, Snapchat Expects a Better Offer," *New York Times*, November 13, 2013, accessed March 12, 2014, http://www.nytimes.com/2013/11/14/technology/rejecting-billions-snapchat-expects-a-better-offer.html?_r=0.

3. Ibid.

4. See John Little, "A Powerful Intellectual Foundation for a Jesuit Business Education that Makes a Difference," *Journal of Jesuit Business Education* 3 no. 1 (Summer 2012): 131. According to Bernard Lonergan, SJ, insight is reached as the result of inquiry that leads one to examine an experience, understand it, judge whether one's understanding is right or wrong, and reach a decision for action. See also Robert A. Miller, "Lifesizing Entrepreneurship: Lonergan, Bias and The Role of Business in Society," *Journal of Business Ethics* 58 (2005): 219–25; and Walter E. Conn, *Christian Conversion: A Developmental Interpretation of Autonomy*

and Surrender (New York: Paulist Press, 1986; reprint, Eugene, OR: Wipf and Stock, 2006).

5. James Wilburn, "Capitalism Beyond the 'End of History,'" in *Business and Religion: A Clash of Civilizations?* ed. Nicholas Capaldi (Salem, MA: Scrivener Press, 2005), 176. See also "Rethinking the Social Responsibility of Business: A Reason Debate Featuring Milton Friedman, Whole Foods' John Mackey, and Cypress Semiconductor's T.J. Rodgers," *Reason*, October 2005, accessed March 15, 2014, http://reason.com/archives/2005/10/01/rethinking-the-social-responsi.

6. Segal, "Just Manic Enough."

7. Ibid.

8. See the author's PowerPoint presentation of "Entrepreneurial Discipleship" at http://necddre.org/images/Entrepreneurial_Discipleship.pdf. See also the Fordham University graduate course entitled, "Entrepreneurial Discipleship," http://www.fordham.edu/campus_resources/enewsroom/inside_fordham/february_14_2011/in_focus_faculty_and_professor_uses_busin_78209.asp and http://www.fordhamfab.com/drupal6/content/program-startup-casestudy.

9. For the former, see works by Matthew Fox and, more recently, Clayton Christensen, particularly Clayton Christensen, James Allworth, and Karen Dillon, *How Will You Measure Your Life?* (New York: HarperCollins, 2012). For the latter, see works by David Whyte about spirituality and corporate America.

10. See Maria Kinnikova, "The Open-Office Trap," *The New Yorker*, January 14, 2014, accessed March 17, 2014, http://www.newyorker.com/online/blogs/currency/2014/01/the-open-office-trap.html.

11. Regarding these and related issues, see Francis, *Evangelii Gaudium: On the Proclamation of the Gospel in Today's World,* Apostolic exhortation, November 24, 2013, accessed March 17, 2014, http://www.vatican.va/holy_father/francesco/apost_exhortations/documents/papa-francesco_esortazione-ap_20131124_evangelii-gaudium_en.html; Benedict XI, *Caritas in Veritate: On Integral Human Development in Charity and Truth*, Encyclical letter, June 29, 2009, accessed March 17, 2014, http://www.vatican.va/holy_father/benedict_xvi/encyclicals/documents/hf_ben-xvi_enc_20090629_caritas-in-veritate_en.html, which presents a "logic of gift" and a theology of "gratuitousness"; John Paul II, Encyclical letter, *Laborem Exercens: On Human Work on the Ninetieth Anniversary of Rerum Novarum,* September 14, 1981, accessed March 17, 2014, http://www.vatican.va/holy_father/john_paul_ii/encyclicals/documents/hf_jp-ii_enc_14091981_laborem-exercens_en.html; and Jeffrey Scholes, *Vocation and the Politics of Work: Popular Theology in a Consumer Culture* (New York: Lexington Books, 2013). For crony capitalism, see David Stockman, "The Great Deformation: How Crony Capitalism Corrupted Free Markets and Democracy," lecture, Fordham University Wall Street Council, October 22, 1013, http://www.fiasi.org/event-calendar/339-speaker-seriesoctober-22-2013.

CHAPTER SEVEN

Ministering to the Spiritual Side of Trade: The Sacred Language of Advertising

Andris Berry

The Language of Advertising

"I Am What I Am." "Honor Thyself." "We Bring Good Things to Life." "You're in Good Hands."

At first glance, you might think these quotes were lifted from a page of scripture rather than the slogans of Reebok sneakers, Johnnie Walker whiskey, General Electric, and Allstate Insurance. Why is it that so much advertising is theological in nature? If you are in need of faith, get behind the wheel of a Hyundai, since "Driving Is Believing." If you're in need of miracles, "Bayer Works Wonders." If you are searching for a life and find it, you can also have a beer, because "Where There's Life, There's Bud." If you have a concern about your place in eternity, DeBeers will have you know that "A Diamond Is Forever."

These ads are particularly revealing in their choice of words. There is a strong link between religion and advertising, because they both require our attention and emotion to draw us into closer relationships. Whereas the role of religion is to develop a relationship between God and people, the goal of modern advertising is to create relationships between brands and consumers. Whether or not they use religious language to promote their message, all advertisements work toward the same basic aim: to generate sales. Advertisements and commercials, in particular, are the most ostentatious display of consumerism—the material religion of our time.

In this chapter I explore parallels between marketing and religion. Our attention and our emotions are the substance of a sort of tender, a currency that is sought for acquisition by marketers. Whereas the market needs dollars, percentages, and profit margins, people ultimately need to feel trust and love. The needs of people are exploited by the market to fulfill its own wants. Even though God is conspicuously absent from the marketplace, the language of advertising reveals that it wishes to occupy the role that God has traditionally held in people's lives.

Creating a Layer of Tacit Authenticity

When I began working on commercials in Hollywood, I did not suspect that I was getting involved in a ministry. I never thought to look for the Great Mystery behind the scenes on a Coke commercial or while filming a Ford Mustang at the beach or in the dressing room of any of the various celebrities I encountered. I started as a production assistant and the days were long, 16 hours on average, and the pace breakneck, so I didn't think to step back and reflect on the larger forces at play. There wasn't much glamor either. Making commercials involves a lot of heavy lifting and navigating an environment full of competing egos. What piqued my interest were the methods and means used to create commercials. The images that we see each day on our televisions are oftentimes elaborate fabrications involving scores of crew members and various locations around the city.

A construction site was the location for a typical commercial I worked on some years ago. The product we were shooting was a large pickup truck with a comfortable high-end interior. The main scene from the ad sounded simple. It involved the pickup driving through the construction site and getting doused with mud by another passing truck. The main actor was a handsome middle-aged man with salt-and-pepper hair and a rugged jaw line. He was the driver of the truck and probably offered a faithful representation of the commercial's target demographic. Before we could shoot the driving scene, a front-loading tractor removed the top layer of dirt from an existing dirt road and replaced it with higher quality dirt that we had delivered. My colleagues and I dug a hole in this road and filled it with water and specially refined mud, the sort preferred in strip clubs for mud wrestling, I was told. Using a custom-built hydraulic mortar, the special-effects crew shot this mud onto the shiny-clean pickup truck, just as it drove over the mud puddle and passed another truck going the opposite direction. It took some trial and error to make it look like the opposing truck was causing the mud spray rather than the mortar. This took some timing.

For the better part of the day, we filmed the exploding mud hit the truck from multiple angles. The director shot the scene at 500 frames per second, so when the mud spatter was played back in slow motion, it had a tranquil, epic sort of beauty. After each pass, the truck had to be cleaned and the puddle and makeshift cannon reset for the next take. By the end of the day, my colleagues and I looked like we just crawled out of a swamp.

This particularly dirty job involved several days of preparation and resulted in a 30-second ad. When it was all edited, with a soundtrack, special effects, graphics, and voice-over, the commercial would be seamless. A viewer would never imagine the mess and the expense that went into the making. What they would see was a beautiful truck with a luxurious interior that could take a beating on the job site. For some reason, mud adds a layer of tacit authenticity to all things manly.

I don't know how effective this commercial was, but it had all the elements that make for a good ad. First, it was attention-grabbing. The mud in slo-mo was visually engaging. Second, and perhaps more important, it had emotional touch-points to connect with viewers. The actor looked like the ideal middle-aged man. He appeared to be comfortable in his surroundings and had the semblance of someone who had put in the time to earn his grey hairs and the spacious upgrades that the pickup's plush interior provided. The backdrop of the construction site conjured up the hard-working get-'er-done Spirit of America. Who wouldn't want to identify with that?

A Currency of Attention

The job at the construction site, like so many others, brings to mind the old adage, "time is money." I certainly wouldn't have been up to my knees in mud all day if it wasn't my job. When I go to work, like many Americans, I get paid by the hour. My labor is valued and rewarded with a wage proportional to my time on the clock. Wages in the United States are wildly diverse. There is a gap between the minimum wage and the top earners that would make the pharaohs blush. Suffice it to say that a $5 cup of specialty coffee looks a lot different to someone pushing a broom than it does to someone trading stocks for a living. The unequal distribution of money is a facet of the capitalist consumer economy, and no one, either at the top or the bottom of the income ladder, seems to have enough. However, there is something that we all possess an equal amount of, and that is attention. Attention is our presence of mind at any given moment. There is power in our ability to pay attention and according to marketers; it is a commodity that is much more valuable than we might have expected.

Viewers tend to think of television entertainment as the main course and commercials as the filler, but it is actually the other way around. Advertisers finance the "free" content so that they can have our attention. For them, programming is a sort of bait to get us to watch the ads. Television entertainment (and news for that matter) in the open media market is there to serve the advertisers. Whether it's the newest drama, the cable news, a sit-com or rom-com rerun, each broadcast has its price tag, and advertisers foot the bill. We may try to mute the volume or ignore the commercials, but somehow they still manage to be effective. Otherwise, the advertising industry would not have shelled out an estimated $170 billion[1] on advertising in the United States in 2013. How ads convince us to buy things is one question, but there can be no argument that they are effective. Advertising budgets increase each year as do our spending habits.

In 2014, $4 million was the price of a 30-second commercial during the Super Bowl. Over 111 million people watched the game, so it was a good opportunity for companies to reach out and connect with viewers. It cost roughly 0.035 cents per person for these companies to get their message across. This actually seems like a good deal, considering they purchased a third of the nation's undivided attention. Advertisers understand the true value of our attention. They pay for it, and we give it freely so that we may be entertained. For them each moment of life is an opportunity for a sale, and there are too few opportunities, so the cost of advertising continues to rise.

Seth Godin is former Vice President of Direct Marketing for Yahoo! and author of *Permission Marketing: Turning Strangers into Friends, and Friends into Customers*. He outlines a world wherein scarcity and surplus are guiding principles in human behavior. You need two things to have a bustling economy, he says: "people who want things, and a scarcity of things they want. Without scarcity, there's no basis for an economy." The scarce resource he says, is attention: "there's a vast shortage of attention. This combined shortage of time and attention is unique to todays information age. Consumers are now willing to pay handsomely to save time, while marketers are eager to pay bundles to get attention."[2] This gives the phrase "paying attention," a new significance an it is no coincidence that 6.4 million children between the ages of 4 and 17 have been diagnosed with Attention-Deficit/Hyperactivity Disorder.[3]

Attention is an essential requirement of any religious practice. Fasting, prayer, meditation, group worship, and charity all require mindful participation. As far as I know, there is no shortcut, no outsourcing, no app for the smartphone that can achieve a personal relationship with the Almighty. While it's not easy to find statistics on many religious practices, the figures on church attendance in the United States are somewhat varied. A Gallup poll indicates that close to 40 percent of Americans attend church,[4] but other polls suggest that less than 20 percent of Americans do so.[5] Either way, it is a low figure in a country where the average American watches 3–4 hours of television a day.[6] When it's all added up, the average American will have watched television for nine years of her life and seen over 2 million commercials by the age of 65.[7] How many churches can boast such a clear statement of loyalty and devotion? Neither sports, or any other activity comes close to our consumption of television. And meanwhile, marketers are eager to find new ways to attract more of our attention. The Internet is an open frontier in this rush to colonize mental space.

In his book, *Lovemarks: The Future Beyond Brands*, Kevin Roberts, CEO Worldwide of the marketing firm Saatchi & Saatchi, writes of the saturation of television channels, movies, radio stations, and other media that make it difficult for marketers to reach consumers. "People are overwhelmed by the choices they face. Forget the Information Economy. Human attention has become our principal currency. Job number one for any marketer these days is competing for attention. . . . And once you've captured that attention, you've got to show you deserve it. . . . Emotional connections with consumers have to be at the foundation of all our cool marketing moves and innovative tactics."[8] But his follow-up question is most revealing. He asks, how can marketers "convince people to commit for life?"[9]

Faith in Branding

If attracting attention is the just the initial part of the advertising equation, the second essential part is creating a relationship with consumers. In his book *Emotional Branding*, the late President, CEO, and Executive Creative Director of d/g* worldwide, Marc Gobé counsels marketers "get to know who your consumers really are, what really matters to them, and show them that you feel the same way."[10] Relationships are built on trust. Once we become emotionally engaged with a brand, the relationship starts to develop, and may possibly evolve into loyalty.

Harry Beckwith, popular lecturer and author of theologically sounding titles like *Selling the Invisible* and *The Invisible Touch: Four Keys to Modern Marketing*, writes that brands "are not simply tools for attracting business." Rather, they are able to "convince clients that they got just what the brand promised—even when they didn't." He counsels his readers to "Build a brand. Services are sold on faith, and brands create faith.[11]"

Kevin Roberts uses the phrase "loyalty beyond reason" to describe a sort of faith-based relationship between brands and consumers. He writes, "My thinking started to crystallize around a line Tide used back in the 1970s. 'Tide for cleaning you can count on.' I thought, 'Something you could always count on. That would be hugely valuable. That *would* be Loyalty Beyond Reason.' And the first word that came to me was trust."[12]

Emotional branding and "loyalty beyond reason" speak of a type of advertising that goes way deeper than the label on a box or a single commercial. It speaks of identity and not so much that of the product as of the consumer. Much as a cattle owner's hot iron is used to burn his mark on the flesh of his property, brands today seek to possess consumers' hearts, minds, and wallets with a "til death do us part" kind of relationship. Loyalty, faith, trust, and love are just some of the popular catchphrases among marketing gurus for building consumer relationships. The McDonald's slogan, "I'm Lovin' It," perhaps sums up advertising's holy grail: to design brands we love so much, we think we cannot live without them.

The Stuffed Calf and the Golden Fleece

On a visit to Ethiopia, my wife and I traveled to a rural farming community about two hours walk from the nearest road or electric wire. Rolling grassland stretched for miles in all direction, dotted with small family farms. Some farms had a cow or few sheep. All the homes were small and round and made of mud and thatch. Inside one of these homes, we broke bread with a family. When lunch was finished our host took down from the rafter where it hung something about the size and shape of a large dog. It had stiff legs and scruffy hair that looked like it had been coming off in patches for some time. We couldn't tell by looking, but soon discovered it was the remains of a baby calf that had undergone some kind of homespun taxidermy. I waited while our laughing host told the story to my wife's cousin before he could translate it to me. The calf had been stillborn and its mother had, as a result, refused to produce milk. The farmers, searching for a way to salvage an unfortunate situation, had stuffed the calf and brought it to the mama cow, hoping its scent and likeness would trick her into lactating. It must have been a bizarre sort of puppet show, but somehow the ruse worked, and the mother cow responded by giving milk. It was a great win for the family and a great story that had obviously been told many times with pleasure.

Some years earlier, I had worked on a commercial in downtown Los Angeles that involved a number of cows. I don't remember what product the ad was supposed to be selling, probably some sort of breakfast cereal, but the concept was elaborate. It required a crane to hoist the cows off of the ground and film them dangling in midair, suspended by a sling and wires. We did the filming in a parking lot but had erected a green screen as a backdrop so a landscape could be digitally inserted in postproduction. After plenty of digital effects, the commercial would portray a stack of cows, standing on top of one another, probably in an idyllic green field, and there would be a funny punch line. In reality, cows are not anatomically designed to be lifted 10 feet off the ground by a crane, and their discomfort was anything but idyllic. The pressure of the hoist caused them to cry out and send cascades of manure down to the hot pavement where we waited with shovels and trash cans. I once spent a summer worked on a dairy farm and shoveling manure has never bothered me, but watching the poor bewildered heifers dangling in midair gave the whole job a bad smell.

Stories connect us to one another. The stories told in commercials are designed to connect people with products and convince people to go out and buy. The trick is, how do you get someone to believe your story in 30 seconds? If you can make them laugh or find some other way to stick in their mind, you've done your job. The bizarre illusions created in our cow commercial probably made an effective pitch, but something like that would seem ridiculous in other parts of the world where hunger is rampant and food does not need to be advertised to be sold.

I found something sacred in the story of the farmer in Ethiopia. He may have been poor by Western standards, but he had a wealth of creativity. He created an illusion that helped to feed his family, and the story retold continued to produce joy. I couldn't help but compare his story to ours. Our commercial created an illusion of a different sort, one designed to generate profit. Even though there may be nothing wrong with doing business this way, it seems our stories have drifted away from the source of life.

The God of the Bible seeks a relationship with people, and the Old and New Testaments trace the evolution of that relationship. Other religions are also relational, seeking to bridge the gap between human beings and the Great Mystery. Advertisers also seek a relationship with people. That relationship, as any, requires our time and attention, both limited resources. A worldview in which people are related to the Almighty is quite different to a worldview where people are seen as nothing more than consumers of goods and services. But the language used by marketers, the things they profess to value, their selling points, contain the same words and phrases, and offer the same rewards as religious leaders and texts. Advertising speaks to something fundamental about human nature and our spiritual needs, even if it encourages us to respond in a way that can never satisfy those needs. So many of the stories in consumer culture are told so as to transform spiritual needs into material desires, while religious texts are full of stories of people seeking spiritual fulfillment through material gain and failing.

Consumption as Religion

In *The Call to Conversion*, Jim Wallis points out that "Material goods have become substitutes for faith. It's not that people literally place their cars on the altar; rather, it is the function of these goods in a consumer society. They function as idols, even though most affluent U.S. Christians, like rich Christians throughout history, would deny it."[13]

Consumption operates a lot like a religion in capitalist societies. This isn't an recent idea, but has been echoed by both critics and supporters of advertising for nearly a century. Calvin Coolidge, U.S. president from 1923 to 1929, noted, "Advertising ministers to the spiritual side of trade. It is great power . . . part of the greater work of the regeneration and redemption of mankind."[14]

In 1955, economist Victor Lebow penned the often-quoted statement:

> Our enormously productive economy demands that we make consumption our way of life, that we convert the buying and use of goods into rituals, that we seek our spiritual satisfactions, our ego satisfactions, in consumption. The measure of social status, of social acceptance, of prestige, is now to be found in our consumptive patterns. The very meaning and significance of our lives today expressed in consumptive terms. The greater the pressures upon the individual to conform to safe and accepted social standards, the more does he tend to express his aspirations and his individuality in terms of what he wears, drives, eats- his home, his car, his pattern of food serving, his hobbies.[15]

Similarities between religion and consumption can be found throughout popular culture. Malls are designed like houses of worship, carefully using the religious symbols of water and light to influence consumer behavior. Shops line the corridors like little meditation chapels. Advertisers, like priests, minister to our desires by offering us affirmations that the newest products will bring us happiness, security, freedom, or a better tomorrow—in short, heaven. The sacred rite and duty of consumption is shopping, and the altar of the religion is the television. A good study on the subject is Jon Pahl's *Shopping Malls and Other Sacred Spaces*, in which he writes,

> At least with traditional religions, you know you're getting sold a product you have to take on faith—whether it's heaven, or nirvana, or whatever. Traditional religions are also quite up-front about the reality of suffering in the world, and they do much to remedy it. But the marketers of our domestic religious practices, ironically, lead us to think that we're actually choosing to spend hours with scrubbing bubbles and that through such choices we'll be "saved" from dirt.[16]

Consumerism is ritualistic, but advertising must constantly innovate to maintain the culture of consumption. Even though companies may "own" the earth's natural resources, they cannot, at least in theory, own our desires. Our relationship with brands must be constantly reaffirmed for them to remain viable. Consumers have short memories and are prone to feel more strongly about something they encounter frequently.

Advertising is the public face of enterprise, prompting us to believe in, buy, invest, engage, and connect with interests who market themselves. Politics is not exempt from this engagement. More often than not, the candidate with the best advertising and biggest budget wins the election. It is not that we are powerless in the face of clever marketing, but it does the job it is supposed to do and we are convinced. The more often a message is repeated, the more likely we are to believe it. The more often we see a product or person advertised, the more familiar we become with him, her, or it, the more we think about it and the more it becomes connected to our life. These are simple rules of living and apply to anything in our mental sphere.

In a consumer economy, people make discretionary choices as to how they will spend their money. The U.S. Bureau of Economic Analysis reports that 2012 personal consumption expenditures topped 11 trillion dollars.[17] It is the discretionary nature—the choice—of how the dollar will be spent that makes tools of influence so important to companies.

The Transformative Power of Thought

A commercial is just a simple tool, but taken in aggregate, and within the context of the entire spectrum of advertising, there emerges a much larger picture of a great struggle for our time, attention, devotion, love, and life-force. Americans altogether spend an estimated 250 billion hours in front of the television annually. If that time were translated into working wages of $5 an hour, we would earn extra $1.25 trillion dollars.[18] If that time were translated into helping others or visiting with friends, who knows how happy we could become?

My work behind the scenes on commercials prompted me to study them and the nature of images, influence, and mindful living. Every thought that passes through the mind has two parts: one is knowledge and the other is feeling. Knowledge is important, but I only act in proportion to feeling. I may know that there are starving people in the world, but if I do not know any of them personally, it is less likely I will feel connected to their suffering, and I will be less likely to act. On the other hand, if someone or some ad suggests that I look shabby and need a makeover, I am far more likely to feel something about that piece of knowledge, even if it is a lie. Because feeling empowers knowledge, emotion, properly instructed, is a powerful tool. Emotion leads to action.

I have noticed that what holds my attention becomes a part of my life. We have the power to change things in this world. What we devote our attention to is of profound importance. The challenge isn't to isolate oneself from advertising, though that may be a good idea. Rather, we need to become highly aware of our thoughts and emotions, becoming tireless gatekeepers for the substance of our consciousness, for out of it come the issues of life.

Religion, for all its failings, points the way to God. It attempts to address suffering in the world and calls us to have compassion for others. Prayer and fasting call us to contemplation. Worship and charity call us to community. Whatever feel-good, funny, or dire messages they may express, the role of advertising is all the same, regardless of the product: advertising calls us to buy things. The transaction is, on their end, purely financial. On the other end of the relationship, "consumers" trade time for money and money for the things that are advertised. It is a trade-off of life force for material.

I have never sought God in commercials, but I have become convinced that they are part of a ministry in the service of commerce. Popular culture is dictated by the medium through which it arrives. Television is funded by advertising, and programming is put there in an attempt to persuade us to buy things. Every representation of God in popular culture must be viewed with care. Pop culture as expressed through mass media has the mandate to be entertaining in order to draw viewers and sell advertising. Some portrayals may originate in a genuine search for meaning, but all content is subordinate to the system which is dominated by money.

The advertising world rarely references God, but it religiously uses sacred language. What does that say? Perhaps religion and advertising both attempt to communicate with the most profound and mysterious elements of the human experience. There is something intangible that they both attempt to connect with in the human mind and they have to use similar language to do it. What is the underlying truth behind both the materialism of the secular world and the spirituality of the religious world? What are they both addressing? Wherefrom do they draw their power? Toward what are they both pointing? What does it say about us and what we truly possess?

Notes

1. "US Total Media Ad Spend Inches Up, Pushed by Digital," eMarketer, August 22, 2013, http://www.emarketer.com/Article/US-Total-Media-Ad-Spend-Inches-Up-Pushed-by-Digital/1010154#irRPlOy5AVufpZVk.99.

2. Seth Godin, *Permission Marketing: Turning Strangers Into Friends, and Friends into Consumers* (New York: Simon and Schuster, 1999), 42.

3. "Attention-Deficit/Hyperactivity Disorder (ADHD)," Centers for Disease Control and Prevention, last updated November 13, 2013, http://www.cdc.gov/ncbddd/adhd/data.html.

4. Frank Newport, "In U.S., Four in Ten Report Attending Church Last Week," Gallup Politics, last updated March 15, 2014, http://www.gallup.com/poll/166613/four-report-attending-church-last-week.aspx.

5. Rebecca Barnes and Lindy Lowry, "7 Startling Facts: An Up Close Look at Church Attendance in America," Church Leaders, accessed March 15, 2014, http://www.churchleaders.com/pastors/pastor-articles/139575-7-startling-facts-an-up-close-look-at-church-attendance-in-america.html?p=1.

6. "Economic News Release," Bureau of Labor Statistics, United States Department of Labor, last modified June 20, 2013, http://www.bls.gov/news.release/atus.t11.htm.

7. "Television and Health," Internet Resources to Accompany *The Sourcebook for Teaching Science,* 2007, http://www.csun.edu/science/health/docs/tv&health.html#tv_stats.

8. Kevin Roberts, *Lovemarks: The Future Beyond Brands* (New York: Powerhouse Books), 33–34.

9. Ibid., 36.

10. Marc Gobé, *Emotional Branding: The New Paradigm for Connecting Brands to People* (New York: Allworth Press, 2001), 298.

11. Harry Beckwith, *The Invisible Touch: Four Keys to Modern Marketing* (New York: Warner Books, 2000), 103.

12. Roberts, *Lovemarks*, 66.

13. Jim Wallis. *The Call to Conversion: Recovering the Gospel for These Times* (San Francisco: Harper, 1992), 49.

14. Calvin Coolidge. BrainyQuote.com, accessed March 15, 2014, http://www.brainyquote.com/quotes/authors/c/calvin_coolidge_3.html.

15. Victor Lebow, "Price Competition in 1955," *Journal of Retailing* 31 (Spring 1955): 3.

16. Jon Pahl, *Shopping Malls and Other Sacred Spaces: Putting God in Place* (Grand Rapids, MI: Brazos Press, 2003), 108–109.

17. "Personal Consumption Expenditures by Function," U.S. Department of Commerce, Bureau of Economic Analysis, last revised August 7, 2013, http://www.bea.gov.

18. "Television and Health."

CHAPTER EIGHT

Theologizing Together: Media as Mediator of Meaning

Paula J. Lee

The purpose of this chapter is to reflect on the state of the engagement of contemporary journalism with religion. How has the relationship between religion and the media evolved? Are journalists being adequately trained in religion reporting? In what ways do contemporary media mediate the religious/spiritual meaning-making process after tragedies and other important events? Is it possible for the media to offer the complexity necessary for any sort of responsible care for persons? Are the needs of people being adequately met or instead impeded in this effort? Finally, what are the implications for pastoral theology?

To the question of whether the secular media should even cover religion, Gayle White, past president of the Religion Newswriters Association, says "yes," because along with sports, science, and politics it is an important part of life for many people. "Often, religion provides the 'why' in the equation of a story,"[1] she writes. Citing the role of religion in events around the world, religion's influence on voting, the arts ,and issues of life and death, she suggests that religion and/or ethics have application to a wide variety of news stories. Freelance writer and media consultant Kim Sue Lia Perkes writes about the challenges of balance and fairness in religion reporting that occur because one is often writing about beliefs versus facts that can be proven. She suggests that "fairness" should trump the journalistic concepts of "objective" and "subjective." The difficulties of this approach are obvious, and Perkes advises careful checking for biased jargon and true representation of both sides of a story. "The fairness of a good religion story relies on . . . [your skill] to explain intangible concepts held as real truth and sacred fact to those who believe them."[2] Fairness has not always been a standard in religion reporting, so a brief historical overview may prove helpful.

Historical Overview and Literature Review

Doug Underwood takes us back to the author of *Adventures of Robinson Crusoe*, Daniel Defoe, who is acknowledged for his role in the development of both journalism and novel writing. Underwood suggests Defoe was a "transitional figure who blended deep religious faith with the increasingly secular values of commercial publishing."[3] Believing in God's involvement with world events, Defoe wrote about the 1665 plague in England, which he experienced as a young man. He believed there was a message from God in this event, and he reflected on what this message might be both in his journalistic writing (*Due Preparations for the Plague*) and his fiction (*A Journal of the Plague Year*).

Scholar Marvin Olasky highlights the importance of journalism for 17th-century Puritans saying "events were their report card signed by God, and they wanted to know where they stood, for better or for worse."[4] Puritan journalist Increase Mather reported on natural disasters as "ordered by the Providence of God."[5] Underwood suggests that Deists and Enlightenment-influenced thinkers began to challenge this religion-centric worldview, even as they often unwittingly operated out of traditional Judeo-Christian moral thinking themselves. Controversy over religious ideas became increasingly prevalent in journalism, with publications backed by political factions and writers using pseudonyms as they hashed out religious issues.

As the newspaper industry became industrialized in the 1830s, religion coverage began to decline in the popular press, becoming primarily the domain of the religious press, who charged commercial newspapers with worldliness and abandoning religious tradition. Religion coverage, in the midst of scientific discovery and a more "objective" approach to news writing, became marginalized, "particularly as Darwinian theory arose to offer a competitive cosmological account of the origins of life found in the Bible."[6] The values of journalism became more aligned with commercialism and sensation-seeking than the speculative reflections of Defoe. Contrary to this trend were the "muckrakers" of the late 19th and early 20th centuries; investigative journalists who exposed corruption in order to correct the ills of society. Underwood says they were motivated by religious ideals, especially by Jesus as a promoter of social justice, but they did not necessarily believe in institutional religion.

Moving into the mid-20th century, Christian religion writers were focusing on issues more directly related to their own denominations. "Religious conservatives came to identify the mainstream press as an enemy of traditional religious beliefs, and surveys throughout the twentieth century often have shown reporters and editors to be political liberals (at least in the cultural and social sense, if not always in economic terms)."[7]

As religious and political stories became increasingly sensationalized, Robert Park and John Dewey called for "a richer and more intelligent form of journalism that utilized the techniques of social science to provide context and perspective to the day's events."[8] For Dewey and Park, a focus on community versus commercialism in communication was more true to Christian values. Their plea has seemingly fallen on deaf ears as evidenced by the pervasive vitriol we seem to accept as the norm on issues such as war, partisan politics, and social issues including gay marriage, abortion, and gun control. Interestingly, counteracting the move away from reporting on religious issues, Underwood says that at the end of the 20th century, in a response to market research that showed that there was reader interest in religion-related stories, American secular newspapers began publishing more of these in an effort to boost circulation.

Contemporary Journalism

Some important attention is being paid in the field of journalism to religion reporting and the formation of journalists. The Religion Newswriters Association (www.rna.org) is a support and advocacy group that describes itself as follows:

> RNA was founded in 1949 to advance the professional standards of religion reporting in the mainstream media and to create a support network for religion reporters. The Association's primary projects include an annual conference, contests for religion reporting, membership resources and mentoring. RNA envisions religion reporting and commentary informed by civility, accuracy, fairness and insight.

The Poynter Institute (www.poynter.org) is a journalism school offering courses on a variety of learning platforms covering reporting on all issues, including religion. A recent course offering, taught by Diane Winston, was "Religion, Culture and Society: Getting Beyond the Clichés." Winston is a scholar and journalist specializing in religion and the media. She teaches at the Annenberg School for Communication and Journalism at the University of Southern California. In addition to teaching and writing, her website (www.trans-missions.org) offers world news stories related to religion and resources for religion reporters.

Winston says, "The real issue is not the lack of trained religion reporters, but rather Americans' widespread ignorance about religion."[9] She suggests there never was a time "when the press provided smart, in-depth, contextualized coverage of religious leaders, issues, ideas, and communities,"[10] because it was sensationalism that brought in the advertising dollars and sold papers. Citing the lack of secular religious studies in schools and colleges, she claims that many otherwise well-educated people are ignorant of even the most basic religious issues and says this also impacts religion reporting.

In a 2012 article, Winston and writer John Green wrote about the public's faith in religion reporting based on a joint project of the Knight Program in Media and Religion at the Annenberg School and the Ray C. Bliss Institute of Applied Politics at the University of Akron.[11] The study surveyed journalists and media consumers to find out how effective the media is in this area. Noting the majority responses from both constituencies that the news media "does a poor job of explaining religion in society,"[12] the authors cite "lack of expertise" as a cause. "Half of those surveyed say they don't know a lot about religion. Only a fifth claimed to be 'very knowledgeable,' and most in that small segment said their information was from their own religious practice, self-study and their family background."[13] Both groups acknowledge the impact of religion on popular culture, politics, and global and environmental issues; however, they also see religion as a source of conflict. Winston remarks, "One might think, then, that the news media would be filled with thoughtful stories that explore the complexity and ambiguity of religion in society. But since that's not the case, journalists, lacking strong feelings of their own, may be opting for what's easy."[14]

Religion reporter Terry Mattingly says, "At the moment, the state of religion coverage is somewhere between "evolving" and "on life support." "Cutbacks in top 40 newsrooms—organizations that once had the resources to support a variety of specialty reporters—have sent many veteran scribes into early retirement. More than a dozen print newsrooms have reduced or eliminated their religion-news jobs in the past three years."[15] The editors of *Christianity Today*, in a 2010 editorial on religious reporting, describe "an impoverished media environment that values outrage and eyeballs above all else."[16] In the same editorial, they report on a panel at a recent meeting of the Religion Newswriters

Association where members applauded increasing online reader interest in religious issues while also noting that the majority of "clicks" went to divisive and inflammatory stories versus nuanced, meaningful reflections.

Some see value in the ongoing changes in the way religion is reported. Doug Underwood, author of *From Yahweh to Yahoo!: The Religious Roots of the Secular Press*, believes taking religion reporting out of the "ghetto" of the Saturday page and integrating it with news of other important issues will improve the coverage and make it more relevant to peoples' lives.[17] Still others believe religion reporters need to accept the fact that the ecosystem of religion is evolving and journalists need to present issues in a way that "the non-religious, at least some of the time, find themselves."[18] Smith insists that religion be covered as it is really experienced. "Properly understood, our beat has become more important than ever precisely because traditional religion is in eclipse."[19]

Meaning-Making

The debate continues, but so does the news. Whether it's a school shooting, subway bombing, or a natural disaster such as a hurricane or tsunami, contemporary media provide us with an intensive and intimate view, sometimes more than we can bear to watch. An important part of the journalist's job is to disseminate the facts, informing the public about exactly what happened and who was affected by the event. It is difficult enough, as we experience with increasing frequency, to get these basic facts on the table, what with instantaneous videos and rumors and suggestions taken as truth. In the rush to be first with breaking news, errors are made, errors that can themselves cause further tragedy. Citizens active on Twitter, Reddit, and other social media platforms also contribute to the confusion, not always taking into account the moral and ethical implications of the information they share. After the 2013 Boston Marathon shooting, a Brown University student was falsely identified as one of the suspects. His name and picture went viral, followed by threatening emails, phone calls, and news teams descending on his family members, despite the fact that there was no evidence tying him to the shooting. The student was later found dead in the Providence River. It is believed that he took his own life, and it is not known whether this happened before or after the Boston Marathon, as he had been missing and known to be depressed before this event. Regardless, his family had to endure additional grief and stress from the hype that one imagines was not greatly relieved by Reddit's formal public apology.[20]

Once and if the facts are presented, the next step is an analysis of the event. What led to it? What was the motivation for violence? How are those affected working through it? What do they have to say about it? At this point in the process, news reporting takes widely divergent paths, depending on viewers/readers, political bent, financial backing, and the level of the source's commitment to quality journalism presented by well-trained professionals.

As the power and presence of the media in its many forms continues to evolve, R. S. Sullender writes about the growing role of the media in mediating the grieving process after very public tragedies. "The media increasingly plays the role of a maker of meaning or an attributor of various diverse meanings . . . a role traditionally reserved for theologians, politicians and historians."[21] He suggests that the media actually shapes the way grief happens, using the example of the public's anger and perception of a lack of response by the Royal Family to the death of Princess Diana. The media highlighted this, leading to a change in behavior and protocol. Sullender argues that in the experience of "collective sorrows, we often look for an emerging grief leader, who can speak on behalf of us all, speak to and about the feelings, the pain and the meaning of the unfolding events."[22] Fulfilling this need is predicated on trust in the wisdom and discernment of the leader, which is not necessarily what we have come to expect from media pundits.

Our ability to feel connected to events far away from us through images and personal narrative is enhanced by the omnipresence of media options that invite our involvement in tragedies we previously might not have been aware of, which has implications for both our personal and communal psyches. The proliferation of hyperreporting techniques and news anchors repeating the same sound bytes as they wait for the continuing development of a story has driven many to the satirical "fake news" sources of late-night comedy. Jon Stewart's *Daily Show* and Stephen Colbert's *The Colbert Report* have taken on credibility as entertaining and reliable sources who point out hypocrisy in political, social, and religious contexts. Schofield Clark and Dierberg write about the method of truth-finding employed by contemporary news satirists. Citing Jeffrey Jones, they name the method "'redaction' . . . the taking apart and reassembling of facts within a different frame to create a new meaning."[23] In this way, Schofield Clark and Dierberg suggest, the programs are "performing a function formally assigned to journalism, encouraging people to become aware of how both punditry and mainstream news are constructed to create a particular narrative, and how the facts within a narrative might be alternately assembled to create a different, sometimes competing, meaning."[24]

The purpose of this redactive technique is to create meaning and arrive at some approximation of "the truth" (or "truthiness" as Stephen Colbert names it). The meaning-making quest of these satirists and other late night talk show hosts extends into tragic events as well. A few days after September 11, 2001, Jon Stewart, in his first television appearance since the event, addressed it directly with authentic tears as he asked his audience, "Are you okay? We pray that you are and that your family is." He went on to acknowledge what many of his viewers were experiencing, that "we've had an unendurable pain, an unendurable pain, and I just . . . I just wanted to tell you why I grieve—but why I don't despair," through choked-back tears. [25] In this opening, Stewart played the role of Sullender's "grief leader," and for many, with the gravitas and credibility needed to be of service.

After the Aurora movie theatre shooting in July of 2012, Stewart once again acknowledged the shared pain of his viewers. This time, he quickly moved into the political arena, questioning recent pundit comments that this was not the time to address gun control and accusing those who wanted to address it as "politicizing" the tragic event. His intense and articulate analysis of this moved him beyond the role of grief leader and into action for justice.

Late Late Show host Craig Ferguson devoted the opening of his show the day after the Aurora shooting to a serious reflection on the state of the world, drawing on his not-often-seen philosophical bent. He said the opening monologue that had been recorded the previous day referred to the Batman movie and was totally inappropriate to be shown this evening. He asked the question, "How do we make sense of anything like this?" and went on to say in a halting and heartfelt way, "if you are any way connected to this awful business; I'm sorry. I'm sorry that that happened. I know it's just awful, and my thoughts and my sympathies go to the families and to the people who were there. And just remember that we are all diminished by this. Every time something like this happens, we are all diminished by it."[26] Although Ferguson would likely not label himself a "grief leader," there are probably people who did not have his question "How do we make sense of anything like this?" posed to them in any other venue, and his articulation of this may have provided an opportunity for some form of contextual theologizing, even if it was not named as such.

The influence of these comedians with something to say about the repercussions of tragedy and social issues can reach beyond their television shows. Stephen Colbert, a self-proclaimed practicing Catholic, broke character and testified before a subcommittee in the House on the issue of migrant workers. He quoted Matthew 25 ("Whatsoever you do . . .") in reference to the injustices these individuals face. He regularly contextualizes religious topics on *The Colbert Report*, criticizing unjust power structures and calling out an inconsistent approach to moral issues. Using his conservative religious and political persona, he is able to skewer these inconsistencies, shifting thought and leading to a better understanding of issues. From a segment on the Christian Coalition: "On those subjects (reproductive rights and gay marriage), Jesus was very consistent. He never said a thing about either of them. So it's easy to know what he thought . . . [it's] whatever the Christian Coalition says he thought! You can trust that, 'cause no one thinks more right than them."[27] Schofield Clark and Dierberg suggest the contemporary lack of deference shown to religious issues, especially on satirical news shows, is not all bad. "As Colbert's persona bumbles his way through the worst of the United States' religious hubris and insensitivities, perhaps the public is invited to reconsider and tend to its own proclivities for similar human failings."[28]

Precritical Reporting

In reporting about natural disasters one notices the frequency of the word "miracle" or "miraculous" in describing survival stories. CNN reporter Wolf Blitzer was excoriated in a piece on *Slate.com* in May 2013 for comments he made to a survivor of the tornado in Moore, Oklahoma. Discussing her escape, Blitzer said, "'I guess you got to thank the Lord, right?' The woman hedged and looked down at her baby. 'Do you thank the Lord? For that split-second decision?'" Blitzer continued to push for an answer until the woman politely told him she was an atheist.[29] The interview ended awkwardly. Mark Stern writes, "Blitzer's behavior may seem startlingly condescending, insensitive, and mawkish. But in fact, mentions of God, miracles, and prayer have become the argot of post-disaster reportage. They shouldn't be. If you want to pray for Oklahoma or thank God it didn't kill more people, go ahead. But please, especially if you're a journalist, keep it to yourself."[30]

Stern makes a heartfelt plea; however, he goes on to reveal the lack of nuanced understanding so prevalent in media reporting on God, religious experience, and religion in general, when he writes, "Any God powerful and attentive enough to save survivors' lives should also be powerful and attentive enough to stop the catastrophe in the first place. It's insulting, futile, and distracting from the reality of natural disasters to inject your god into a calamity like Oklahoma's."[31] He speaks from his embedded theology, and it resonates with many people who also operate from precritical ways of reflecting on suffering and tragedy; however, it has little to offer a thoughtful or nuanced dialogue.

After the attacks of September 11, 2001, a common public response from religious leaders was to focus on God's presence in those who saved lives, rescued people, offered support to others, and cleaned up in the years following. This was helpful to many; however, the question of God's implication in the attacks themselves was not adequately addressed by theologians in the public forum. Had it been, new language and different paradigms for interpreting these events might be commonplace or at least referenced after new disasters, and this is not happening. Certainly, scholars wrote for other scholars and theologians; however, the message was not fully received or discussed by the average person, who doesn't often think about God or religion, except during times like these when the old and worn phrases are pulled back out again with no apparent development or growth in the public thought process.

Jerry Falwell, Pat Robertson, and other representatives of the Religious Right insist that tragedies such as the attacks of September 11 are God's punishment for human sins such as abortion and promiscuity. This is a religious interpretation that is not relevant or meaningful for most contemporary people who are not part of conservative evangelical circles, and the continuing rehashing of this understanding of who God is serves only to further alienate the public, reinforcing their belief in the anti-intellectual stance of religion in general. The lack of complexity or any attempt at cocreating a deliberative theology that would prove meaningful and life-giving does not do justice to the public voice these figures have.

Fox News general assignment reporter Kelly Wright (an ordained minister and former cohost of *Fox & Friends Weekend*) recently wrote a story about Morgan Lake of Dunkirk, Maryland. She was rear-ended by a tractor trailer on the Chesapeake Bay Bridge in July 2013 and ended up in the Bay. Lake believes God intervened during her time of panic, calming her enough to unbuckle her seatbelt, pull herself out of the car window, and swim to shore where she was rescued. Wright's story centers around the media's handling of Lake's ordeal. Her mother accused the media of leaving out her daughter's references of gratitude to God in their reporting. Wright said, "She (Lake) wanted me to let you know how God's supernatural power gave her superhuman strength to break free from a watery grave. So here's the rest of the story."[32] Wright accuses "some news organizations" of distancing "themselves from any reference to God, Jesus, or miracles, even when it's germane to the story. In this age of cynicism and abandonment of faith, Morgan's story is a dramatic reminder that God is real. Miracles happen every day; they're just not reported."[33] Lake's story is compelling;

however, Wright's simplistic religious approach lacks nuance just as much as Mark Stern's does.

Pastoral Theology

What illumination can the field of pastoral theology offer? In her discussion of *Compassion as a Practical Theodicy*, Wendy Farley writes, "Religious accounts of the human condition are largely defined by the desire to understand, intellectually and experientially, how it is that human beings find themselves in an existence torn by the extremes of love and beauty on the one hand and abysmal and seemingly meaningless pain, destruction, and injustice on the other."[34] Farley articulates the existential human situation in a way that makes us appreciate the contribution of pastoral theology as we bemoan the current state of much of religion reporting. How often do we read news stories that provide us with meaningful frameworks for developing our capacity for this type of reflection? (I realize this is beyond the scope of many journalists, but encourage us to continue to think about how pastoral theology can join the conversation at this level.)

In her discussion Farley holds the Buddhist and Christian notions of compassion as a response to evil as opposed to the justifications and expositions found in traditional theodicies. Through compassion, Farley says, we move beyond our own egos into an agapaic love and concern for others into a *practice* (italics mine) of theodicy, which means "participating in a compassionate response to evil rather than trying to justify it."[35] In an earlier work, Farley reminds us of the foundational importance of appreciating the humanity of others if we are to continue to evolve beyond mere moralism to an ethical existence. "One may feel pity or obligation toward another person but not toward 'filthy Communist swine' or 'lazy drug-addict welfare mothers.'"[36] This insight adds more urgency to the potentially harmful consequences of Winston and Green's suggestion that busy and uninformed journalists may be "opting for something that's easy,"[37] especially as it relates to generalizations and labels.

I am not suggesting that media or journalists are responsible for pastoral care; however, they do contribute to the meaning-making process, so a reflection on a pastoral theological approach to responding to tragedy may provide a helpful contrast. Larry Graham suggests three responses in an effort to meet the needs of people who have experienced catastrophic disaster: "First, by lamenting the world that was lost; second, by interrogating the social, moral, and cosmic order giving rise to catastrophic disasters; and, third, by reclaiming life through an enduring strategic outpouring of justice-based communal, political, economic, and spiritual assistance over time."[38]

Media outlets certainly provide a platform for lamentation; telling one's story and expressing the pain and loss that have been experienced. This narrative process often brings us to vicarious grief that moves us with sympathy and "serves as a reminder of our own losses and thus re-activates our own unfinished grieving";[39] this is reflected in the displays of public mourning that have become so prevalent in recent times. It also provides the impetus to move people to respond in the form of monetary or physical assistance, the erecting of shrines, and the offering of prayer. Graham says this process "provides the basis for moral outrage, social protest, and for engaging and revising theological interpretations of God and the world."[40]

Lamentation over a catastrophic event or anything that shakes our basic beliefs about how the world "should be," leads us to a "painful struggle to create new meanings from the rubble of shattered beliefs and assumptions."[41] This provides an opening for the coconstruction of a deliberative theology; the offering of a framework and guidance for a public process that would not, of course, replace individual work but would enrich and complexify the often-simplistic approach offered in the journalistic landscape of meaning-making, which may provide the only reflective opportunity for many people. As an example, in writing about the media response to the Fort Hood shooting in 2009, Michele Rosenthal says this event "demonstrates the ways in which civil religion remains dependent on the small screen."[42] The shooter at the U.S. Army base was identified early on as being of Middle Eastern origin; however, most of the major news networks did not mention this, instead focusing on posttraumatic stress disorder and stories of those affected by PTSD. *Fox News* did take the religious-terrorist route and were critical of the other networks for their choices and of President Obama for his cautious response. Up to and including the memorial service at Fort Hood that followed the shootings, the President framed the tragedy in a way that did not employ evangelical rhetoric or the further advancement of a culture of fear. "'Drawing upon a tradition of civil religion that embraces unity and diversity', he declared powerfully: 'We are a nation that guarantees the freedom to worship as one chooses. And instead of claiming God on our side, we remember Lincoln's words, and always pray to be on the side of God.'"[43] Graham acknowledges the conflict and potential further dislocation that can occur "when belief systems, theological meanings, and moral codes become public discourse for the purpose of interpreting catastrophic disasters. . . ."[44] He wisely counsels sensitivity and the careful choice of words while encouraging pastoral theologians to engage with these issues.

Graham's third step is reclaiming goodness, which he describes as helping "ourselves and others reconstruct lives that are meaningful in the aftermath of disaster."[45] Sullender's conclusions suggest this effort may be impeded by an increasing media focus on trauma, both on a personal and collective level. He asks, "Does the media's over-exposure of death, violence and tragedy desensitize us to the real dramas and needs that surround us, sometimes in our immediate neighborhoods?"[46] From television dramas to intensive and repeated graphic videos of violent world events, we are exposed as never before to depictions of a world that does not seem conducive to or coherent with "the existence of truth and beauty that are harmonized within actual community practice,"[47] as described by James Poling. By its nature, reporting focuses on the dramatic events themselves and little is written about the grief process, which may lead to "a death-denying and grief-avoiding culture,"[48] as well as a desensitization to suffering and tragedy. Media coverage may well be working against the process of reclaiming goodness, despite its potential to facilitate it.

Graham says disaster and tragedy "generate the possibility of an intense human solidarity by which we are sustained and from which we might generate meaning and hope."[49] This coming together in the face of suffering may be a connection point for the media and pastoral theology, although they have different aims. We have seen how quickly the original sense of solidarity we experience after a tragedy can degenerate into blame, choosing camps, and divisive theological claims. Journalists often escalate this process because as we have seen, many are operating out of precritical understandings of suffering, sensationalism sells, and human nature keeps us moving forward in our quest for answers and reasons. Pastoral theology is concerned with meaning-making that emerges though the exercise of caring relationships, utilizing both present and prior lived experience. It seems that these are two divergent paths; however, the sustenance, meaning, and hope Graham identifies in "intense human solidarity" is worth holding onto. Perhaps a focus on this place of possibility would serve both groups, providing the opportunity for the cocreation of meaning and news stories that move beyond the simplistic.

Individually and as societies, people need care after tragic and disturbing events, and many don't have ties to religious communities that traditionally provided this care. These events must be reported on in a way that provides knowledge; however, the complexity and meaning-making possibilities of these events cannot be abandoned out of ignorance or laziness. Together, journalists and pastoral theologians have the potential to provide the framework and resources for life-giving postmodern religious interpretations from a place of solidarity and commitment to care.

Notes

1. Gayle White, "Secular Media and Religion," ReligionLink, June 2, 2013, http://www.religionlink.com/faqs/secular-media-and-religion/.

2. Kim Sue Lia Perkes, "Balance and Fairness," ReligionLink, June 16, 2013, http://www.religionlink.com/faqs/secular-media-and-religion/.

3. Doug Underwood, "Religion in Print Media," in *The Oxford Handbook of Religion and the American News Media* (New York: Oxford University Press, 2012), 113.

4. Marvin Olasky, *Telling the Truth: How to Revitalize Christian Journalism* (Wheaton, IL: Crossway, 1996), 103–106.

5. Ibid.

6. Underwood, "Religion in Print Media," 121.

7. Ibid., 122.

8. Ibid., 123.

9. Diane Winston, "The Myth of News Media as Secularist Conspiracy," *Religion Dispatches*, April 16, 2013.

10. Ibid.

11. John Green and Diane Winston, Good News? Media Consumers and Producers on Religion Coverage University of Southern California and University of Akron, April 5, 2012, http://annenberg.usc.edu/~/media/PDFs/winston-bliss.ashx.

12. Diane Winston and John Green, "Do You Have Faith in the Media?," Washington Post, April 5, 2012, http://www.washingtonpost.com/blogs/guest-voices/post/do-you-have-faith-in-the-media/2012/04/05/gIQALA2fxS_blog.html.

13. Ibid.

14. Ibid.

15. Terry Mattingly, "State of the Godbeat 2010," Patheos: Hosting the Conversation on Faith, April 19, 2010, http://www.patheos.com/blogs/tmatt/2010/04/state-of-the-godbeat-2010/.

16. Editor, "Burned by the Qur'an Burning," *Christianity Today*, November 2010.

17. Sarah Pulliam, "Religion Sections Deleted," *Christianity Today*, April 2007.

18. Peter Smith, "The Facts of Faith," Religion Newswriters Association, July 15, 2013, http://www.rna.org/?page=eextra_2013_07_15.

19. Ibid.

20. Daily Mail Reporter, "Parents' Agony as They Wait for Confirmation on Whether Body Pulled from River Is Their Son, the Missing Brown Student Who Was Wrongly Accused in Marathon Bombing," The Daily Mail, April 2013, http://www.dailymail.co.uk/news/article-2313870/Sunil-Tripathi-Police-body-missing-college-student-falsely-accused-Boston-Marathon-bomber-internet-sleuths.html.

21. R. Scott Sullender, "Vicarious Grieving and the Media," *Pastoral Psychology* 59 (2010): 196, doi:10.1007/s11089-009-0227-5.

22. Ibid., 195.

23. Jeffrey Jones, *Entertaining Politics: New Political Television and Civic Culture* (Lanham, MD: Rowman and Littlefield, 2004).

24. Lynn Clark and Jill Dierberg, "Late-Night Comedy as a Source of Religion News," in *The Oxford Handbook of Religion and the American News Media* (New York: Oxford University Press, 2012), 99.

25. Jon Stewart, "The Daily Show," *The Daily Show with Jon Stewart* (New York: Comedy Central, 2001).

26. Craig Ferguson, "The Late Late Show with Craig Ferguson," July 2012.

27. Stephen Colbert, "The Colbert Report" (Comedy Central, December 5, 2006).

28. Clark and Dierberg, "Late-Night Comedy as a Source of Religion News," 108.

29. Mark Joseph Stern, "There Is Nothing Miraculous about a Tornado, Wolf Blitzer," *Slate.com*, May 22, 2013.

30. Ibid.

31. Ibid.

32. Kelly Wright, "Morgan Lake's Story Dramatic Reminder That God Is Real, Miracles Happen," FoxNews.com, July 24, 2013, http://www.foxnews.com/opinion/2013/07/24/morgan-lake-story-dramatic-reminder-that-god-is-real-miracles-happen/.

33. Ibid.

34. Wendy Farley, "'The Pain-Dispelling Draft': Compassion as a Practical Theodicy," *Perspectives in Religious Studies* 26, no. 3 (Fall 1999): 291.

35. Ibid., 296.

36. Wendy Farley, *Tragic Vision and Divine Compassion: A Contemporary Theodicy* (Louisville, KY: Westminster John Knox Press, 1990), 37.

37. Winston and Green, "Do You Have Faith in the Media?"

38. Larry Kent Graham, "Pastoral Theology and Catastrophic Disaster," *The Journal of Pastoral Theology* 16, no. 2 (Fall 2006): 2.

39. Sullender, "Vicarious Grieving and the Media," 193.

40. Graham, "Pastoral Theology and Catastrophic Disaster," 7.

41. Ibid., 9.

42. Michele Rosenthal, "Commercial Television News, Crisis, and Collective Memory," in *The Oxford Handbook of Religion and the American News Media* (New York: Oxford University Press, 2012), 142.

43. Ibid., 152.

44. Graham, "Pastoral Theology and Catastrophic Disaster," 10.

45. Ibid., 12.

46. Sullender, "Vicarious Grieving and the Media," 198.

47. Graham, "Pastoral Theology and Catastrophic Disaster," 12.

48. Sullender, "Vicarious Grieving and the Media," 199.

49. Graham, "Pastoral Theology and Catastrophic Disaster," 15.

CHAPTER NINE

A Shared Critical Ethic for Media Images and Liturgy

Jann Cather Weaver

Do not remember the former things, or consider the things of old. I am about to do a new thing; now it springs forth, do you not perceive it?
—Isaiah 43:18–19

And the one who was seated on the throne said, "See, I am making all things new."
—Revelation 21:5

This chapter will initiate a shared critical ethic for liturgy and the media images of visual culture. This critical ethic has concise rubrics for the creation of both media images and liturgies in postmodern "realities": a Tillichian understanding of implicitly and explicitly religious content in form and style;[1] a substance of significant meaning and just purpose; a decentralized authority; an understanding of community as incarnational as well as virtual and viral;[2] and, a nonessentialist understanding of theological aesthetics as politically and culturally contextual. With this shared critical ethic, we can perceive and participate in media images and liturgies of substance, which God is making new, now.

The Link between Media Images and Liturgy

Media images and liturgy hold comparable power and authority. They make or break communities. They proffer meanings for life and provide orderings for values and mores. Both, however, can be Kierkegaardian "twaddle."[3] Or, in this day, we could call them, analogously, "Twitter-iffic."[4] Media images and liturgy share a common bed; their pillow talk is about the human condition in crisis and crux, in fear and flux, accompanied by arguments about authority, responsibility, and "reality."

A shared critical ethic for media images and liturgy begins with understanding that they are both media. Media images and liturgy are intervening instruments for storing and/or communicating expressions of significant content in order to participate in the ongoing creation with God of a responsible world in right relationship (righteousness). They mediate the Sacred, the Ultimate Concerns, the Numinous, God, the meanings, the messages, the mediocre, and/or the twaddle.[5] Media images and liturgy mediate that which the church and/or culture deem as the implicitly or explicitly religious—be it consumerism, patriotism, or humanity's relationship to creation. They point to themselves (signs) or beyond themselves (symbols); we participate in and with them; and, they "reveal something which otherwise does not enter into our consciousness."[6]

Liturgy functions as explicitly religious in form/performance and content, in that it explicitly mediates the Sacred or Ultimate Concern.[7] Liturgies, for instance, which promote affluence ("prosperity theology/ prosperity gospel") as evidence of God's favor, use liturgy to mediate the Ultimate Concern of wealth by using language of economic blessings, perhaps purposefully using expensive technological media to produce high-definition and entertaining images to manipulate emotions. Liturgies, however, that mediate an encounter with the Sacred/the Ground of Being (Paul Tillich)/the Divine, use liturgy that has compelling, challenging theological substance—the liturgies "make it plain."[8] Images in these liturgies do not manipulate emotions; rather, they mediate transcendence. In our consumer culture, media images function both/and as explicitly and implicitly religious. Unless explicitly religious, most mass media images are implicitly religious in content, in that they mediate what the producers of the images want us to consider as our Ultimate Concerns: cars, McMansions, and/or the latest smartphone.

Media images are mediated images via digital or print form. Images by definition are a representation of a portion of various realities. (I say, "realities" because "reality" in postmodern thought and theology is a construction of interpretations with shared meanings and is contextually biased and socially constructed.[9]) Mass media images mediate varying interpretations of realities. We experience the "message," that is, the effect or consequences, of media images. This is what Marshall McLuhan meant by the catchphrase, "The medium is the message."[10] The media images in our lives mediate a message with consequences, that is, an effect, that shapes what we, consciously or unconsciously, should consider our Ultimate Concern. For example, historically, the ubiquitous 19th-century missionary image of Jesus as Caucasian with blue eyes led to the common belief in the superiority of the Caucasian race, that is, the race most similar to Jesus.[11] Consequentially, Western colonization of Africa and Africans seemed divinely stamped to both the colonizer and the colonized. Similarly, the medium of liturgy, when created and performed as an art form with substance, mediates participatory encounters with God, transforming us and generating agents for just action.

Presuppositions

In visual culture, many people meet media images with passive, uncritical attention. Media images deluge our visual field. As David Freedberg claimed in his 1989 book, *The Power of Images*, we have a "new abundance" of "low-level imagery."[12] Their focus is more on sensory appeal than significant content. "Substance gives way to sounds and sights."[13] In 1994, George Barna claimed that we "have been seduced by breadth rather than depth, by quantity rather than quality, by style rather than substance."[14] "Making it plain," that is, making our images compelling, challenging, and substantial in message, is not a commonly shared rubric in our visual culture. Freedberg made his claim decades before high-definition, digitally relayed images, ubiquitous digital cameras in phones, Facebook, Flickr, blogs, YouTube, GodTube, and online streaming of shows offered by Hulu, Netflix, and HitBliss. Truly, a "new abundance" of "low-level imagery" does not "make it plain."

The privileged media images today are not significant in content or aesthetic. Rather, media images are "vast, diverse, and . . . incapable of being tamed," all bearing a complexity of responses.[15] As an analogous parallel to Moore's Law of 1965, the "law" that predicts exponential growth of technology in form and bandwidth every two years, we can likely expect exponential growth of media images as technology exponentially advances every two years the means for mediating these images to us.[16] Our cultures' "high art" is increasingly more removed from daily life, more elite, and is far outnumbered and in competition with untamed media images.[17] Ubiquitous media images today do not "make it plain."

In the ecclesiastical world, speaking specifically about mainline American Protestantism, many liturgies lack substance, style, or any significance of the Sacred. Liturgies vacillate between boring, stale, static orders or distracting pop-liturgical experiments. Liturgists speciously compartmentalize worship styles into traditional, contemporary, or blended in flawed attempts to retain and attract new members. Without forethought of liturgical theology, a typical order of worship becomes pot-holed with hip moments of film clips and/or theologically vapid visual displays. Worship focuses more on MTV appeal than substantial content.[18]

Mainline American Protestantism seems to swing between seeking the Sacred in sentimentality and privileging the staid practices.[19] Rather than question the current state of liturgy with participatory, responsible, and theological inquiry, liturgy, in its extremes, has trendy frenetic enthusiasts ripping it to unrecognizable shreds—or it remains hermetically sealed from any refreshing spirit. Instead, our liturgies need to evoke awe, contain delight, inspire hope, tell the truth, and "make it plain" with passion and theological substance.[20]

In our media images and in our liturgies, we are, as Franky Schaeffer says, "addicted to mediocrity." This deficiency has removed us from the impulse of the Sacred, "making us ineffectual" in the world.[21] Mediocrity lacks substance of meaning and just purpose. In contrast, the Sacred, God, and/or the Numinous, is substantially diverse, beautiful, interconnected, contextual, and participatory in its ongoing webs of creativity, enjoying beauty with hope and justice in detail and complexity. Encountering God moves us to responsible, just action in creation's community. Mediocre media images and liturgies lack an encounter with the Sacred, failing to move us to responsible and just agency in creation's community. They reduce us to nonparticipants with no authority or accountability.

Qualities of Postmodernism and Poststructuralism

Poststructuralism is one aspect of what may be a larger societal shift called postmodernism. Postmodernism is a new cultural, social, and economic shift in Western societies in which fundamental aspects of the older modern world have changed to such a degree that a new historical world is upon us. That the phenomenon of postmodernism even exists, let alone what its nature is, is highly debatable and has spawned an enormous literature mainly in social and cultural studies.[22]

Postmodernism, a highly contested system of thought, defies definition by the defining nature of radical postmodernism itself. Postmodernism, at its core, is multiplicity and diversity. Art, literature, philosophy, science, theology, and social science all have different understandings of postmodernism. Postmodernism extends from philosophers as Jean Baudrillard, Jacques Derrida, Michel Foucault, Jacques Lacan, and Jean-François Lyotard to artists, theologians, and scientists as John Cage, Ethan and Joel Coen, Umberto Eco, Carlos Fuentes, Michio Kaku, Thomas Kuhn, Toni

Morrison, Robert Rauschenberg, Salman Rushdie, Mark C. Taylor, and Kurt Vonnegut—to name a few. Postmodernism as a thought system—and methodology—that dialogues and debates across disciplines about realities and dissonant contradictions. By definition, postmodernism is postmodernisms.

Poststructuralism, one aspect of postmodernism, is a group of theories "concerning the relationship between human beings, the world, and the practice of making and reproducing meanings." Poststructuralism recognizes that the origins of our worldviews are not the language or images we recognize, but are rather products "of the meanings we learn and reproduce." ("The message is the medium.") Churches and cultures teach worldviews to be learned and reproduced. Poststructuralism understands that meaning is contextual and malleable, because humans can intervene and alter once–taken-for-granted meanings, norms, and values.[23]

A shared, critical ethic for media images and liturgy, which I am presenting, comes from a poststructuralist, postmodern, Jewish, Christian, and interfaith perspective. This does not necessarily neglect the concerns of people who name themselves atheists, agnostics, humanists, or uncategorical, as they also have Ultimate Concerns. In poststructural and postmodern thought and theology, theological aesthetics and liturgical experiences are not known in "universal" or essentialist ways.[24] Context in postmodernism determines content, and, thereby, experience. Postmodernism decentralizes authority, and we see a loss of any central authority determining content and who participates in content creation. Other critical qualities of poststructuralism and postmodernism include the following:

- Agency becomes local and nonhierarchical. All media is participatory and localized in creation (production) and content.
- Media is embodied, virtual, and viral. Emerging media overlaps with multiple other forms of media.
- Meanings, interpretations, and realities diverge, even within a common or shared experience.
- Mediation and negotiation of "truths" operate within a paradigm of both/and rather than a Platonic dualism of either/or.
- Nonhierarchical participation, as well as constant negotiation of content and its purpose, prevent postmodernism from becoming a new form of relativism.
- We experience and participate in community in embodied, virtual, and viral ways.

Content in poststructuralist postmodern societies and institutions is radically decentralized and thoroughly distributed throughout old, new, and emerging methods of delivery, that is, media. The form and style of media are responsible for content: The form and style of media serve the purpose of the content; content determines the form and style of the media. The forms and styles of media create divergent meanings, interpretations, and realities. The former centralizing parties have lost control (authority) of content to localized, individual, or small group self-generated production and distribution processes. We no longer have a center, a hierarchy, a periphery, a margin of expanse, or culturally definitive directions or mores. We have shifting centers, endless expansions, twisted webs of meaning, squiggly complex polyhedra, multilateral untidy negotiations of realities, and a multiplicity of controls.[25] Both/and rather than either/or speaks about how content interacts. Whoever declares responsibility, declares authority for making plain their particular content production and reproduction according to a particular, sometimes negotiated, nonuniversal.

A postmodern world order of media images transforms the very conditions of our lives and consciousness.[26] We live in image-centric economic societies, a characteristic of postmodern realities where the "word" no longer can claim ascendancy. This essay, as it is written and presented, is not participating in a postmodern modality. Rather, it is dependent upon the centrality of the "word," and its presentation is nonparticipatory with its audience. Books like Mark C. Taylor's *Imagologies* begins to participate in postmodernism in its unorthodox presentation of content in "word designs," giving space on each page for the reader to interact with pen or pencil with the content.[27] Yet, a postmodern world order will shelve many books in museums; content—word and image—will be made and delivered in various interactive media forms and modes of delivery. Books and academic dissertations will be virtual, interactive websites with wikis and interactive blogs. Liturgies will be created within the interactive moment of the embodied, virtual, and viral communities' traditions and will be composed of immediate contextual content, rather than designed to be passively followed in prewritten forms found in books of worship.

A Shared Ethic for Media Images and Liturgy

In a shared ethic for media images and liturgy, content is significant and substantial: It is made plain and we perceive it. Significant and substantial content evokes, invokes, and converts us to just, participatory agency and action, locally and in the world; it has the grand Vision of God/the Numinous/the Sacred in mind, implicitly or explicitly, and contextualized.[28] Significant and substantial content is not mediocre or Twitter-iffic litter.

Christian liturgy in postmodern realities is decentralized from the clergy, requiring not only participation but also interactive feedback before, during, and after the liturgy. Liturgical language and formulas are contextualized and particular. Liturgy is not confined or defined by deterministic architecture; rather, liturgy determines architecture. The "Word" becomes a sacrament and the Sacraments belong to the people. Tradition is reformed by placing it in relationship to the future, the already-but-not-yet Vision of God. The core of tradition becomes uncertain, multidoctrinal (if doctrinal), and reforming in relationship to God's eschatological In-Breaking revelations. God is making all things new as the eschatological future impinges on us.

Let us examine contextualized and particular liturgical language and formulas versus universalized liturgical language and formulae. The *Common Book of Prayer* becomes *many* contextualized common books of prayer. Required liturgical formulas, for example, the Trinitarian Formula for baptisms, become "relanguaged" in significance to particular contexts. For instance, in a matriarchal society, the Trinitarian Formula of the Western Patriarchal society fails to signify meaning. Churches will come to recognize people as baptized even when the currently "required" triadic "Father, Son, and Holy Spirit" baptismal formula is not used at their baptisms.[29] Moreover, baptism formulas may not even remain Trinitarian or triadic. Rather, formulas may incorporate pre-Trinitarian baptismal formulas, such as "In the name of Jesus Christ" (which is among the earliest baptismal formulas of the Christian church[30]) or Augustine's formula, "in the name of the Triune God, from whom, through whom, and in whom all things exist, now and forever."[31]

Another illustration of a relanguaged contextualized and particular liturgical formula is what communities of faith have already done with the wording of the traditional "Lord's" Prayer. I was a member of a church in Berkeley, California, in the early 1990s, where, as a community, we relanguaged the prayer of Jesus to contextualize the prayer to the community's realities. In lieu of "thy Kingdom come," we relanguaged this particular line to "your Future come," which had specific significance in our faith community that had a number of members dying from complications due to the HIV virus. We all needed to know that the immediate Future contained God's new enduring Presence, now.

Authority for content of media images has the similar qualities of decentralized authority for liturgy: authority is interactive, localized, and contextual. The "once-marginalized" populations produce media-image content, and the distribution/dissemination system is available to a majority of the people. Virtually, given the simplest technological resources, anyone today can be a producer, creator, and distributor of media images with significant content. (Google Chromebook™ laptops are available for around $200 USD.) Authoritatively, everyone can offer critical, substantial feedback and commentary, that is, "make it plain."

A shared ethic supports, claims responsibility, and develops new literacies and skills in media images and liturgy that involve participatory community.[32] Liturgical literacy and authority is decentralized from the clergy and books of worship. Liturgy truly becomes the "work of the people," lay and ordained, from its creation as an art form to preaching the word to reading the Gospel. All participants are liturgically, theologically skilled and literate. As liturgical artisans, they create theologically sound, holistic, tied in tradition yet contextualize liturgies. All are "experts." "'Performance' is improvisation and discovery."[33]

The new literacies and skills for liturgies are applicable also to the creation of media images.[34] These new literacies and skills require multilateral and weblike evaluative critique. Media-image consumers are nonpassive, interactively active in critique and feedback. Play becomes improvisation and discovery; play is a modality of learning and gaining knowledge. Content is collaborative and networked; it is contextually substantial and significant in meaning and purpose. Multitasking skills necessitate scanning, sampling, and remixing significant content for production of new media images (or alternative liturgies). Media-image consumers collect, create, "mash-up," and share media tools and skills for localized production. (YouTube has many videos where people teach new skills to remix media forms, as well as instructional videos on how to use new media-creating applications.)

In a shared ethic, community is broadened to embrace embodied/incarnate, virtual, and viral realities for both media images and liturgies. The YouTube video of Susan Boyle on "Britain's Got Talent" was redistributed and watched by a viral community.[35] The poignant YouTube video of Neda of Iran dying from a gunshot wound on June 20, 2009, also went viral.[36] In cyberspace, we find online liturgical communities and liturgies, much like the formerly televised liturgies performed throughout the day on religious channels in the United States. Liturgy no longer requires an immediate, embodied community of people—as oxymoronic as that sounds. Church liturgies are archived and are available for download 24/7. They are virtual, where time is frameless and placeless. The Antiochian Orthodox Basilica of St. Mary in Livonia, Michigan, for example, has archived its sermons and service bulletins, available for download and viewing, allowing anyone to "participate" in the liturgy in the privacy of their computer screen.[37] The Vatican in 2005 established a YouTube channel to control its online image by offering videos of papal events and news of special liturgies.[38] These are not oddities; it is the current state of liturgy and community. Utilizing a critical ethic will help us examine this current state of liturgy and community; just because something can now be accomplished does not mean it has a lasting and substantial purpose.

In critique, Presiding Bishop Katharine Jefferts Schori, leader of the Episcopal Church of the United States, claimed in an interview in 2008 that "[i]t is hard to build a faith community in a deep sense on the internet. We deal with caricatures; we deal with perceptions and positions rather than full human beings sitting in our presence. . . . [People] hunger for intimate community . . . that is only possible in the physical proximity of other human beings. Some of it can be served on the internet but the incarnate piece is missing."[39] Yet, for online religious communities, their paradigm understands "incarnation" differently.[40] Whereas physical presence seems necessary in most religious understandings of human community and liturgy, the embodied, physical incarnational element does not necessitate "that intimacy and care will be achieved in community. . . . [T]he incarnational nature is also about what people bring to the table to create the environment and that this can be intentionally built and maintained in a "disembodied" context [online].[41] Embodied and virtual communities both have a sense of incarnational presence; they are different in some qualities, yet they are experienced as real for participants.

Self-proclaimed "church nerd" Kimberly Knight, for instance, had a congregational ministry as pastor of the online church Koinonia Congregational Church of Second Life.[42] Her congregation of personalized "avatars" met weekly for worship in a virtual 3D-rendered sanctuary in the global virtual world of Second Life.[43] Koinonia Congregational Church was a virtual, engaged, and interactively connected community of faith. "Opening its doors and heart to people of various theologies, sexual orientations, and faith experiences, Koinonia practices God's extravagant welcome to all."[44]

I, personally, attended many worship services in Second Life for years. I participated in Sunday morning worship with the Anglican Cathedral in Second Life, evening prayers at St. Luke's, and visited United Methodist and Presbyterian services of worship. All of them are, unfortunately, virtual reflections of traditional worship services in "first life." I did experience the Sacred during these times with people gathered from around the world; I sensed an incarnational-ness during the virtual services. What disappointed me most, however, was that the liturgies did not utilize the capabilities of the virtual world of Second Life to be interactive and participatory with a decentralized authority. The liturgies were rote and right out of books of common worship. Even the architectural design of the worship spaces mirrored "first life" with pews and stained-glass windows.

One church I experienced as most revelatory met in a circle on a virtual shoreline with flowing waterfalls and verdant mountains as our backdrop. I stopped participating in this Second Life church when they built a traditional church and moved the service inside to rows of pews. I believe, however, and other scholars have confirmed that a virtual space such as Second Life can offer the possibilities of a church community that "embodies" a shared postmodern critical ethic.[45] Again, however, we can apply a critical ethic to perceive if such online religious communities have substance and serve a purpose. Just because we can "worship" in a variety of forms in Second Life does not mean we must.

In a shared critical ethic, theological aesthetics of beauty and our experiences of beauty, to borrow from scholar Kimberly Vrudny, have qualities that are true, good, just, wise, and compassionate.[46] Notice, however, that I did not note these qualities as *The* True, *The* Good, *The* Just, *The* Wise, or *The* Compassionate. The qualities of beauty are nonessentialist, nonuniversal, and not definitive in definition: truth, good, just, wise, and compassionate are contextually contingent. The qualities of beauty in theological aesthetics are politically and culturally contextualized, expressing the diversity of realities of God's concerns.

Therefore, in our media images and liturgies—if we are to be true, good, just, wise, and compassionate—we cannot neglect, ignore, or sentimentalize realities that are ugly, oppressive, historically unjust, prejudicial, hegemonic, and hierarchical;[47] for these are formidable realities about which God is concerned, toward which we must be contextually truthful, good, just, wise, and compassionate. For our media images and liturgies to be beautiful, they must "make it plain," making known and making visible both the ugly and the beautiful contextualized realities of God's concerns without sentimentality or partial truth-telling.

Our media images and liturgies are to convert people, systems, and institutions to be the responsible agents of contextually significant change. This entails ensuring equal access to the creation of media images and our liturgies by the suffering, the marginalized, "the least" among us, and the vulnerable. We recognize that vulnerable people are the experts for contextually significant change; not the well-intentioned "expert" or "professional" people. Our media images and liturgies, thereby, hold a multiplicity of conflicting voices with equal authority, and they enhance, advocate, and negotiate an open exchange of worldviews. Our media images and liturgies bring forth an understanding of life that interprets people realities as "thick" with contextualized, agent-producing meaning, significance, and substance—that might lead to encounters with God and God's Vision. God is making all things new—do we not perceive it?

Conclusion

In this proposed shared critical ethic, media images and liturgies convert people, cultures, and institutions to live and work in God's Vision. In this eschatological, already-but-not-yet-realized Vision, we do not profit from greed, and the suffering of others does not stem from a profligacy of consumeristic narcissism. Rather, through our media and liturgies, we become advocates for unconditional, unearned liberation from the oppressions of economic tyranny and privilege; we become apostles for deliverance from global poverty and its diseases; we become living examples of liberation from individualistic "success" and self-centered "excellence"; we become disciples dismantling the perpetuation of dehumanizing stereotypes and prejudices; and we become upholders of justice to never again allow physical, spiritual, and psychic suffering, torture, and abuse in church and world.

This shared critical ethic for our media images and liturgies, with the wisdom and power of the Sacred, will generate an enduring hope for the Realm of God's concerns. In this hope, we will not "remember the former things, or consider the things of old"; rather, we will behold that God is eschatologically about "to do a new thing." Together, we shall "perceive it" and "make it plain" for all to see and be made new.

Notes

1. See Paul Tillich, "Art and Society," "Existentialist Aspects of Modern Art," and "Religious Dimensions of Contemporary Art," in *On Art and Architecture*, ed. John Dillenberger and Jane Dillenberger, trans. Robert P. Scharlemann (New York: Crossroad, 1987), 11–41, 89–101, 171–87. A condensed explanation of Paul Tillich's theology of art is to see his discussions as talking about explicitly religious and implicitly religious art in style and content. While accurately accused of a specious dualism, we can use Tillich's categories within a postmodern, both/and framework. Explicitly religious art, in Tillich's categories/dimensions, would be either art with religious content yet nonreligious in style, such as traditional Sunday School cartoons or art with religious content and religious in style (e.g., Matthias Grünewald's *Crucifixion* (1512–1516) panel in the Isenheim Altarpiece). Implicitly religious art would be art with nonreligious content yet religious in style, such as Pablo Picasso's *Guernica* (1937).

> When we hear the words, "religious art," we usually believe that one refers to particular religious symbols like pictures of Christ, pictures of the Holy Virgin and Child, pictures of Saints and their stories, and many other religious symbols. [Explicit religious art.] Now this is one meaning of religious art; but

there is another following from the larger concept of religion, namely, art as an expression of an ultimate concern. Naturally, it will be an esthetic [sic] expression, an artistic expression, but it will be an expression of ultimate concern. [Implicit religious art.] . . . [W]e distinguish these two ways in which art can express religion . . .

Tillich, "Existentialist Aspects of Modern Art," 92.

2. A "viral" community is that which is created by "viral" media. "Viral," in media speak, is "contagious media," i.e., "content that [is] consciously *made to spread*. The 'viral', whether e-mail or website or song or video, [is] gradually emerging as a new genre of communication, even of art. . . . [W]here TV success was a passive thing, success in viral culture is interactive, born of mass participation, defined by an awareness of the conditions of its creation." Bill Wasik, *And Then There's This: How Stories Live and Die in a Viral Culture* (New York: Viking Adult, 2009), 7–8. Wasik notes the success of the new viral culture as having four key attributes: speed ("incredible rapidity"), shamelessness for attention's sake, duration ("assumed to be ephemeral"), and sophistication (interactive, "built . . . upon what one might call the *media mind*") (8). See also David Rees, "Diagnosis: The Spread of Viral Culture—A PowerPoint Analysis by an Internet Has-Been," June 17, 2009, accessed March 2, 2014, http://nymag.com/arts/books/bookclub/then-theres-this/index5.html.

3. Søren Kierkegaard, *The Point of View for my Work as an Author* (Gloucester, MA: Peter Smith, 1983), 39. "And one thing the author must not forget, namely, his purpose, the distinction between . . . the religious as the decisive thing and the aesthetic incognito [the deceit or deception]—lest the criss cross [sic] of dialectics end in twaddle."

4. A pun on the Twitteriffic™ application for Twitter users.

5. "Mediocre": "Middle French, from Latin *mediocris*, from *medius* middle + Old Latin *ocris* stony mountain; akin to Latin *acer* sharp." *Merriam-Webster*, accessed March 5, 2014, http://www.merriam-webster.com/dictionary/mediocre. "Medium": "Latin, from neuter of *medius* middle." *Merriam-Webster*, accessed March 5, 2014, http://www.merriam-webster.com/dictionary/medium.

6. Paul Tillich, "Art and Society," in *On Art and Architecture*, ed. John Dillenberger and Jane Dillenberger, trans. Robert P. Scharlemann (New York: Crossroads, 1987), 37.

7. "Performance" is not entertainment. I use the word "performance" to note "a way of thinking and being revealed in the act of doing, carrying out, or putting into effort." Performance requires practice, the taking on of *habitus*, that is, "habits of thinking and dispositions of the practice." Charles R. Foster et al., *Educating Clergy: Teaching Practices and Pastoral Imagination* (San Francisco: Jossey-Bass, 2006), 158.

8. For "Ground of Being," see Paul Tillich, *Systematic Theology*, vol. 1 (Chicago: University of Chicago Press, 1951), 155–56. "Make it plain," is a phrase from the African American preaching tradition. "In many black churches, when

the preacher delivers the word in an especially compelling fashion, someone in the pews is likely to declare, 'Make it plain, preacher, make it plain.'" Vernon E. Jordan, Jr., *Make It Plain: Standing Up and Speaking Out* (New York: Public Affairs, 2008), xii.

9. On socially constructed realities, see Peter L. Berger, *The Sacred Canopy: Elements of a Sociological Theory of Religion* (New York: Anchor Books, 1990, 1967).

10. Marshall McLuhan, *Understanding Media: The Extensions of Man* (New York: McGraw-Hill, 1964), 7–21.

> [T]he medium is the message. That is merely to say that the personal and social consequences of any medium—that is, of any extension of ourselves—result from the new scale that is introduced into our affairs by each extension of ourselves, or by any new technology. . . .
>
> For the "message" of any medium or technology is the change of scale or pace or pattern that it introduces into human affairs. . . .
>
> "[T]he medium is the message" because it is the medium that shapes and controls the scale and form of human association and action.

McLuhan, *Understanding Media*, 7–9. "With telephone and TV it is not so much the message as the sender that is 'sent,'" accessed March 5, 2014, http://www .marshallmcluhan.com/mcluhanisms/.

11. For instance, the missionaries to Africa in the 19th century used paintings of Jesus's life by German painter Heinrich Hofmann (1824–1911). *The Portrait of Jesus: A Shade of Difference*, directed by Madelene Pretorius (New York: Manhattan Center Studios, 1994), VHS.

12. David Freedberg, *The Power of Images: Studies in the History and Theory of Responses* (Chicago: University of Chicago Press, 1989), xxv.

13. Arthur W. Hunt, III, *The Vanishing Word: The Veneration of Visual Imagery in the Postmodern World* (Wheaton, IL: Crossway, 2003), 21.

14. George Barna, *Virtual America* (Ventura, CA: Regal Books, 1994), 147.

15. David Freedberg, *The Power of Images: Studies in the History and Theory of Responses* (Chicago: University of Chicago Press, 1989), xxv, xxiii.

16. Gordon Moore's Law predicted in 1965 the exponential growth in the number of transistors placed inexpensively on an integrated circuit every two years. Moore was cofounder of Intel Corporation. Imagine how archaic the first release of the iPhone by Apple in 2007 will seem at its 10th or 20th anniversary. Furthermore, who could have imagined how ubiquitous the iPad by Apple (and other tablets) would be in less than four years from its 2010 release? "Moore's Law, after all, is not a law of physics. It is merely an uncannily accurate observation on what electrical engineers, when organized properly, can do with silicon. Companies that can keep their tech teams humming will reap profits and power. Those that can't will fade away." Michael Kanellos, "Myths of Moore's Law," *CNET*, June 11, 2003, accessed March 5, 2014, http://news.cnet.com/Myths-of-Moores -Law/2010-1071_3-1014887.html.

17. Since the early 1990s, shopping malls and airports worldwide have designated exhibit spaces for "high art," expanding the function of art museums as places for the curation and the dissemination of "high art" into the common, public square.

18. Hunt, *The Vanishing Word*, 23.

19. Many current images used in liturgy are sentimental and cute, equating sunsets and sunrises, footprints in the sand, and mountain ranges with God and with experiencing God. While these images are pretty, they lack substance of meaning or significance to life's harsh realities. The pretty images evoke nonsustaining sentiment.

20. See Don E. Saliers, *Worship Come to Its Senses* (Nashville, TN: Abingdon Press, 1996).

21. Frank Schaeffer, *Addicted to Mediocrity: 20th Century Christians and the Arts* (Westchester, IL.: Cornerstone Books, 1981), 16.

22. Jeff Meyerhoff, "Poststructualism and Postmodernism," in *Bald Ambition: A Critique of Ken Wilber's Theory of Everything"* (IntegralWorld.Net, 2005), accessed March 5, 2014, http://www.integralworld.net/meyerhoff-ba-7.html.

23. Catherine Belsey, *Poststructualism: A Very Short Introduction* (New York: Oxford University Press, 2002), 5, 7.

24. "Universal," as understood in a metaphysical, nonphysical entity "-ness, -ity, or -hood" sense. . . . [P]hilosophical universalism claims that the presence of common traits testifies to a common purpose. It says that the form of the ideal human community can be determined by reference to a universal human nature. Richard Rorty, "Who Are We?: Moral Universalism and Economic Triage," in *Global Ethics: Seminal Essays,* ed. Thomas Pogge and Keith Horton (St. Paul, MN: Paragon House, 2008), 314.

Diana Fuss asserts that essentialism "is most commonly understood as a belief in the real, true essence of things, the invariable and fixed properties that define the 'whatness' of a given entity. . . . [Essentialism is understood as] a set of preexistent human essences [that] constitute the subject." Diana Fuss, *Essentially Speaking: Feminism, Nature and Difference* (New York: Routledge, 1989), xi–xii.

25. Ideas derived from Mark C. Taylor and Esa Saarinen, *Imagologies: Media Philosophy* (New York: Routledge, 1994).

26. Terry Semel, president of Warner Brothers, quoted in ibid., front flap.

27. Ibid.

28. By "the grand Vision of God," I mean the shared, interfaith vision of a reconciled and reconciling time for humanity and creation. In the Christian tradition, this is known as the eschatological, full realization of God's Kingdom, Kindom, Realm, and/or Reign.

29. World Council of Churches, "Baptism," in *Baptism, Eucharist and Ministry: Paper #111 (Faith and Order)* (Geneva: World Council of Churches, 1982), V:17. See also World Council of Churches, *Baptism, Eucharist and Ministry (Faith and Order Paper no. 111, the "Lima Text")*, accessed March 13, 2014, http://www.oikoumene.org/en/resources/documents/wcc-commissions/faith-and-order-commission/i-unity-the-church-and-its-mission/baptism-eucharist-and-ministry-faith-and-order-paper-no-111-the-lima-text.

30. Hans Conzelmann, *An Outline of the Theology of the New Testament*, trans. John Bowden (London: SCM Press, 1969), 49. For a fascinating and scholarly treatment of the Trinitarian baptismal formula, see Ruth Duck, *Gender and the Name of God: The Trinitarian Baptismal Formula* (Cleveland, OH: Pilgrim Press, 1991).

31. This Baptismal Formula is an interpretation of Romans 11:36. Gail Ramshaw, *God Beyond Gender: Feminist Christian God-Language* (Minneapolis: Fortress Press, 1995), 87, 91.

32. See Henry Jenkins, *Confronting the Challenges of Participatory Culture: Media Education for the 21st Century*, John D. and Catherine T. MacArthur Foundation Reports on Digital Media and Learning (Chicago: The MacArthur Foundation, 2006), 1, accessed March 13, 2014, http://digitallearning.macfound .org/site/apps/nlnet/content2.aspx?c=enJLKQNlFiG&b=2108773&cont ent_id=%7bCD911571-0240-4714-A93B-1D0C07C7B6C1%7d¬oc=1.

33. Ibid.

34. Ibid.

35. "Susan Boyle—Britains [sic] Got Talent 2009 Episode 1," April 11, 2009, YouTube, accessed March 13, 2014, http://www.youtube.com/watch?v= RxPZh4AnWyk.

36. "Young Girl Shot by Iranian Police Dies on Camera," June 20, 2009, YouTube, accessed March 13, 2014, http://www.youtube.com/watch?v=mZf9nl5zrp0&NR=1.

37. "The Antiochian Orthodox Basilica of Saint Mary," accessed March 13, 2014, http://saintmarylivonia.com/home/.

38. "The Vatican—English," YouTube, accessed March 13, 2014, http://www .youtube.com/user/vatican?blend=1&ob=4.

39. Heidi Campbell, "Can Online Community Be Incarnational?" When Religion Meets New Media, January 19, 2009, accessed March 10, 2014, http:// religionmeetsnewmedia.blogspot.com/search?q=Can+online+communty+be+inc arnational. Also see Heidi Campbell, *Exploring Religious Community Online: We Are One in the Network* (New York: Peter Lang, 2005).

40. Some online religious communities include the Anglican Cathedral in Second Life (http://slangcath.wordpress.com/about/), tangle (http://www.GodTube .com/), and Church Online at LiveChurch.tv (http://churchonline .lifechurch.tv/who-we-are/what-is-church-online/).

Tangle understands themselves in the following way: "tangle.com is about community—real community. As a global technology company, our primary focus lies in the development of new and innovative tools that help you reconnect with old friends and make new ones. . . . We help you connect, interact and grow. If it's part of your life, it can be part of tangle.com. . . . [T]angle is also about expression. You can create, personalize and showcase everything that makes you, you. . . . When you express your thoughts, hopes, dreams, fears and disappointments, you allow others to share their lives as well. And this is where real community begins." "Tangle," accessed June 27, 2009, http://www.tangle.com/support/aboutus.

Church Online at LiveChurch.tv claims they are "a community of people all over the world experiencing God and connecting with one another like never before in history. What does that mean? It means you have found a place to encounter God and people who care about you—just as you are, anywhere in the world." "What Is Church Online?" Church Online, accessed March 10, 2014, http://churchonline.lifechurch.tv/who-we-are/what-is-church-online/.

41. Campbell, "Can Online Community Be Incarnational?"

42. Kimberly Knight, "Kimberly Knight," Patheos: Hosting the Conversation on Faith, n.d., accessed March 15, 2014, http://www.patheos.com/blogs/kimberlyknight/about/. See also "Koinonia Church of Second Life," Facebook, accessed March 13, 2014, https://www.facebook.com/koinoniaSL?group_id=0; and Jill A. Oglesby Evans, "Sacred Space in Cyberspace: The Koinonia Congregational Church of Second Life," sermon, Emory Presbyterian Church, Atlanta, GA, September 18, 2011, accessed March 13, 2014, http://www.emorypresbyterian.org/sermons/KoinoniaChurchOfSecondLife.pdf.

43. "Second Life Official Site: Virtual Worlds, Avatars, Free 3D Chat," accessed March 13, 2014, http://secondlife.com. Second Life avatars are virtual and personalized graphic 3D representations of persons who virtually live and interact with other avatars from across the globe. Avatars can chat, hug, dance, and even own a home in Second Life. Each avatar represents a person's personality in a graphically rendered body. Avatars attend live concerts, go to church, dance to music, shop for clothing, join support groups, travel to different "countries," and befriend each other, all under fictitious names and with pseudo-anonymity. The level of interaction between people as avatars is intense and long lasting. Many people who meet in Second Life become "first-life" friends.

44. Kimberly Knight, "Sacred Space in Cyberspace," *Reflections* 96, no. 2 (Fall 2009): 43–46.

45. See Stephen Jacobs, "Virtually Sacred: The Performance of Asynchronous Cyber-Rituals in Online Spaces," *Journal of Computer-Mediated Communication* 12, no. 3 (April 2007): 1103–21, accessed March 14, 2014, http://onlinelibrary.wiley.com/doi/10.1111/j.1083-6101.2007.00365.x/abstract; Ralph Schroeder, "The Sacred and the Virtual Religion in Multi-User Virtual Reality," *Journal of Computer-Mediated Communication* 4, no. 2 (December 1998): 1, accessed March 14, 2014, http://onlinelibrary.wiley.com/doi/10.1111/j.1083-6101.1998.tb00092.x/full; Nicole Stenger, "Mind Is a Leaking Rainbow," in *Cyberspace: First Steps*, ed. Michael Benedikt (Cambridge, MA: MIT Press, 1991), 55.

46. Kimberly Vrudny, "30/30: Documenting a Pandemic," accessed June 30, 2009, http://30years30lives.org. See Kim's blog, Ububele, accessed March 13, 2014, http://ububele.wordpress.com, on the photographic project she did on HIV infection in Cape Town, South Africa, in 2009 with her family. "'Ububele' is the Xhosa word for 'kindness' and 'generosity.'"

47. Theologian Paul Tillich, in writing about a sacramental religious experience, states that even the "lowest or ugliest" are included in the sacramental quality of holiness. Paul Tillich, "Art and Ultimate Reality," in *On Art and Architecture*, ed. John Dillenberger and Jane Dillenberger, trans. Robert P. Scharlemann (New York: Crossroad, 1987), 143.

God and Popular Culture

CHAPTER TEN

God in the Smartphone: Sacred or Sacrilege?

Joyce Ann Konigsburg

Introduction

Telephony is one of the fastest evolving sectors in the marketplace, advancing in recent decades from mere communication devices requiring human intervention when establishing connections or managing person-to-person and collect calls to an evolving and sophisticated array of personal tools and functions. The latest technologically portable devices known as "smartphones" are themselves the intermediaries that directly dial other phones or connect to the Internet for almost instant access to other people, data, and new experiences from a variety of software applications. With these "apps," people passively watch movies and live sporting events or actively research the Internet for facts and figures; communicate with other people via voice, text, or email; and participate in competitive games and other interactive group activities. Many of these apps focus on spiritual themes and promote sacred experiences. All smartphone application experiences, however, occur independently of physical proximity, face-to-face interpersonal interaction, and customary relationality. Sociologists have only begun to investigate how the latest smart-technology phenomenon is influencing human relationships, behaviors, and societal norms. Likewise, theologians ask similar questions but narrow their inquiries to how this technology affects the divine-human relationship. Stated another way, do smartphones and their associated religious software applications bring people closer to God or distract them from God?

Religious Experience

Smartphone technology combines cell phone functionality with portable access to the Internet and a minimal operating system for executing software applications. Computer programmers create "apps" (shorthand terminology for "applications") with a limited or specific purpose, such as watching a movie or receiving weather alerts via smartphones. Consequently, numerous customized apps exist for diverse interests, hobbies, and online pursuits, including religion-related activities. Several apps enable users to read sacred texts, pray, perform rituals, and worship the divine. Through a prudent selection and use of software apps, one's smartphone facilitates the possibility of achieving an authentic religious experience.

Sacred Writings

Reading and downloading data from the Internet is a standard activity on smartphones, so accessing the sacred writings of God is a relatively simple task. If a copy of the text is on the Internet, then people are able to find it in diverse forms, translations, and languages. Instead of carrying one printed copy of the Christian Bible, for instance, a number of smartphones have the ability to download more than 300 versions from websites such as "YouVersion.com," which "gives access to the Bible in 160 versions in 51 languages" and offers reading plans and study applications to "leverage technology to its fullest to advance the gospel" so that "this could become the most Bible-engaged generation in history."[1]

With revolutionary parallels to movable type, smartphones change the way people read, analyze, and study sacred texts. Using the appropriate apps, people download to their phones a collection of wisdom from most religions, thereby having immediate access to texts from the Torah, the Bible, the Qur'an, the Buddhist text *Dhammacakkappavattana Sutta*, and writings from many other faiths. A simple "Google" Internet search yields more than 112 million results for the term "Bible," 52 million for "Qur'an," 6.8 million for "Torah," and in excess of one million each for Buddha quotes and Hindu Vedas and sacred writings.[2] In fact, the Internet is a great equalizer for promoting one's message; the "pagan communities were among the first to find a voice on the Web" along with more nimble spiritual communities, while "traditional religious practices were a bit slower on the uptake" but now have a presence that extends beyond their local boundaries.[3]

Even with different versions, languages, and analytical tools, the smartphone-savvy millennial generation who read religious texts needs "an interactive media format in snippets—short learning experiences. It has to be something that somehow connects with their life," so software programmers develop apps like Glo Bible, which "illuminates the full text of Scripture through HD [high definition] video, high-resolution images, zoomable maps, 360-degree virtual tours, and customizable reading plans," thus providing a more complete bible study encounter.[4] Other smartphone apps also bring other religions' holy texts interactively to life. The "Pocket Torah" displays Jewish scriptures and law, while "Talmud Directory," an app for reading the story of Esther during Purim, enables smartphone faithful to hear and customize the sounds that noisemakers (groggers) utilize to drown out Haman's name at appropriate times.[5] Muslims access the Qur'an (Al Mus'haf app) and Allah's 99 names online, while the *Bhagavad Gita* is available in English, Hindi, and other languages. From a website called "Buddha Doodles," people sign up to receive a cute, uplifting cartoon, and a daily Buddha affirmation on their smartphones.[6] As a result, new technology interactively engages the religious audience in novel and contemporary ways without necessarily altering the meaning or message of traditional sacred writings.

Prayer

Similar to sacred writings, locating prayers from different religions in textual form is straightforward with Internet search engines. Hindus access the "Digital Puja [prayer]" app, Hebrew blessings exist for almost all occasions, and the Christian *Common Book of Prayer,* and the specific Catholic Breviary that includes prayers to the saints, liturgical prayers, and the rosary are all available online. Once again, what the smartphone brings to the prayer experience is interaction. By pressing an app button on the smartphone, one hears blessings in Hebrew and English. Subscribing to Azan Alarm Clock or Adhan Alarm alerts Muslims in time for prayers and by setting reminder programs, Christians recite the Liturgy of the Hours or the rosary at appropriate or scheduled times. Several interactive Buddhist apps exist, including a few that spin a prayer wheel when a person shakes the smartphone and the "Buddha Box" app, which enhances prayer with various images, chants, singing, and soothing sounds for meditation.[7] The application also includes a gong timer to begin and end one's contemplative state.

Through smartphone apps, the faithful send prayers and receive wisdom from anywhere in the world. One Jewish app emails prayers to a Jerusalem location where a person prints them and places them, according to tradition, in cracks in the Western Wall. Text messages are popular as well; in India, people send text messages to "a Bombay temple where they are offered to the Hindu god Ganesh," and from Rome, the Catholic pope texts his prayers and "thoughts for the day" to faithful worldwide.[8] Texting and multimedia apps provide spiritual guidance as well. Deepak Chopra, author of *The Seven Spiritual Laws* series, sends daily sayings, images, and support to his subscribers. He finds it "amazing that people can find solace in something so short. People just need a little nudge so that they can have a reflective experience."[9]

Some applications imply that they have direct prayer access to God. The app "Note to God" enables people to gather their thoughts, write a personal note to the divine, and the press a button on the phone to send it. Application users then wait a few seconds for a confirmation to their smartphone that the "note was sent successfully to God"; the app additionally stores the note in a database and then displays the most common words from all notes in a "prayer cloud."[10] Furthermore, the divine answers prayers or at least fortifies people spiritually with words of inspiration from an app called "Reminders from God," which produces daily messages from various religious and spiritual sources and sends the notes from God to subscribed users.[11] Perhaps some people find comfort or reassurance in the generated note content or in the act of writing their thanks or requests to God, even though most of them understand the interaction is computer generated.

Finding God

Smartphone apps locate different religious prayers and texts, determine the direction toward Mecca with compass apps, and even reveal what God is doing at this very moment. A humorous smartphone-accessible website named "god-was-here.com" searches email, text messages, and tweets for the word "god," identifies God's location on a map, classifies what God is doing from surrounding words and phrases such as "damn," "oh my . . . ," or "thank God I . . . ," and then places the results on a constantly undated website whose purpose is "tracking god and all that he does in real-time."[12] Watching God move around the country damning things, expressing surprise, being thanked, or matchmaking/meddling is an amusing, although not necessarily moving, religious experience. Other smartphone apps offer more spiritually meaningful engagements with the divine. One example is the NewLife application that supplies Bible downloads but also explores the ultimate questions regarding God, truth, morality, purpose ,and specific topics such as faith, prayer, sin, church, and Jesus Christ.[13] Several smartphone apps present Buddhist enlightenment at one's fingertips, describes ways to create sacred space, and suggest a variety of meditation trainer, music, and timer programs. In addition, special apps find the nearest synagogue, church, mosque, and even the nearest kosher restaurant using the smartphone's GPS (global positioning system) application to identity locations and then coordinate and calculate the distances and propose directions.

Prior to finding God, one must determine if God exists. Smartphone applications supply evidence, strategies, and pithy comebacks for both sides of the debate. For atheists and skeptics, the "BibleThumper" app supplies "the most funny and irrational Bible verses right in their pocket," while believers use apps such as "Fast Facts, Challenges & Tactics," "The Atheist Pocket Debater," "One-Minute Answers to Skeptics," and "Answers for Catholics" to prepare arguments based on logic and with less reliance on biblical text.[14] Application providers claim they are helping people see the truth from opposing perspectives, yet "most applications focus less on scholarly exegesis than on scoring points."[15] Union Theological Seminary President, Dr. Serene Jones thinks these apps turn the discussion into a game where "both sides come to the discussion with fixed ideas, and you have what amounts to a contest between different types of fundamentalism."[16] Nevertheless, if these apps entice people to debate religion on the Internet as they discussed it in the marketplace centuries ago, then perhaps the current cyber-dialogue contributes a little value in the search for truth.

Worshipping God

Apps also support worship activities by converting general calendars to the specific needs of diverse religions and researching the times and nearby locations for religious services. Furthermore, participating in worship services is possible through a smartphone and an app that receives Internet broadcasts from churches, synagogues, mosques, or other religious places. One may choose to join a variety of religious services from anywhere on the planet at any time of the day or night. Similar to watching a television program, a person need not be part of the actual community or faith to take part in religious practices in cyberspace. Some Internet virtual worlds create detailed facsimiles of reality that include worship centers in which one's Internet image or representation called an avatar, a term borrowed from Hinduism that means an incarnate manifestation of a deity or soul, attends and partakes in various virtual rituals. One of the original and more robust websites called "Second Life" currently contains 23 "spirituality and belief" destinations ranging from models of St. Columba's

Chapel (Ireland), St. Mary Abbotts Church (Kensington, U.K.), and the Basilica of St. Peter the Apostle (Italy), to Grace Baptist Church of Second Life, First United Church of Christ, Seventh-day Adventist Community Church, Church of Jesus Christ of Latter-Day Saints, a Ganesh Temple and Gardens, Buddha centers and Zen retreats, a monastery, and a Wiccan Learning Center.[17]

In addition to attending religious services, interactively participating in ritual activities and rites is possible from one's smartphone. Apps enable Jews to light menorah candles at Hanukkah. Hindu worship sites exist where the devout leave virtual incense, fruits, flowers, and other offerings to the gods at Internet temples or computer-generated home altars. People in China burn images of smartphones "to ensure their dead relatives are fairing [sic] well in their parallel lives," while others bring their smartphones to Buddhist monks to receive blessings against evil forces.[18] Experiencing Christian sacraments such as Baptism and Eucharist is difficult because pouring actual water or distributing edible hosts is not possible on a smartphone; however, a couple of apps exist for the Catholic Sacrament of Penance and Reconciliation. Neither app actually administers the sacrament or absolves the faithful from their sins, but one app provides customized spiritual guidance for examining one's conscience in preparation for the sacrament. As the first known smartphone app to receive a Catholic bishop's imprimatur (formal approval usually for printed materials), the Apple app "Confession" presents a "step-by-step guide to the sacrament," which coaches and guides those unsure of or unfamiliar with the new rites and "invites Catholics to prayerfully prepare for and participate in the Rite of Penance."[19] The other app solves the problems of too few priests available to perform the sacrament of Penance and Reconciliation in addition to the lack of privacy when making an appointment to confess one's sins. Known as "myconfessor," the app allows priests to log in and list when and where they will be available to hear confessions.[20]

Playing God

Apparently a strong software application market exists not only for worshipping God but for actually being a god. More than 25 games offer different ways of playing god thus making the god game "a genre unto itself, varied in style and theme but always giving players the ability to change the world around its tiny virtual people and creatures—subverting their free will but seldom denying it."[21] With names like "Pocket God," "Doodle God," "GodFinger Deluxe," "Babel Rising," "Virtual Villagers," and "Meteor Smash," players control the weather and perpetrate disasters, manipulate creatures' lives, create new worlds, destroy the entire universe, combine novel chemical substances, and manufacture new life forms.[22] Application programmers even include some theology in their products. The creation-oriented game called "The Sandbox" is "kind of like a Lego set crossed with a junior chemistry kit" and "Artificial Life" has several game mode options where "you [interactively] create your own animalcule and see how long it survives" or "you set the parameters for the universe and watch over it like a distant Deist god."[23]

Religious Reactions

The ability to "play god" from one's smartphone seems to exemplify humanity's prideful yearnings, for as Pope Benedict XVI says, "from the beginning, men and women have been filled—and this is as true today as ever—with a desire to 'be like God,' to attain the heights of God by their own powers."[24] He further cautions that while "the achievements of technology are liberating and contribute to the progress of mankind," humanity must develop and use it with clean and pure hearts by seeking God's love and the truth.[25] Likewise, the Second Vatican Council decree, *Inter Mirifica* (The Means of Social Communication) and its companion pastoral instruction, *Communio et Progressio*, recognize the value and potential of social communication and recommend prudence when employing such influential capabilities and functions. Although the two documents primarily address broadcast media (radio and television) and media arts (movies, magazines, and books) the definitions are perhaps purposely vague in order to extend their relevance and therefore include emerging technologies such as the Internet and smartphones. The documents place responsibility on the Church to monitor, on media professionals to produce, and on consumers to choose social communications and programming that will not cause "spiritual harm" to themselves or others.[26]

The Dalai Lama agrees that numerous Buddhist apps are fine to use in one's spiritual life.[27] However, he cautions that contemplation and the principles of virtue must guide the rapid development of smartphones, software applications, and other technologies. Without clear vision, dignity, and concern for others, "technology can prey on us, detecting our weakness or lack of resolve" or can distract from the "nowness . . . it seduces us for a few minutes, which become hours, days, months and years."[28] If a person's actions using a smartphone leave one dull and drained of energy, then one is being used by technology; instead, feeling satisfied and positively uplifted indicate control of technology and "a complete karmic act."[29]

Even though various religions cautiously support the use of smartphones and their applications, rabbis, pastors, priests, imams, and other religious leaders express mixed reactions. Rabbi Emanuel Carlebach of the House of Israel Congregation in St. Agathe, Quebec endorses using smartphones for prayer and worship. He accesses "Psalms in his Palm" and other apps to read scripture because "There is a principle that the Torah teaches us: We are supposed to utilize everything in the world to serve God."[30] A response to a question on www.askimam.org indicates that the Qur'an may exist on a smartphone provided that all other videos, apps, and text uphold Shari'ah law and the sanctity of the holy book.[31] On the other hand, an interfaith coalition of religious leaders from "the National Council of Churches, the United States Catholic Conference of Bishops, and the Islamic Society of North America" for the past several years have called for a "Screen-Free Week" usually coinciding with the Christian Holy Week between Palm Sunday and Easter Sunday.[32] Out of a growing concern that people are spending too much time staring at their smartphone or computer screens and not enough time fostering meaningful relationships, the coalition calls people "to enter into the 'brave old world' of unmediated connection . . . with one another, with God's creation, and with the God of many names."[33]

Some religious groups see almost no redeeming value to smartphones and Internet technology. For years, the ultra-orthodox Jewish Haredim has been urging followers to disconnect from the Internet and lately smartphones and other mobile devices are under attack. In Jerusalem, rabbis encourage smartphone owners to smash their devices in a form of ritual cleansing, and one rebbe (rabbi) of a Satmar Hassidic sect in New York "laid down an ultimatum for his followers: Get rid of their smartphones within a month or find a new rebbe."[34] He cites a rule that forbids people to connect to the Internet via computers or smartphones, except for employment in very limited circumstances and then only when using restrictive Internet filters.

Interestingly, several theologians, scholars, and observers consider fanatical stances for or against smartphones to be a form of idolatry. Rabbis who issue ultimatums or encourage people to smash their smartphones ceremonially to reach a higher spiritual level "are not *Tikkun olam* (repairing the world)" but "attributing supernatural qualities to a device [which] is idolatry" because "a mere device is viewed by the rabbi as a small, dangerous deity."[35] Moreover, such edicts reveal very little faith in people and their ability to make good choices. The smartphone is only a tool; its owner chooses whether to use the device and its appropriately selected applications for the greater good (enhancing business productivity or strengthening one's relationships with God and others) or to become a slave to the gadget.

Many people do choose to establish and maintain unhealthy or idolatrous relationships with their smartphones to the exclusion of God and others. An early smart-technology device called a BlackBerry® quickly assumed the derogatory nickname "crackberry" because its users exhibit symptoms similar to crack-cocaine addicts.[36] These behaviors include a compulsion to check for messages and texts frequently, an obsession with responding to any input immediately, and panicked feelings of isolation and loneliness when messages and texts were not forthcoming. One's mobile device becomes the first item a technology-obsessed person seeks in the morning and one's last interaction before bed at night. In between waking and sleeping, the smartphone is a person's continuous companion. Studies show that smartphone users are more active than non-smartphone users at engaging popular Internet applications such as email (45 percent to 28), Facebook (23 percent to 12), and Twitter (5 percent to 2).[37] Hence, the present generation of smartphones becomes one's personal amulet; that is "a sacred object to be held and caressed and constantly attended to" and through constant devotion, users "engage in a form of idolatry."[38]

A number of theological reasons exist to explain the idolatrous behavior of a person's attachment and attention to smartphones. For example, from God's gift of intelligence, humanity develops an object and reveres it instead of the divine Gift-Giver. People moreover fail to perceive themselves as humble cocreators, thereby neglecting the actual Creator of all things. By opting to substitute the seemingly unlimited knowledge and virtual world of the Internet for the Ultimate Reality, humans avoid any accountability to God. This idolatrous behavior however generates anxiety and stress from worshiping something material and temporal rather than the eternal divine.

A Question of Relationship

Modern technology and the Internet provide powerful opportunities to connect nations and their inhabitants around the globe. Many people perceive this unifying function as a graced opportunity for humanity, whereas others express concern about the Internet's influence. Thus, appropriate use of and respect for the capabilities of smartphones is necessary to utilize them toward good ends. Monitoring one's time and properly selecting applications, especially religious apps, has the potential to create and develop relationships with others and God. Yet the relationships people establish via these devices and the Internet differ from conventional interactions. These anomalies include privileging the long-distance other over face-to-face encounters, extending notions of social interactions, and affecting communal worship activities with the introduction of virtual worship practices.

Privileging the Internet Other

The smartphone connects its user to others on the Internet even as it discourages nearby interaction with others or God. Consequently, social practices seem to be shifting as smartphone owners isolate and dehumanize proximate people while privileging distant others. A recent survey illustrates that almost 20 percent of American smartphone users "would never hide the fact that they are using their mobile device, no matter where they are" and disclose that they use their smartphones to avoid others (35 percent), to look busy and important (33 percent), and to research information to prevent appearing ignorant (41 percent).[39] More than half (62 percent) the smartphone owners use their phone around friends and 58 percent during quality time with their families.[40] Within intimate relationships, 28 percent of people employ their devices while on dates with their significant others, and surprisingly, "77 percent of smartphone owners admit they would openly use their phones while in bed with someone else."[41] Another statistic that privileges no one is the 75 percent of smartphone owners who are not ashamed to use their phones in public restrooms.[42] One reason for such behavior is that smartphone users "are less exposed" to others, which results in altering their interactions with people, and they admit "because we are not face-to-face, we might say or do things that we would not normally say or do."[43]

Social Interaction

An unusual form of social interaction occurs online between smartphone users. Teenage users consider talking to someone as too personal and consequently use text messaging more frequently in their Internet interactions with others. Across the Internet, text messages are surrogate gifts to be "'exchanged in performances that have specific meanings in young peoples' daily lives and are played out with the intent to cement social relationships."[44] Smartphone-mediated relationships suggest that being physically close is no longer a requirement for interpersonal intimacy. Marshall McLuhan, philosopher of communication theory, posits that technology is an extension of a person's body, mind, and senses, and so smartphone users engage in emotional relationships that seem authentic.[45] Sociologist and psychologist, Sherry Turkle, questions the actual connectedness of online relationships as merely psychological because the only tangible relationship that exists is between the user and one's smartphone.[46] Turkle's thinking seems to parallel existential philosopher Martin Buber's I-It experience, while McLuhan's notion implies extensions to Buber's I-Thou experience in which two people encounter and acknowledge each other. Two people in the same room, for instance, who independently utilize their smartphones and thus ignore each other certainly exhibit different relational aspects than the text "conversation" one of them is having with friends online or if both are, instead, on a coffee break interacting in dialogue with each other.

Communal Worship

Being present to God and others is a key component to devotional prayer and worship. Yet the LG Smartphone Survey reveals that 48 percent of owners "would be comfortable using their devices in a place of worship."[47] The real issue of concern is whether people employ their smartphones during services to praise and honor God or as a distraction. Are the people praying with the congregation or answering their email and texting during service? Legitimate ways to enhance the worship service include following the liturgy using online text, researching the building's art or architecture to further appreciate the worship space, investigating the meaning of a particular ritual for greater understanding and reverence, or perhaps taking notes on a sermon to reflect upon at a later time. Moreover, on-call physicians, police, and firefighters, or a traveling salesperson whose pregnant wife is close to delivery are examples of people who have justifiably ethical needs for being online. Because social interactions and relationality are important elements in communal worship that intensify the graced religious experience, religious leaders frequently deliberate the advantages and disadvantages between absent faithful verses those who physically are present but disengaged.

External or formalized prayers and rituals "enhance and reinforce private devotional orientation" even as they produce communion and institute religious socialization.[48] Furthermore, humans tend to share religious rituals "so that the experience can be articulated for oneself and validated by others."[49] People participate and practice rites and rituals because these acts have significance and generate meaning for themselves and the community. A single woman who lights Sabbath candles every Friday, thus emulating her mother, remembering her childhood, and engaging in religious tradition, is fully present and experiencing a sacred moment. Her pious actions nevertheless take on additional significance and deeper meaning when performed with family or within a community of friends. Likewise, reading one's Bible at bedtime offers a different religious experience than attending church, hearing the Word of God, and reflecting on a homily or sermon among the assembled faithful. Engaging in similar activities through a handheld electronic device with no physical or actual interaction with people introduces yet another form of worship experience.

Virtual Worship

Through smartphone applications, people perform religious rituals in two ways. The first is by virtual representation within an online community. However, the definition of participation differs in virtual worship services and poses several questions about the authenticity of the religious experience. When entering a virtual mosque, for instance, the online community agrees that visitors should remove their virtual shoes as part of observing rituals. What about the shoes on a person manipulating the avatar from one's smartphone? Should they be removed too? How important and enriching is the religious experience when a person is virtually but not physically engaged in the rituals? Attending worship services via smartphone requires very little effort or involvement from the device holders. A person need not sway, bow, or kneel at appropriate times nor respond to prayers or sing and therefore is more of an observer than participant in the ceremony. Even if a smartphone owner manipulates an avatar to participate fully in worshipping God, the virtual person does not actually interact with others or experience the divine; only the smartphone owner is real and in relationship with God. Do an artificial community, pseudoidentity, and simulated interaction satisfy an actual person's social, religious, and psychological needs?

The second way a person performs religious rituals is though smartphone apps that imitate actual ceremonial signs and symbols that engage people, convey meaning, and promote shared experiences. Because people are both bodily and spiritual creatures, religious symbols engage all five human senses to more effectively reveal God's presence and grace.[50] Offering virtual gifts to a deity or lighting representations of candles or incense loses the vital sight, smell, and touch components that contribute to the rite's meaning, imagination, and lasting memory. Moreover, engaging in rituals via a smartphone requires no sacrifice on the participant's part. If one need not physically be present to attend a service, then social and relational requirements regarding conduct, dress, or behaviors are no longer necessary. Worshiping in public demands presence; it discourages people from arriving ungroomed and wearing fuzzy slippers or only boxer shorts. Communal devotional services also deter people from multitasking; it is difficult to participate in public rituals and rites and to cook dinner, watch TV, or do sit-ups at the same time. As for one's relationship and graced experience with the divine, how much awe and glory for God can a smartphone generate after vibrating in one's pocket all day or being retrieved after accidently dropping it in the toilet? Respect and inspiration derive from sacred spaces, tangible ceremonies, and community participation, not necessarily from a small, handheld device.

Sacred space and time along with performing traditional rituals all create meaning and foster individual or communal religious experiences, thereby enhancing one's relationship with God and others. Until the arrival of portable technology, people communicated, worshipped, and gathered together to adore and venerate the divine in consecrated places at particular times. Smartphones however afford users the opportunity to worship and experience God online, and as a result, technology is mediating ritual communication, redefining worship practices, and reestablishing sacred spaces and infrastructure on the Internet. The newest devices and software programming function as a bridge between the real and the virtual and associate the physical with the spiritual. By blurring lines between the concrete and the abstract, smartphones and their applications may influence people to recognize and accept new encounters with the sacred. Through virtual and actual interactions with others and the divine, one builds a religious story or reality describing personal experiences of God's revelation. Hence, any reality may initiate a grace experience, so perhaps "meaning can be found in a digital space just as in a physical one."[51]

Conclusion

The latest smartphone technology has the potential to develop a deeper relationship between the user and the divine. By selecting appropriate religious applications, people read sacred texts, pray, perform rituals, and attend virtual worship services interactively. The Internet and assorted smartphone apps represent diverse religious beliefs and institutions that interpret the signs of the times and adapt to new technologies, tools, and communication methods. Several religions connect the secular with the sacred and therefore accept that grace and the divine presence may be experienced in the real and the physical as well as in the abstract and the spiritual; thus God may be known in actual and virtual worlds.

Numerous smartphone apps increase business productivity and improve peoples' lives. Likewise, prudent use of email, social media, and other programs connect people to each other. Obsessive use of other apps nevertheless wastes one's time and distracts the user from God, others, themselves, and the world around them. To the detriment of higher priorities, people become engrossed in email, Facebook, Twitter, YouTube videos, movies, live sporting events, and a large selection of games and activities supporting a variety of interests and preferences. The fact that smartphone apps are convenient, easy to use, and fun contributes to people's fascination with the technology.

The smartphone and its associated applications are tools that humans create and develop with their God-given knowledge and ingenuity. Like any tool, the devices are neither good nor evil; people determine how to utilize smartphones and their associated applications. Human free will and its subsequent choices take center stage to resolve if smartphone technology and software apps bring people closer to God or distract them from God. People choose to purchase the latest technological devices to make life easier. They select which applications to download and they decide when, where, and how often to engage those apps. If a person decides to check email frequently, one can also choose to spend time reading sacred text. If an app sends daily reminders to pray or meditate, then a person is opting to integrate sacred time for communication with the divine into one's busy life. Actions, tradeoffs, and results all hinge on priorities and choice. Smartphones distract people from God only if people choose to permit it or the devices may strengthen graced divine-human experiences through good choices and efforts to encourage flourishing relationships.

Notes

1. Robert C. Crosby, "The Social Media Gospel: How Interconnectivity Helps Us Better Engage the Bible," *Christianity Today* (June 2012): 38.

2. Results of an Internet search from http://www.google.com,February 10, 2014, 5:30 p.m. EST.

3. Grady Booch, "Deus ex Machina," *IEEE Software* (November/December 2013): 15, accessed February 10, 2014, http://www.computer.org/software.

4. Crosby, 39. For more information, refer to http://www.globible.com.

5. Anav Silverman, "Smartphone App Has Text of Megillah and Drowns out Haman's Name," *The Jewish Press* (February 24, 2013), accessed February 10.2014, http://www.jewishpress.com/news/smartphone-app-has-text-of-megillah-and-drowns-out-hamans-name/2013/02/24.

6. For more information, refer to http://www.buddhadoodles.com.

7. Tom Heneghan, "Faith and Smart Phones Commune in Religion Apps," *Reuters* (August 3, 2010), accessed February 11, 2014, http://www.reuters.com/article/2010/08/03/us-usa-religion-smartphones-idUSTRE67211X20100803.

8. Elizabeth Biddlecombe, "Cell Phone Users Are Finding God," *Wired.com* (August 2004), accessed February 11. 2014, http://www.wired.com/culture/lifestyle/news/2004/08/64624.

9. Ibid.

10. For more information, see https://itunes.apple.com/us/app/note-to-god/id323043623?mt=8.

11. For more information, see http://remindersfromgod.net.

12. For more information, see http://www.god-was-here.com.

13. For more information, see http://www.newlifeapp.ca.

14. Paul Vitello, "You Say God Is Dead? There's an App for That," *New York Times* (July 2, 2010), accessed February 10, 2014, http://www.nytimes.com/2010/07/03/technology/03atheist.html?_r=1&.

15. Ibid.

16. Ibid.

17. For more information and a full list of religious affiliations and spiritual destinations, see http://www.secondlife.com.

18. Biddlecombe, "Cell Phone Users Are Finding God."

19. For more information, see to https://itunes.apple.com/gb/app/confession-roman-catholic/id416019676?mt=8.

20. For more information, see http://www.myconfessor.org.

21. Richard Moss, "10 iOS Games That Make You All-Powerful," *MacLife*, accessed February 10, 2014, http://www.maclife.com/article/gallery/10_ios_games_make_you_allpowerful.

22. A few of the websites that describe and critique god games are: http://www.maclife,com/article/gallery/10_ios_games_make_you_allpowerful, http://appcrawlr.com/ios-apps/best-apps-play-god, http://www.wired.com/reviews/2012/09/app-god-games/, and http://www.stuff.tv/10-best-god-game-apps/news.

23. Lore Sjöberg, "I Am Your Overlord: 3 God Games for iOS," *Wired* (September 2012), accessed February 10, 2014, http://www.wired.com/reviews/2012/09/app-god-games/.

24. Benedict XVI, "To the 'Heights of God' He 'Wanted to Lift Every Human Being,'" *Pope's Palm Sunday Homily* (April 17, 2011), accessed February 14, 2014, http://www.zenit.org/en/articles/pope-s-palm-sunday-homily.

25. Ibid.

26. Vatican II decree, *Inter Mirifica,* December 4, 1963, accessed February 14, 2014, http://www.vatican.va/roman_curia/pontifical_councils/pccs/documents/rc_pc_pccs_doc_04121963_inter-mirifica_en.html, para. 9; See also http://www.vatican.va/roman_curia/pontifical_councils/pccs/documents/rc_pc_pccs_doc_23051971_communio_en.html#Nota%201.

27. Heneghan, "Faith and Smart Phones."

28. Sakyong Mipham Rinpoche, "Karma and Smartphones: How to Use Technology from a Buddhist Perspective," *Huffington Post* (June 2, 2013), accessed February 11, 2014, http://www.huffingtonpost.com/sakyong-mipham-rinpoche/karma-and-smartphones-how-to-use-technology-from-a-buddhist-perspective_b_3365310.html.

29. Ibid.

30. Biddlecombe, "Cell Phone Users Are Finding God."

31. For more information, refer to http://www.askimam.org/public/question_detail/25388.

32. Nate Anderson, "Ditch Your 'Jesus Phone': Churches Call for Screen-Free Holy Week," *Arstechnica,* April 18, 2011, accessed February 19, 2014, http://arstechnica.com/tech-policy/2011/04/ditch-your-jesus-phone-churches-call-for-screen-free-holy-week/.

33. Ibid.

34. Kobi Nahshoni, "Haredim's war against World Wide Web intensifying with Internet disconnection taskforces and ultimatums: Rid yourselves of smartphones, or find a new rebbe," *Ynetnews,* June 3, 2012, accessed February 19, 2014, http://www.ynetnews.com/articles/0,7340,L-4236936,00.html.

35. Ariana Melamed, "Smartphone-smashing at synagogue shows rabbis consider these devices to be dangerous deities," *Ynetnews,* October 12, 2012, accessed February 19, 2014, ttp://www.ynetnews.com/articles/0,7340,L-4291320,00.html.

36. BlackBerry is a registered trademark of Research In Motion, Limited (RIM).

37. For more information, refer to http://www.marketingprofs.com/charts/2011/4702/smartphone-ownership-drives-hyper-email-facebook-use.

38. Andrew J. Bacevich, "Selling Our Souls—Of Idolatry & iPhones," *Commonweal,* July 29, 2011, accessed February 14, 2014, https://www.commonwealmagazine.org/selling-our-souls.

39. The following statistics and quotes in this paragraph are from results of an LG Smartphone Survey conducted between September 30 and October 7, 2013 among 1,152 nationally representative Americans ages 18 and over with a margin of error +/-3.5. For more information refer to http://www.prnewswire.com/news-releases/three-fourths-of-smartphone-owners-admit-they-would-be-comfortable-using-their-device-in-a-public-restroom-and-77-percent-would-openly-do-so-while-in-bed-with-someone-else-231583291.html and www.lg.com.

40. Ibid.

41. Ibid.

42. Ibid.

43. Rinpoche, "Karma and Smartphones."

44. Alexander S. Taylor and Richard Harper, "The Gift of the *Gab?*: A Design Oriented Sociology of Young Peoples' Use of Mobiles," *Journal of Computer Supported Cooperative Work,* 12, no. 3 (2003): 271.

45. Marshall McLuhan, *Understanding Media* (Cambridge, MA: The MIT Press, 1994, reprint from 1967), 9.

46. Sherry Turkle, *Alone Together: Why We Expect More from Technology and Less from Each Other* (New York: Basic Books, 2011), 3.

47. LG Smartphone Survey.

48. Andrew M. Greeley, *Religion: A Secular Theory* (New York: Free Press, 1982), 109–13.

49. Ibid., 119.

50. For more details on the Christian perspective of symbols mediating God's graced, sacramental presence through the senses, see Louis-Marie Chauvet, *The Sacraments: The Word of God at the Mercy of the Body* (Collegeville, MN: The Liturgical Press, 2001.

51. Booch, "Deus ex Machina."

CHAPTER ELEVEN

"In Jesus Christ, the Medium and the Message Are Fully One and the Same"[1]: Deriving a Media Theology from the Works of Marshall McLuhan

David E. Beard and David Gore

Marshall McLuhan was the consummate academic for the mass communication generation—with appearances across radio, TV, and in motion pictures. And if Stanley Fish exhorts academics (in *Professional Correctness*[2]) to avoid media appearances because we become tools to speak the messages that the media want spoken (and so open no space for media criticism), McLuhan is the counter-exemplar: He used the media as the tool to advance his critical agenda.[3]

As a result, McLuhan, more than nearly any other thinker in the 20th century, was able to frame the interpretation of his work. He was able to frame popular responses to his ideas, which in turn became the starting point for academic and critical responses. Most notably—McLuhan's self-representation of his own theories was strategic—it was a deeply secularized version of his theories that erased the religious dimension of his thought. McLuhan represented himself as the innovative creator of a secular theory for the analysis of secular media and technology.[4]

Scholars have only begun to recover the religious dimensions of McLuhan's thought, dimensions that McLuhan effaced in his work as a public intellectual. McLuhan is thinkable as a secularist media scholar, but he is also thinkable as a Catholic intellectual who was deeply interested in how his insights on media and technology could inform religion and aid the Church in its mission. This latter dimension is almost entirely lost in most secular accounts of McLuhan's work. This is more certainly even more true in pedagogical terms. That is to say that there is obviously a lot of McLuhan's own writing about Catholicism[5] and scholarship about that writing,[6] but almost none of it makes its way into the traditional *paideia* regarding McLuhan in our time.

This chapter begins a recovery of the religious, specifically Catholic dimensions of McLuhan's work. In doing so, it revises our understanding of McLuhan's theoretical and critical project. We believe that McLuhan's aphorisms and maxims were, in the end, Trojan horses. In its barest statement, you cannot read "The Medium is the Message" as a maxim, a flash of theoretical insight, in quite the same way if you recognize that, for McLuhan, in Jesus Christ, the medium and message were one. This revision of McLuhan's thought can be an exemplar for the broader reintegration of the religious dimension into media and popular culture studies, into what we are calling a "Media Theology."

In section one of this chapter, we show that the recovery of the religious tradition was, for McLuhan, part and parcel of the recovery of the richest details of the intellectual tradition of the West. Catholicism became a lens that enriched his reading of the great works of philosophy and of literature. In section two, we revise McLuhan's media theory in light of his religious commitments. McLuhan's religious commitments include claims that the media environment has become an envelope that seals us away from God, revelation, and salvation. We are alienated from religious experience. That said, we are not without hope. As McLuhan criticizes the Church for failing to understand the consequences of media, he nonetheless hopes to encourage a return to the unmediated experience of the divine. These dimensions of his reflections on media theory force us to reexamine his media theory as we have inherited it. We hope that his work will point toward a "media theology."

Finally, we assess the state of media studies in what Charles Taylor has called a "secular age, and point to the necessity of a "media theology" as an alternative hermeneutic for the 21st century. Drawing from Charles Taylor's analysis of the historical roots and contemporary condition of secularism,[7] we define our secular age and the secular hermeneutic we have brought to all aspects of our age, including our interpretations of McLuhan. We argue that the rich dimensions of McLuhan's theory, when we account for his faith, can become a model for a richer engagement with the religious dimension of media culture through the development of a "media theology." We think a media theology, rooted in McLuhan's thought, should take notice of the fact that theology is a multifaceted and multilayered field today, cognizant of the impressive challenges of theologizing in a secular age. This awareness allows scholars to recognize that discourse about God and ultimate ends is a human imperative. Within the religious perspective, the symbolic life of English speaking peoples is permeated by God's presence, even if, and especially when, our active and political lives attempt to exist at considerable remove from the sacred or the religious.

The challenge facing a media theology is to cultivate awareness of religious motives and effects in understanding media and thereby to improve our capacity to theorize, that is, to *see* the operations of religious, divine, and sacred experience in the communication landscape. To put it another, more secular, way, the challenge of media theology is to acknowledge that God, as a perception or conception, may play a role in the construction and interpretation of messages. This acknowledgement may not require the media critic to ditch her critical tools, but it may be more significant than merely adding a few more tools to the toolkit. Media theology might empower media theorists to look for anchors in an unstable environment, as religion seemed to anchor McLuhan in the "Satellite Environment" of the late 20th century.[8] We think media theology can at least provide new ways of thinking about media and thus add a few tools that are not regularly employed and deployed at present.

McLuhan's Discovery of the Catholic Tradition for Literary and Media Studies

Marshall McLuhan did not begin as a media critic; in the first decades of the 20th century, as he completed an undergraduate and an M.A. degree in English literature at Winnipeg, there was no such area of study. In beginning study at Cambridge in 1935, McLuhan was required to complete an additional year of undergraduate work, typified by attendance at public lectures and completion of individual exams (some of those lectures were under the tutelage of I. A. Richards, whose work on *Practical Criticism* helped expand McLuhan's horizons from the relatively narrow study of literature common to the English degree into nonliterary discourses. McLuhan did not begin graduate study until 1936. Shortly thereafter, he received a teaching appointment at University of Wisconsin–Madison, eventually to return to Cambridge in the middle of World War II (1940) to complete his M.A. and begin his Ph.D. (completed in 1943). McLuhan's dissertation, on the trivium (*The Classical Trivium: The Place of*

Thomas Nashe in the Learning of His Time) as the context for the writings of Thomas Nashe, at once a dissertation grounded in the study of literature, but beginning to open the door to more, by virtue of its broad account of the history of rhetoric, grammar, and logic.[9]

If Cambridge was where McLuhan began to break the boundaries of traditional literary scholarship, it is also where he began an intellectual investigation of religion. The contest between religion and atheism constituted the core of the intellectual climate at Cambridge. On the one hand, the shadow of Bertrand Russell's atheism loomed large at the University. Russell's protests (claiming that college events should not occur in the chapels because the work of the faculty was not compatible with the religious function of the chapels) defined the tensions over religion.[10]

At the same time, within the Cambridge context, McLuhan's readings in literary criticism and *belles lettres* introduced him to Christian apologetics and Catholic thinkers like G. K. Chesterton. In Chesterton's Catholicism, McLuhan discovers a religious experience that is generative of the fruits of culture: "games and philosophy, and poetry and music and mirth and fellowship . . . Catholic culture produced Chaucer and his merry storytelling pilgrims . . . Don Quixote and St. Francis and Rabelais."[11] In a letter, McLuhan writes that "Clara Longworth . . . produces an enormous amount of evidence to show how all of Shakespeare's friends were Catholics" and that Shakespeare was penalized by the Anglican Church, paying "about $2,000.00, in our money, to the local Anglican bishop for the privilege of being married by a priest."[12] He also notes that Shakespeare was harassed by Sir Thomas Lucy until he fled to London. McLuhan is convinced that Anglican intellectuals reshaped history to transform England's greatest literary figure into a man without religious convictions, and this irritates McLuhan, perhaps it drives his to work harder to unearth the Catholic traditions in English literature.

McLuhan explored more than just Catholicism; he excavated Rosicrucianism and Masonry as backdrops to English poetry (recorded in his letter to Ong in *The Medium and the Light*).[13] Even though McLuhan's conversion created a preference for the history of Catholicism (a history he believed suppressed in favor of Protestantism), his eyes were opened to the positive interpretive power that comes from rich and diverse religious cultures. In many ways, this openness is the model for what we would articulate as a media theology, because we do not hold that a media theology must be practiced by a believer in a particular faith. Like McLuhan's investigations of multiple faith traditions, beyond Catholicism, for their influences on the literary tradition, a media theology should be open to investigation from multiple perspectives.

McLuhan never genuinely abandons literary criticism, working on literary critical projects for the length of his career (collected, for example, in *Through the Vanishing Point: Space in Poetry and Painting*[14]). Nevertheless, McLuhan's reputation is, first and foremost, as a media critic. His first major monograph, *Mechanical Bride*, was a work of media criticism.[15] In that work, McLuhan was a sharp and powerful critic of mass culture. In works like *Counterblast*, McLuhan insisted that mass communication was destroying human social life.[16] And in works such as the *Gutenberg Galaxy*, McLuhan made his scholarly reputation and crafted his popular persona as a secular critic of the media.[17] In this capacity, he becomes a foundational figure in media ecology—a "media ecologist."[18]

Less visibly, McLuhan also took a role in critiquing media in the Catholic Church—as we see it, becoming a foundational figure in media theology. In that role, McLuhan recounted that he "felt like a man who has been arrested for arson because he turned in a fire alarm."[19] This feeling was magnified many times over when it came to his efforts to convince the Catholic Church that it was in the middle of a media revolution the effects of which would surpass Gutenberg. The pace and scale of the information explosion is debilitating (and this was in the late 20th century, when computers still operated with punch cards and magnetic tape). McLuhan expressed anxiety that we live at a time when culture travels at the speed of light, "when we can live a century in ten years, when every day of our lives can pass through at least a hundred years of historical development."[20] McLuhan raises critical questions designed to bring Church leadership into action, to respond to the changing media environment. McLuhan intended to provoke a sacred response to the problems created by new media forms.

The Catholic Church, in McLuhan's view, was uncritically adopting new media technologies. In McLuhan's view, amplifying sound in liturgies was not a harmless way to reach those seated in the back; it changed the relationship between the priest, the parish, and the Mass. Similarly, broadcasting the Mass on television did not only make it accessible to shut-ins and to those geographically remote; it, too, changed the experience of the Mass. The nuanced nature of McLuhan's reflections on changes to the Mass is visible in his critique of the decision to discontinue the Latin Mass. McLuhan believes that the Church's failure to see the losses entailed in a move to a vernacular Mass is striking: This "alteration or innovation strikes to the psychic core by the resonance of the auditory imagination."[21] Changing from the Latin Mass to a vernacular one was justified as a move to make the text of the Mass accessible and comprehensible to the parish. But in making the text of the Mass more accessible, an important aspect of the ritual was lost, an aspect that made more than just the Mass itself sacred. By changing the Mass from Latin to vernacular forms, the amplifying power of the interface between two tongues was lost. It was not the "Latin" of the Mass that mattered, but the presence of Latin in English, Spanish, Italian, and French that was magnified so many times over by the Latin Mass and that really captured the imagination of Catholics.[22] By McLuhan's account, the language of the Latin Mass infuses the language of the everyday, and so hearing Latin echo in everyday speech encourages the Catholic to believe that the sacred infuses the everyday as well. In so many ways, McLuhan believed that the Church was unreflective in it media practices: In much the way that the Church missed the meaning of the communication revolution in the 16th century, it might be missing the significance of its contemporary media practices.[23]

Given the dominance of the Church as a historical force, McLuhan asks critical questions that ask the Church to account for its influence on the media landscape: McLuhan asks, probingly, whether the Church itself has been responsible for much of "the secular technology that has shaped the Western psyche?"[24] Insofar as the Church has been an agent of literacy for several hundred years, we may now feel that we know that the answer is yes—but if it is, what is the Church's obligation to understand its impact on the Western psyche? When McLuhan asks, "Why has Western man, and why has the Catholic Church, no theory of communication that can also account for secular psychic change?" he is asking the Church to take intellectual responsibility for its social impact.[25] In much the way that media studies today sometimes circles the analysis of media institutions and the political economy of media, a media theology informed by McLuhan's model may take up critique of religious institutional practices.

The Church could, in McLuhan's view, offer solace and even strength in the face of the changing media environment. We are no longer "within the world" or "on the earth"—rather, in McLuhan's terms, we inhabit "the satellite environment of the earth which for the first time makes the earth the content of a man-made container."[26] ("Satellite environment" is McLuhan's term for the media-saturated environment in which we live; there is no spot on the earth that is not saturated by broadcast signal. We cannot live outside the satellite environment.) Secular interpretations of McLuhan have emphasized the effects of living in this man-made, media container: loneliness, the decline of collective life (like the life offered by membership in the Church), the increase in individualism fostered by technological advance.[27] Even more importantly, this new media environment obscures our experience of the divine: "The satellite environment has completely altered the organs of human perception."[28] McLuhan explains:

By its mediated effects it constitutes a new world that *appears as if we are perceiving reality directly* when in reality we are only encountering the masked concepts of others, many others. That which originated in the minds of media producers is, through the medium, presented to us as if it were a revelation. The medium lies to us. It pretends to reveal, when in reality it serves only to conceal. It conceals the fact that what is presented, what is pseudo-revealed, is really nothing more than the productions of many men and women.

The media alienate us from revelation and from God, in McLuhan's terms.

This rapid transformation of the context of our lives means we need something solid—and religious experience and religious institutions offered that solidity. As he claimed, "The Church, which offers to man and demands of him a constant change of heart, wrapped itself in a visual culture that placed static permanence above all other values."[29] As the culture accelerated through technological change, the church could play a role in grounding human experience. Perhaps, even, through the Church, we can restore our access to the divine—we can recover revelation and so recover contemporary religious experience. McLuhan hoped that Catholicism might even yet find a voice to respond to "electric man," "who has no bodily being" and is "literally dis-carnate."[30] A media theology for the 21st century must also address the intersections between community life, participation in religious institutions and communities, and the media effects traditional conceived as the proper realm of media criticism.

Conclusion: Toward a Media Theology

McLuhan is not, we believe, an outlier in the tradition of studying media and popular culture. His religious turn is not idiosyncratic; rather, scholars in communication and popular culture studies do not recognize the role of religion in our work.[31] When we address religion, we do so awkwardly. We define homiletics as one on a spectrum of rhetorical genres, no different from the campaign speech or the business proposal. We define scriptures as one on a spectrum of texts, sandwiched between mythology and poetry and philosophy, without difference. We define churches along a spectrum of human social institutions. And we understand the experience of media (within the context of religious life) as if the experience of the *700 Club* was no different from an infomercial.

The impulse to erase or efface religious experience is symptomatic of the larger culture. Charles Taylor's *A Secular Age* traces the development of secularism. Under secularism, where earlier humans were enchanted by a wonderful and sacred world and deeply embedded in practices, rituals, songs, and work that allowed them to participate in creation, modern humans quickly reimagined their circumstances. Rather than stand in awe at the signs of an awesome creation, we moderns developed an instrumental relationship to nature. The new disembedded and disenchanted social order was coherent and uncompromising. It brought a new uniformity of purpose and principle. It tended toward individualism rather than collectivism, and it created distance between us and our emotions.[32] Gradually, secular society obscures the theological and religious aspects of our nature, precisely because these aspects seem to serve so little instrumental purpose. We do not understand what we have lost in losing access to religious experience as intellectuals generally, and as scholars of media studies in particular.

In such a context, it becomes easy to (mis)read McLuhan as a secular thinker, partly because he wanted to write in such a way that sometimes obscured his moral and religious opinions, beliefs, and judgments, and partly because our secular age is tilted toward such misreadings. McLuhan is one of a handful of major thinkers of the late 20th century who has understood the power of religion (specifically the Christian tradition) as an integral component of understanding human experience. If we are to think our way through these questions, we may turn to him, first, for help in constructing a media theology.

We can begin by rethinking McLuhan's central thesis, at least as it disseminated into the popular imaginary. The idea that McLuhan thought of Jesus Christ as "the one case where the medium and the message are fully one and the same"[33] has a number of implications for how his work might be received in mass media theory. First, McLuhan seems to have theorized of religion as a kind of anchor in the ever-deepening ocean of media technology and mass production. Both the pace and scale of the information explosion are debilitating and perhaps a turn toward religion, especially toward Catholicism, would function one some level as a corrective to modernity's love affair with disembedding people from their traditional communities and ways of life. The rapid transformation of the context of our lives means we need something solid, something we cannot find in the media of our time. A media theology would recognize that very human hunger and it would account for the ways that religious communities meet these needs and complicate our assumptions about media ecology.

McLuhan's centering of Christ in media studies allows us to imagine an ideally suited medium and message, a medium that is also the message, a message that is also a medium, an intercessor, a mediator. McLuhan no doubt saw every other medium as a hermeneutic puzzle, a Hermes trickster. Thus, the various media were not to be trusted because they were not trustworthy. Like Hermes, sometimes they delivered the message precisely to leave the wrong impression, other times they delivered a message quite contrary to the intended message, but through inventive interpretation the gods got exactly what they wanted. By concentrating on the sacred image of Christ at the center of media studies, McLuhan was not only revealing his own personal commitment to the life of a Christian, but he was illustrating the utility of theology to media studies. Not only is a mediated existence deeply upsetting to traditional ways of life, but it also invokes a future that appears fundamentally light-minded and unaware of its peculiar preoccupations. By wrapping creation in a man-made container, rather than seeing it as a gift from out of the middle of nowhere; that is, the vastness of space, humanity is fundamentally altering its capacity to theologize. Once the power to theologize is lost or simply obscured from the view, human experience is rendered thin—a media theology and media ecology must hold onto the ways that the very human desires for an unmediated experience of the sacred inflect our understanding of the media ecology.

Finally, many, though certainly not all, religious frames of reference include an eschatology, a looking forward to the end or telos of human existence. If McLuhan thought that the Church risked its own obscurity because it failed to fully grasp the role that technological change was playing, and the role of its own media practices in accelerating or transforming that change, he nonetheless retained a vision of the future with the Church at its center:

> I have never been an optimist or a pessimist. I'm an apocalyptic only. Our only hope is apocalypse. If you are asking about the ordinary secular climate of the Church, or its prospects as a secular institution, I should think the opportunities for survival are a heck of a lot better than those of the United States or any other secular institution. Even in the secular sense, the Church has at least as much survival potential as any existing social or political institution, because, after all, it is not unaided at all times—even on the secular side—by supernatural means.
>
> Apocalypse is not gloom. It's salvation. No Christian could ever be an optimist or a pessimist: that's a purely secular state of mind.[34]

To trust in faith and the possibility of human redemption and salvation was, for McLuhan, about training attitudes toward God. "Today, personal prayer and liturgy (which are inseparable) are the only means of tuning in to the right wavelength, of listening to Christ, and of involving the whole person."[35] Without that faith, modern people were out at sea without an anchor in their lives, and the sea itself was becoming increasingly toxic to the health and survival of their communities.

Perhaps an apocalyptic vision is too pessimistic for contemporary media studies to adopt. (So much of the work in media studies entails struggle, it entails resistance.[36]) But our call for a media theology is a call to reconceive the work of media studies to account for these religious dimensions of human experience, as McLuhan did, including the eschatological.

It is our contention that if media studies were to develop an approach to the problems it seeks to address that could make room for acknowledging problems addressed through theology, the discipline would be better for it. Media studies would be more capable of seeing human beings as whole persons, captivated by the cacophony of voices in our modern, liberal, mediated environments, but also still searching for a voice more meaningful than them all. It might begin to see what's at stake for families and communities that are utterly dependent on communication technologies. It would, along with Albert Borgmann, see that "a culture informed by the device paradigm is deeply inhospitable to grace and sacrament. . . . The union of discipline and grace that marks celebration has been divided by the device paradigm. Discipline has been assimilated to the machinery side and has turned into the strain and exertion of labor. Grace has been absorbed by the commodity side and has degenerated into the gratification of consumption. Celebration has, as a consequence, lost much of its discipline and is too often thought to be a matter of gratification rather than grace."[37] Whatever its merits, a fully secular media studies will not deliver us a vision that can empower us to understand the cultural forces at work in a world where images on screens permeate every aspect of existence.

In this chapter, our exegesis of the works of Marshall McLuhan gives us a sense of the perspective of one of the central figures in media studies and media ecology on these questions. If we restore religious experience to a central place in media studies, for the cause of a genuine media theology, we will produce richer histories attuned to resonances we never felt before. If we rethink contemporary religious experience as a means of perceiving the world, we will enter a far richer conversation and acknowledge the importance of different kinds of voices and different ways of seeing. This is not merely to argue for the tolerance that should prevail in all conversations but to argue in favor of acknowledging the complexities involved in human relationships and in human ways of knowing. It is to call for an appreciation of a richer picture of what it means to be human. At this point, our attempt to reclaim elements of McLuhan's religious conversion raises more questions than it answers about media theology. Without reflecting on more of these questions, conversations about media theory will not likely keep up with emerging conversations in philosophy, history, and economics about the role of religion and belief in our secular age.

Notes

1. Marshall McLuhan, "Religion and Youth: Second Conversation with Pierre Babin," in *The Medium and the Light: Reflections on Religion,* ed. Eric McLuhan and Jacek Szklarek (Toronto, ON: Stoddart, 1999), 103.

2. Stanley Fish, *Professional Correctness* (New York: Clarendon Press, 1995).

3. McLuhan's prolific appearances in the media are captured in, for example, Marshall McLuhan, *Understanding Me: Lectures and Interviews,* ed. Stephanie McLuhan and David Staines (Cambridge, MA: MIT Press, 2003).

4. Perhaps one of the most substantive examples of the secular interpretation of McLuhan is in *Hot & Cool: A Primer for the Understanding of and a Critical Symposium with a Rebuttal by Marshall McLuhan,* ed. Gerald Emanuel Stearn (New York: Dial Press, 1967).

5. McLuhan's religious writings are collected in Marshall McLuhan, *The Medium and the Light: Reflections on Religion,* ed. Eric McLuhan and Jacek Szklarek (Toronto, ON: Stoddart, 1999).

6. Writings about McLuhan's Catholicism have been collected in a special issue of *Renascence* 64, no. 1 (Fall 2011).

7. Charles Taylor, *A Secular Age* (Cambridge, MA: Belknap Press, 2007).

8. The "satellite environment" is developed in Marshall McLuhan and Wilfred Watson, *From Cliché to Archetype* (New York: Viking Press, 1970).

9. Marshall McLuhan, *The Classical Trivium: The Place of Thomas Nashe in the Learning of his Time,* ed. W. Terrence Gordon (Corte Madera, CA: Gingko Press, 2006).

10. The story of Russell's atheism is recounted in many places, including S. T. Joshi, *The Unbelievers: The Evolution of Modern Atheism* (Amherst, NY: Prometheus Books, 2011).

11. McLuhan, *The Medium and the Light,* 15. In some ways, McLuhan learned from Chesterton what contemporary rhetorical and media theorists fail to recognize: that the products of culture can be fruitfully understood against the backdrop of religious experience.

12. Ibid., 27.

13. Ibid., 81.

14. Marshall McLuhan, *Through the Vanishing Point: Space in Poetry and Painting* (New York: Harper and Row, 1968).

15. Marshall McLuhan, *The Mechanical Bride: Folklore of Industrial Man* (New York: Vanguard Press, 1951).

16. Marshall McLuhan, *Counterblast* (New York: Harcourt-Brace, 1969).

17. Marshall McLuhan, *The Gutenberg Galaxy: The Making of Typographic Man* (Toronto, ON: University of Toronto Press, 1962).

18. Media Ecology Association.

19. McLuhan, *The Medium and the Light*, 129.

20. Ibid., 46.

21. Ibid., 125.

22. Ibid.

23. Ibid., 118.

24. Ibid.

25. Ibid.

26. Ibid., 90.

27. Ibid., 121–24.

28. Ibid., 81–83.

29. Ibid., 49.

30. Ibid., 50.

31. As a result, it is Plato's epistemology that interests us, not his cosmogony.

32. Charles Taylor, *A Secular Age* (Cambridge, MA: Harvard University Press, 2007), 139.

33. McLuhan, *The Medium and the Light,* 103.

34. Ibid., 59–60.

35. Ibid., 141.

36. Possibly, this resistant move can be traced to Henry Jenkins' *Textual Poachers: Television Fans and Participatory Culture* (New York: Routledge, 1992), although it is certainly more widespread than that.

37. Albert Borgmann, *Power Failure: Christianity in the Culture of Technology* (Grand Rapids, MI: Brazos Press, 2003), 126–27.

CHAPTER TWELVE

Poets: God's Prophets

Steven Berry

The Present Crisis

In the congregational meetinghouse of my youth I remember standing and singing hymns during Sunday worship. My father said that often a hymn was a poem set to music. He said, "We love hymns and poems for the same reason. They touch a place deep inside us."

Among my favorite hymns was "Once to Every Man and Nation," written by James Russell Lowell, who was an American writer, editor, statesman, professor, and poet. Lowell lived in the 1800s and hailed from my birthtown of Boston. He was one of the fabled "Fireside Poets," which included John Greenleaf Whittier, Oliver Wendell Holmes, Sr., and Henry Wadsworth Longfellow. Some of the works of these poets were introduced to me well before my 10th birthday. It seems odd today to picture a family sitting together reading poems to each other as a form of entertainment. But that is what I experience. My grandmother and my great aunts and uncles introduced me to poetry. They simply read poems. I listened. Then they discussed.

One of the poems they read was James Russell Lowell's "The Present Crisis." A portion of that long poem was used in the hymn I remember singing: "Once to every man and nation/Comes the moment to decide, / In the strife of truth with falsehood, /For the good or evil side; /Some great Cause, God's new messiah, /Offering each the bloom or blight, /And the choice goes by forever /'Twixt that darkness and that light."[1] As I became older, it became increasingly clear that the words of this particular poem are as relevant for my time and me as they were for his time and him.

Does Poetry Have a Place in Popular Culture?

> The changing wisdom of successive generations discards ideas, ques-
> tions facts, demolishes theories. But the artist appeals to that part of our
> being which is not dependent on wisdom; to that in us which is a gift
> and not an acquisition—and, therefore, more permanently enduring.
> (Joseph Conrad, Preface to *The Nigger of the Narcissus*[2])

What I intuited early on was that many poets are truth-seekers. As artists they make their appeal to us out of their passion and pain and sense
of purpose. They can take universal truths, force them into iambic pen-
tameter, and still articulate what lies just beneath the threshold of our
consciousness.

In 1961, Robert Frost, already famous, was further elevated in popularity by being asked to speak at the Inauguration of President John F.
Kennedy. (Presidents Bill Clinton and Barack Obama have followed suit
in their inaugural programs by inviting poets.) When he was unable to
read the intended poem because of the sun's glare, Frost recited "The Gift
Outright," reminding, "The land was ours before we were the land's." Frost
presented Kennedy with a manuscript copy of "Dedication," the poem
he'd intended to read, and wrote to the newly minted president, "Poetry
and power is the formula for another Augustan Age."[3]

This idea is jarring. In our culture, putting poetry and power together is
odd and incongruous. Is poetry possible as an expression within popular
culture? I can't quite picture the appeal of "poetry slams." But poetry is still
taught in our schoolrooms. We still sing our poems in churches. Parents
and grandparents still share poems with the generation that is growing-
up. Our states have poet laureates who travel throughout the country.
Billy Collins, former poet laureate of the United States gave a reading at
my church in 2006. American Public Media features a weekday program
called "The Writer's Almanac," in which radio personality Garrison Keillor
recounts the day in history and then reads a poem or two. Poets are indeed
part of popular culture.

To illustrate, we begin with poet Walt Whitman's encouraging and
hopeful words, quoted in Peter Weir's 1989 film, *The Dead Poets Society*.
The Apple Corporation reprised these words in 2014 for a Super Bowl
commercial to promote their iPad Air. The voice is that of the teacher
speaking to his class of students:

> We don't read and write poetry because it's cute. We read and write
> poetry because we are members of the human race. And the human
> race is filled with passion. Medicine, law, business, engineering—these

are noble pursuits and necessary to sustain life, but poetry, beauty, romance, love—these are what we stay alive for.
To quote from Whitman:
O me, O life of the questions of these recurring.
Of the endless trains of the faithless, of cities fill'd with the foolish,
What good amid these, O me, O life?
Answer:
That you are here. That life exists and identity.
That the powerful play goes on, and you may contribute a verse.
That the powerful play goes on, and **you** may contribute a verse.
What will **your** verse be?[4]

The advertisement reached 111.5 million people globally—the most people to collectively listen to a poem in human history. The words were wrapped around a celebration of life. Depicting values that make us feel good; the visual images were one's of concord, earthly grandeur, cultural inclusivity, racial diversity, harmony, and peace. For those who believe in God, the poetry and pictures evoked a profound sense of the holy. For those who don't—the commercial was still deeply satisfying on a purely human level. The poem and pictures transcended differences. They are universally resonant. They appeal to our collective sense of beauty and remind us that we are interconnected.

I find that poetry is a means through which I can connect to my deeper self. This is true of other expressions of art as well. At their best, they all seem to have the ability to collapse space and time. A poet may entertain us. But as with other art, a poem can also shake us. Poems can be vehicles of revelatory thought. They can express the almost inexpressible. Poems find ways to shout out even when they are being repressed. That is precisely what happened in a culturally rich program, which took place in 2003.

The 2003 White House Poetry Reading

First Lady Laura Bush, a former librarian and advocate for reading, had invited poets to the White House to read. The poetry symposium was on schedule when word came to Mrs. Bush that some of the poet invitees might actually recite or read poems other than the works of Emily Dickinson, Langston Hughes, and Walt Whitman, whose works were being celebrated that year.

As the First Lady was preparing to host the event, the drumbeats preceding the war in Iraq were sounding. What if some poets came and objected to the war and voiced their opposition? It would be embarrassing.

Mrs. Bush, only four months before the poetry reading, had made a public statement that was reported by Elisabeth Bumiller in *The New York Times* ("White House Letter," October 7, 2002). Mrs. Bush stated, "There is nothing political about American literature." How is it that Laura Bush could have failed to notice that poets from the time of the Hebrew prophets have always stood up, at risk of death, to corrupting powers and political influencers? It seems incredible that she hosted a Mark Twain symposium in 2001 while being unaware that Twain was cynical about unbridled patriotism and religious fervor that often accompanies support for war. Twain's prose poem titled "The War Prayer," is about as graphic and politically antiwar as a writer can get. Twain, anticipating the power of that poem, wrote, "I have told the whole truth in that, and only dead men can tell the truth in this world."[5] He instructed that his poem be printed post mortem.

Laura Bush's White House Poetry Symposium was scheduled for February 12 and the war her husband the President and Vice President were building toward was to begin at an unannounced time that felt as though it was fast approaching. The poetry reading thus became almost a matter of national security within closed circles. Perhaps it could be described as a low-grade furtive internal Code Orange alert. (One can never tell what poets may say.)

There was a "tip-off." Connecticut Poet Laureate Marilyn Nelson, an invitee, while determining her attire for the soiree, confided to a friend that she had decided that she would wear a silk scarf with peace symbols to catch the First Lady's eye. She stated publicly, "I had decided to go because I felt my presence would promote peace." She continued, "I had commissioned a fabric artist for a silk scarf with peace signs painted on it. I thought just by going there and shaking Mrs. Bush's hand and being available for the photo ops, my scarf would make a statement."[6] That didn't seem to be such an audacious decision. Meanwhile someone in the White House must have actually read a poem by one of the celebrated poets. That would have been good reason to call off the symposium. Firstly, Emily Dickinson's poems challenge manners, complacency, religion, and conformity. Whitman's poems are radically democratic. For all the speech about wanting the world to be free and experience democracy, what the Bush/Cheney Administration had in mind would have appeared to Whitman as a sham and charade. Read aloud, his poems could have made that embarrassingly clear. Hughes's poems criticize the American system of injustice, privilege, and racism.

Had Laura and her staff considered the poetry of the said poets prior to the Poetry Reading, other poets probably would have been selected in a war year because Dickinson, Whitman, and Hughes would not have supported the portentous bombing of Baghdad.

Poets in the grand tradition of the scriptures are prophets. They are harsh social critics. They speak words of judgment. They confront injustice. Those in power hate the prophets because they refuse to be silenced. They rile up what might otherwise be calm waters. They agitate, they irritate, and they infuriate. They inflame for change. Clearly, at the White House trouble was thought to be afoot. Therefore, the prominent American poets who had been invited by the First Lady to the White House were disinvited. Once the event was called off there was no worry about the press getting wind of disaffected poets, that is, until Barbara Morrow, co-owner of the Northshire Bookstore in Manchester, Vermont, saw an article on the canceled poetry reading on a back page of *The New York Times*. Barbara then went to the marketing director for the bookstore, who took one look and said, "You want us to invite the poets? Okay, I'll get on the phone and make it happen!"

From the White House to the Green Mountains

On February 7, 2003 in the Village of Manchester, Vermont, with Laura Bush having officially canceled the poetry symposium, Zachary Marcus began contacting poets.

Now Vermont is a most appealing destination, but coming to Vermont in the *really, really dead* of dead winter is a stretch. Zach was undeterred. Eleven poets, all of whom knew about the dis-invitation from 1600 Pennsylvania Avenue, were pleased to come to Vermont to stand and publically exercise their patriotic right and duty to celebrate free speech. In the new age of the USA Patriot (Uniting and Strengthening America by Providing Appropriate Tools Required to Intercept and Obstruct Terrorism) Act of 2001 following the terrorist attacks of 9/11 this was not a light decision. However, it was the right one as clearly targeting terrorists and those who threatened American citizens was unlike launching a full-scale war. The poets knew there was insufficient evidence that Iraq held weapons of mass destruction; the stated reason for the planned attack.

Zach now had to choose a venue for the event. There is no town hall in Manchester, Vermont. There isn't a large enough room in the local Grange. The VFW? No! The school auditorium would have confounded the school calendar. So Zach cut the process short, went to his friend the local pastor, and got the green light to have the event at the historic, tall-spired, white, landmark First Congregational Church in Manchester Village. The two bantered a bit. Zach asked, "Is the church, which you call a 'meeting-house' really open to everyone?" I responded, "I guess that depends upon how rowdy the poets and the poetry listening crowd is." Zach continued,

"You put the sign out on the front lawn so you must be ready to suffer the consequences?" "I sure am," I said, "I had construction workers remove the stocks before I put the meetinghouse sign-up just in case of a revolt." Zach asked, "What this boils down to is whether the 'meetinghouse' sign is merely a ruse like the seemingly obligatory 'All Are Welcome' signs on church lawns across the country?" I sighed and then asked, "Who comes to poetry readings anyway?" Zach responded, "I was going to ask the same thing about churches—who comes to them anymore?"

"How many people do you expect?" I inquired.

"If we get shitty weather and it's wicked cold, maybe 50 or 60 people . . . if the weather's not too bad, we could double that."

The day of February 16 was chosen for the poetry reading, and it was, in fact, shittily cold. There had been sleet the day before, rendering the roads slick as grass through a goose. By evening, conditions were even worse. The wind chill was minus 70 degrees—or minus 27, depending on who is recounting the evening's event. People started to arrive early. The poets made their way along winding roads from points north, south, east, and west, some from hundreds of miles away. Locals started streaming out from the dark country roads. By 6:15 p.m. my church, which seats approximately 300 people, was half full. Every folding chair was set up in each available space. The choir loft in the chancel, under the stained-glass nativity scene, began to fill up with the guest poets. Middlebury Professor and Robert Frost scholar Jay Parini arrived. Grace Paley, Vermont State Poet arrived. Award-winning poet Donald Hall came in from New Hampshire. Galway Kinnell, a former Poet Laureate of Vermont, took a seat. Poets from north of Montpelier, Jody Gladding of East Calais, and David Budbill from up on the hill in Wolcott were there. The Cofounder of Copper Canyon Press, William O' Daly, came all the way from California's Sierra foothills.

The local residents continued to stream in. By 6:45 p.m. people were lined up at the door and out into the street. By just after 7 p.m. the place was packed—upstairs, downstairs, on the stairs. I had never seen my church so full. We had more than 600 people. I felt that this was using the church's building in a way that was truly relevant for the entire community. It *was* a meetinghouse, made contemporary and pertinent and engaged in popular culture.

Jamaica Kincaid, Julia Alvarez, Greg Delanty, and the venerable Ruth Stone—all had arrived. Here we all were, less than a half-hour's drive from Robert Frost's homestead in the very setting where Vermont poet Walter Hard had grown up in faith. (Carl Sandburg wrote of Hard's poetry, "I find his Yankees more fascinating than most of the Greeks in Greek mythology.

He and I are of the same school in believing that an anecdote of sufficient pith and portent is in essence a true poem. I treasure and reread his volumes."[7])

If Walter had been there in the flesh that night he would have taken joy in seeing the faces of all the people, old and young, and the majority of them from his beloved Bennington County.

The poetry reading was billed as an evening to honor the Right of Protest as a Patriotic and Historical American Tradition. After I made some historical remarks on the place of the meetinghouse in New England society, I introduced Ed Morrow, co-owner of the Northshire bookstore, who offered the following:

> The reasons we have assembled in this place are as numerous as there are people in the room. These reasons have been accumulating over the past many months, largely ignored, cast aside into a vat of seeming irrelevance—a vat now bubbling with a brew that will no longer be contained.
>
> Protest and dissent played an essential role in the founding of our country, and they have been needed to keep our society free and open and governed by the rule of law. Our leaders are accountable to the people; that is a basic tenet in our form of government. Protest and dissent are tools of the people to hold our leaders accountable when we feel they've gone astray.
>
> The generalized fear and sense of vulnerability generated by 9/11 has fostered a great expansion of governmental powers. Power is as corrupting here at home as it is anywhere else in the world. In a democracy, the citizenry is responsible for keeping this power in check, and that involves vocal dissent. Speaking out. Insisting on being heard. Protesting, if necessary. We are not being loyal to our country or our form of government if we refused to protest or dissent when we believe policies are seriously askew. That may be loyalty to the people in office, but not to the country. So we refuse any corrupting dilution of the words "patriotism and loyalty" by honoring today, in this room, not merely the right, but the duty, to protest—to dissent. This we will do peacefully. This we will do together in a most uplifted manner, by sharing in a primary art.[8]

The Poets Read

The speech of dissent is historically the hardest to make for the prophets in time of war. When voices challenge the powers that be their pronouncements may be viewed as seditious, heretical, and dangerous. That is how the powers seek to paint them—when in fact they may be the only voices of reason. Poets and their dangerously dissenting truths are often the only conscience of a community that might be too scared or ambivalent to know how to address life and death issues.

Going in, a poet who protests powers has to be aware and willing to face the consequences of what is going to be unpopular to the majority. However, that night the crowd that had gathered with less than a week's notice, was ready and waiting to hear the minority report. We were prepared for what these warrior poets would share and I was particularly mindful that our erstwhile neighbor from down the road, Robert Frost, was speaking for us when he stated that what we were doing was "*A way of remembering what it would imperil us to forget.*"[9]

Ruth Stone, one of the "Cry Out" poets, stepped up to the pulpit and read from Emily Dickinson:

> I'm Nobody! who are you?
> Are you—Nobody—Too?
> Then there's a pair of us!
> Don't tell! they'd advertise—you know!
>
> How dreary—to be—Somebody!
> How public—like a Frog—
> To tell one's name—the livelong June—
> To an admiring Bog![10]

Ruth then shared from her own poems: "Lesson"; "Eden, Then and Now"; and "Mantra."

When Ruth was finished, poet Donald Hall walked to the pulpit and addressed the congregation. "I am proud to take part in this passionate occasion, sharing the passion with you, and a passion for peace, against our proposed terrible misadventure."

He read a poem by Walt Whitman called "Reconciliation," written in 1865.

> Word over all, beautiful as sky,
> Beautiful that war and all its deeds of carnage must in time
> be utterly lost,
> That the hands of the sisters Death and Night incessantly
> softly wash again, and ever again, this soil'd world;
> For my enemy is dead, a man divine as myself is dead,
> I look where he lies white-faced and still in the coffin—I
> draw near,
> Bend down and touch lightly with my lips the Whiteface in
> the coffin.[11]

Following Donald Hall's reading of his own poem, "1943," Jamaica Kincaid rose, made her way to the pulpit, and stated:

> I would like to thank Mrs. Bush for being so thin-skinned. If she had not been so thin-skinned we would not be sitting here. To think that a woman who goes to bed and sits down and has dinner with a man who is a lord and master of weapons of mass destruction, and plans to use them, could not stand to hear some poets disagree with him. When Walt Whitman and Emily Dickinson and Langston Hughes were chosen, you could see that they were chosen because they were dead, but *we* now bring them back to life. And *we* must never allow people like that to take them again. The next time you're asked by people in power to come and discuss great works of literature with them, you must tell them No![12]

Greg Delanty offered these remarks:

> I'd like to say that I would have welcomed a chance to go to the White House. I'd have put on my collar and tie to show sameness rather than define myself as different, as I do when I attend demonstrations and when I do civil disobedience. We destructively define ourselves by difference all too often, and a demonstration with all of the demonstrators dressed in suits rather than playing out the stereotypical conflict of the Denims versus the Suits would be very effective. I'd say, "Mr. Bush, all fire is friendly fire. You must stop looking at people as terrorists, because sooner rather than later, you'll turn into one yourself. Mr. President, now turn away from homo sapiens the terrorist and attend to the poor, the sick, the flora and the fauna of the world that we are undoing." But tonight I'm especially glad to be on this sublunar, crooked ball spinning through the multiverse of this universe—to be among this verse, this universe.[13]

From the pulpit, Galway Kinnell quoted Walt Whitman's poem, "To the States," which includes the lines:

> Resist much, obey little,
> Once unquestioning obedience, once fully enslaved,
> Once fully enslaved, no nation, state, city, of this earth, ever afterward resumes its liberty.[14]

The evening whirled on. David Budbill stood in the pulpit and shared his poem, "Easy as Pie":

The Emperor divides the world
into two parts:
The Good and the Evil.

The final presenter was Jay Parini, who looked out at the assembly and said, "Poetry really does matter, and it matters most in these times of peril. As Auden said, 'All I have is a voice to undo the folded lie.' And that's what we're working for, we're working to undo that folded lie."[15]

Zach Marcus offered closing comments spoken by President Kennedy at American University on June 10, 1963:

> For in the final analysis our most basic common link is that we all inhabit this small planets, we all breathe the same air, we all cherish our children's futures and we are all mortal.[16]

Thus ended the night of poetry at First Congregational Church of Manchester, Vermont on what turned out to be one of the coldest nights of the winter of 2003. As the doors were open the blast of northern air quickly chilled a sanctuary that had been bubbling over—fired—by the desire for justice and truth to prevail in our land. Some people stayed behind to thank the poets for coming but after three hours of poems, like it or not, it was time to head home.

The poetry reading in Manchester on the grand scale of events had no effect whatsoever. There was some news coverage in popular media and Vermont Public Radio aired some of the event. C-SPAN books covered the event in its entirety for its entertainment and educational value. The *Los Angeles Times* and Fox News cited what happened, but in the grand scheme of things it mattered little. The Iraq war was launched a month later on March 19, 2003. The bombing of Baghdad was witnessed on global television, commencing with a display of "shock and awe" like nothing ever witnessed. The bombing lasted until May 1, 2003, when President Bush landed on board the aircraft carrier USS *Abraham Lincoln* and declared an end to Operation Iraqi Freedom and "Mission Accomplished." Nine years later, in December 2011, the war with cost exceeding $2 trillion paid for by the American people, after 4,486 American deaths and many thousands at home but unable to cope following the stress of war—U.S. troops were pulled out of Iraq. In 2014, the mission has not been accomplished, with a new Islamic State seeking to make the country of Iraq an extremist militant state. The war by all counts was a total failure except for those who have profited from the death and destruction. The monetary cost of the war with Iraq coupled with that of Afghanistan has eclipsed $5 trillion.

The reason given for launching a war against Iraq is now all but forgotten. The Bush Administration presented the clear and present danger of Iraq having weapons of mass destruction. The Administration lied about this to the America people and the poets sought to undo the folded lie.

Years later, in an imaginative act, the citizens of the city of Brattleboro, Vermont, at town meeting in March 2008 voted 2,012 for (1,795 against) indicting George Bush and Dick Cheney for violating the Constitution and issued arrest warrants for the President and Vice President citing: perjury, war crimes, espionage for spying on U.S. citizens, and obstruction of justice for the firing of U.S. attorneys. The warrant would be limited to only the state of Vermont if Bush or Cheney ever entered the state. Kurt Daims, who had organized the town petition to get the indictment placed on the town meeting ballot, stated that "This petition is as radical as the Declaration of Independence, and it draws on that tradition in claiming a universal jurisdiction when governments fail to do what they're supposed to do. We have the full power to issue indictments, conduct trials, incarcerate offenders and do all other acts which independent jurisdictions have the right to do." The criminal indictments carried the following penalties "law of the town of Brattleboro and the Brattleboro police . . . arrest and detain George Bush and Richard Cheney in Brattleboro."[17] This statute remains on the books. Richard Cheney, the former CEO of Halliburton Corporation (the largest supplier of the war goods and services to Iraq), reportedly received a $34 million payday as CEO when he became the Vice President. His stock options reportedly rose 3,000 percent due to the Iraq war.

God: A Behind-the-Scenes Look

Observations: Poets don't get their due. They are something of an afterthought in the culture. If regarded at all, they are, culturally speaking, low people on the totem pole—the Rodney Dangerfields of popular culture. Yet, the poetry reading in Manchester was very relevant because it was a contemporary Feast of Fools event. A tiny social revolution took place, where, at least in a small gathering, the proud and mighty were toppled for a night. The usually voiceless were given a platform from which they could mock the Powers that Be. In the case of poets expressing their right to free speech, the Bush Administration was targeted.

The evening for me punctuated my feeling about how "church" should be done in the 21st century. The bantering back and forth between Zach and myself contains powerful questions about the role of church in popular culture. If the churches and houses of worship represent God's communities on earth then these groupings should want to do nothing more than to represent the best of what it means to be hospitable, welcoming, inclusive and generous. In order to do this they have to be extremely adept students of popular culture. They cannot dismiss popular culture as happened in the 1950s and led to the slow erosion of churches that we have witnessed for the past four decades. The meetinghouse needs to be an intentional community. Each church, which is defined as the people of God, a household—has to make way for people who aren't part of the household. The idea of the meetinghouse came out of the congregations of New England, but each and every individual church should be a meetinghouse open to the community for civic engagement, the arts, and discourse and explorations on how to live together—regardless of whether or not those who enter are believers. The old New England meetinghouse was a place of worship, but it was also the communal place for enacting town business, engaging in education, discussing issues, and bringing people together: In his sermon, *A Model of Christian Charity,* John Winthrop cautioned in 1630:

> If we do not restrain our individual appetites and ambitions, and put the good of the whole before the good of the self, if we are unable to share abundance with those in need, if we are unwilling to take our public responsibility more seriously than our private convenience, then this new society we are seeking to create will be no better than the one from which we are trying to escape. We will be an embarrassment to ourselves and to the world. We will be left out as fools on a foolish errand and we will deserve the ridicule and derision. If we cannot flourish together we will never flourish privately.[18]

They took down the sign "Meetinghouse" when I resigned my post in Manchester. Meanwhile, I have come to this truth, written by James Russell Lowell, in the hymn I still sing:

> Though the cause of evil prosper, / Yet 'tis truth alone is strong, / Truth forever on the scaffold, / Wrong for forever on the throne. / Yet that scaffold sways the future, / And behind the dim unknown, / Standeth God within the shadow / Keeping watch above his own.

I believe those words and these words of Lowell's with which I conclude. (They, as with all the rest in this chapter, are found in his one poem, "The Present Crisis"):

> New occasions teach new duties, / Time makes ancient good uncouth; / They must upward still and onward, Who would keep abreast of truth.

Notes

Notes were derived from video record by Rev. Dr. Steven E. Berry, Senior Minister, First Congregational Church of Manchester, Vermont, and C-SPAN, February 16, 2003.

1. James Russell Lowell, "Once to Every Man and Nation." *Pilgrim Hymnal* (New York: Pilgrim Press, 1980), 441.

2. Joseph Conrad, *The Nigger of the Narcissus* (Charleston, SC: BiblioBazaar, 2007), 14.

3. "Poetry and Power: Robert Frost's Inaugural Reading," Academy of American Poets, 2014, http://www.poets.org/poetsorg/text/poetry-and-power-robert-frosts-inaugural-reading.

4. Tom Schulman, "Dead Poet's Society,"1989, http://moviescriptsource.com/movie-script.php?id=140&script=Dead%20Poets%20Society.

5. "The War Prayer," Mark Twain, 1904, http://www.antiwar.com/orig/twain1.html.

6. Gary Younge, "First Lady Postpones Poetry Talk Over Protest Fear," *The Guardian*, January 31, 2003, http://www.theguardian.com/world/2003/jan/31/books.politics.

7. "Walter Hard Sr. (1882–1966)," *Vermont Today*, 1999, http://www.vermonttoday.com/century/mostinflu/whardsr.html.

8. George Braziller, comp., *Cry Out: Poets Protest the War* (New York: George Braziller, 2003), 15.

9. Ibid., 15.

10. Ibid., 17.

11. Ibid., 27.

12. Ibid., 32.

13. Ibid., 46.

14. Ibid., 49.

15. Ibid., 108.

16. Ibid., 113. .

17. Susan Smallheer, "Brattleboro to Vote on Arresting Bush, Cheney," *Rutland Herald (Vermont)*, January 27, 2008. ·

18. Braziller, *Cry Out*, 13–14.

CHAPTER THIRTEEN

Finding God in Near-Death Experiences, Art, and Science

Paul H. Carr

Religion is the substance of culture and culture the form of religion.
—Paul Tillich[1]

Introduction

What can near-death experiences (NDEs) tell us about God? Can science explain the full range of NDEs? Neurologist Oliver Sacks thinks so. On the contrary, cardiologist Pim Van Lommel's research on hundreds of patients leads him to believe that the current views on the relationship between the brain and consciousness held by most physicians, philosophers, and psychologists are too narrow for a proper understanding of the phenomenon.

When words are inadequate to express the transcendent beauty of NDEs, perhaps art can help. The trend in contemporary art is to express God symbolically. The beauty of nature and of science, with their underlying mathematical order, point beyond themselves to a transcendent and immanent God.

Why do both atheist and believing scientists use the God word?

What Can Near-Death Experiences Tell Us about God?

Near-death experiences have many features in common: out-of-body consciousness, movement through a dark tunnel, entering a world light, meeting an angelic person, God, predeceased relatives, a life review, experience of a barrier, return, and awakening.[2] No two experiences are identical and no single feature is found in every NDE. Over 80 percent of surveyed people who experiences an NDE expressed a strong increase in their concern for others and that life has greater meaning and purpose.[3]

Eben Alexander, M.D., author of the best-selling *Proof of Heaven: A Neurosurgeon's Journey to the Afterlife*,[4] had an NDE in the fall of 2008. Before this, he had thought he understood what happened to the brain when people are near death and had always believed there were good scientific explanations for the heavenly out-of-body journeys described by those who narrowly escaped death. However, after seven days in a coma during which his brain showed complete absence of neural activity in all but the primitive portions, he experienced something so profound that it gave him a scientific reason to believe in consciousness after death. This included meeting his deceased sister whom he never knew he had. He was able to verify this later.

Here is the conclusion of Alexander's *Proof of Heaven*:

> There is no scientific explanation for the fact that while my body lay in coma, my mind—my conscious, inner self—was alive and well. While the neurons of my cortex were stunned to complete inactivity by the bacteria that had attacked them, my brain-free consciousness journeyed to another, larger dimension of the universe: a dimension I'd never dreamed existed and which the old, pre-coma me would have been more than happy to explain was a simple impossibility.[5]

But that dimension—in rough outline, the same one described by countless subjects of NDEs and other mystical states—is there. It exists, and what I saw and learned there has placed me quite literally in a new world, a world where we are much more than our brains and bodies and where death is not the end of consciousness but rather a chapter in a vast, and incalculably positive, journey.

Eben Alexander's answer to Oprah Winfrey's[6] question, "Did you see God?" is similar to many theologians' idea of the Divine. Alexander answered that God is neither a "he" nor a "she," but infinitely powerful, all knowing, infinite love, transcending time and space, symbolized by a brilliant orb of light and expressed by the sound "Om." God does not have a face. Alexander's transcendent experiences are difficult to express in words. He said it is "like trying to write a novel with only half the alphabet."[7]

Can Science Explain Near-Death Experiences?

Neurologist Oliver Sacks, M.D., who considers himself to be a non-militant atheist, ironically chose the title "Seeing God In the Third Millennium" for his article offering a naturalistic, scientific explanation of Alexander's NDE. Sacks beliefs the NDE occurred when Alexander's cortex was returning to its full function. For Sacks, NDEs can occur in 20 to 30 seconds, even though they seem to last much longer because the concept of time may seem variable or meaningless. Sacks put it this way:

> Hallucinations, whether revelatory or banal, are not of supernatural origin; they are part of the normal range of human consciousness and experience. This is not to say that they cannot play a part in the spiritual life, or have great meaning for an individual. Yet while it is understandable that one might attribute value, ground beliefs, or construct narratives from them, hallucinations cannot provide evidence for the existence of any metaphysical beings or places. They provide evidence only of the brain's power to create them.[8]

For Sacks, Alexander's NDE was not proof of Heaven. However, Sacks would, I believe, be open to the possibility of "seeing Heaven in a wildflower," to use William Blake's metaphor.[9]

Let's now examine the decades of NDE research on hundreds of patients, who had survived cardiac arrest, as summarized in Pim van Lommel's book, *Consciousness Beyond Life: The Science of the Near-Death Experience*.[10] Van Lommel provides scientific evidence that the near-death phenomenon is an authentic experience that cannot be attributed to imagination, psychosis, or oxygen deprivation. He shows that our consciousness does not always coincide with brain functions, and that, remarkably and significantly, consciousness can even be experienced separate from the body. Neuroscientists are still investigating the nature and source of consciousness. Progress in this area of research will undoubtedly shed new light on the nature of NDEs.

Religions have a longer historical tradition for finding meaning in death and life than science. The resurrection showed that the transforming power of God's eternal love in Jesus was stronger than death.

The lasting life-transforming effects of NDEs can hardly be explained as neurophysiological artifacts. Finally, no neurophysiological finding can explain the full range of near-death phenomena. Words are inadequate to express the transcendent beauty of NDEs. Perhaps art can help.

How Does Art Portray God?

Theologian Paul Tillich experienced a Divine Presence when seeing the painting of *Botticelli's Madonna with Singing Angels*. His excerpts from his "One Moment of Beauty" are as follows:

> Strangely, I first found the existence of beauty in the trenches of World War I. At 28, I became a chaplain in the German army and served for five ugly years until the war ended. To take my mind off the mud, blood and death of the Western Front, I thumbed through the picture magazines at the field bookstores and discovered Botticelli's *Madonna with Singing Angels*.
>
> After the war, I hurried to the Kaiser Friederich Museum. Gazing up at the painting, I felt a state approaching ecstasy. In the beauty of the painting there was Beauty itself. It shone through the colors of the paint, as the light of day shines through the stained-glass windows of a medieval church. As I stood there, bathed in the beauty its painter had envisioned so long ago, something of the divine source of all things came through to me. I turned away shaken.
>
> That moment has affected my whole life, giving me the keys for the interpretation of human existence, brought vital joy and spiritual truth. I compare it with what is usually called revelation in the language of religion. I know that no artistic experience can match the moments in which prophets were grasped in the power of the Divine Presence, but I believe there is an analogy between revelation and what I felt. In both cases, the experience goes beyond the way we encounter reality in our daily lives. It opens up depths experienced in no other way.[11]

Tillich believed Picasso's *Guernica* (1937) was the greatest Protestant painting of his day because it illustrated the Protestant principle of prophetic judgment and protest. Guernica was a small town in northern Spain where the Fascist countries, Germany and Italy, used saturation bombing to obliterate it. Tillich regarded *Guernica* as profoundly religious because it expressed so honestly and powerfully our anguished search for ultimate meaning and our passionate protest against cruelty and hatred. It did not have, however, any explicit religious content.

Paradoxically Tillich was critical of Dali's *Last Supper* (1955), at the National Gallery of Art in Washington, D.C. This large oil on canvas painting does have religious content. Tillich regarded Dali's representation of Jesus as too idealized and somewhat effeminate, "kitsch," or commonplace. Tillich, who was forced to leave Germany when the Nazis relived him of his academic position in 1933, was not that well versed in English.

He thought that the appropriate translation of "kitch" was "junk." Since Tillich was a respected art critic, the curator of the National Gallery of Art mentioned this in a telephone conversation[11] with Dali in Spain, to which Dali replied that he was not drunk when he made the painting.

Contrary to Tillich, I love Dali's *Last Supper*. I have stood in front of it many times at the National Gallery of Art. Its rectangular dimensions, 66 inches by 106 inches, have the divine proportion. Each time I discovered something new, such as being present with Jesus and his disciples and also the right and left symmetry of the disciples. Jesus's outstretched arms grasping the base of the dodecahedron, a symbol of the universe, is awesome.

Contemporary art is depicting God more symbolically than in the past. The influential Russian abstract painter and art theorist Wassily V. Kandinsky's *Concerning the Spiritual in Art*[12] showed how artists of the early 20th century expressed the Divine through their abstract paintings.

Michelangelo's 1505–1512 Sistine Chapel ceiling showed God as an old man imparting life to Adam. *God as an Architect* (1794) by William Blake was a water colored relief etching of a wise white-haired man symbolically creating and measuring the world with a divider.

In Vincent Willem van Gogh's 1890 version of Rembrandt's *The Raising of Lazarus*, van Gogh depicts himself as Lazarus being raised through the compassionate outreach of two women. Instead of Rembrandt's figure of Christ standing above Lazarus's grave, van Gogh painted the blazing sun—as a symbol of Divine Love. He always said that he only painted what he knew . . . he had never seen Christ, but he believed in the Divine that flowed through Christ. For Van Gogh the sun, as the source of our life on earth, symbolized the Divine Creator.

The neglect of artistic expressions of beauty in many Protestant churches and our neglect of nature's divinely created beauty contributes to the declining main-line church membership. People fill this vacuum by expressions of God in the popular media. Theologian Paul Tillich believed that the Protestant Principle of prophetic judgment should be courageously balanced by Roman Catholic substance and tradition.

Rev. Rob Bell is, in my view, popularizing Tillich's existential theology. Bell's videos give us images of the Divine in the many facets of everyday life. For him *Everything Is Spiritual*.[13] His best-selling book, *Love Wins: A Book about Heaven, Hell, and the Fate of Every Person Who Ever Lived*[14] envisions a loving God who does not necessarily condemn people to eternal torment in the place called Hell. This angered many conservative evangelicals and contributed to Bell's resignation from the Mars Hill megachurch that he founded. His latest book, *What We Talk about When*

We Talk about God,[15] shows how traditional ideas about God have grown stale and dysfunctional. Bell believes that God is with us, for us, and ahead of us.

At the conclusion of Tillich's popular *Courage to Be*,[16] he stated that the source of the courage was the God above the God of Theism. An example of the God who must be transcended is the rhetorical-political abuse of the name of God, as when Saddam Hussein said that he would win the Gulf War because God was on his side. Tillich would have preferred Abraham Lincoln idea that the question is not whether God is on our side, but are we on God's side? For Tillich, the God of theism would be a being but beside other beings (hence finite and provable), an invincible tyrant who controls and determines everything and allows us no freedom. God is not a finite being but the ground and abyss of all being.

Why Do Both Atheist and Believing Scientists Use the God Word?

Tillich, I believe, would have criticized physicist Leon Lederman for labeling the Higgs boson *The God Particle*[17] to gain support for the national expenditure of the billions of dollars required to construct the super particle collider needed to prove its existence. Many physicists dislike the term, including Peter Higgs, who regards it as inappropriate sensationalism. When Lederman was asked why did you call it the God Particle, he answered that there were two reasons: One, the publisher wouldn't let us call it the Goddamn Particle, though that might be a more appropriate title, given its villainous nature and the expense it is causing. And two, there is a connection, of sorts, to another book, a much older one.

Elaine Pagels was more theological when she wrote in *Newsweek*:[18] "It is called the God Particle because you cannot see it and everything depends on it."

Albert Einstein once said, "I want to know God's thoughts. The rest are details."[19] He also said, "I don't try to imagine a God; it suffices to stand in awe of the structure of the world, insofar as it allows our inadequate senses to appreciate it."[20]

Einstein's contemporary, Paul Tillich observed the original unity of science and religion in antiquity.[21] There was no conflict, as science had not emerged from natural philosophy. According to ancient mythology, nature was explained by the action of the gods. Conflicts arose, however, as scientific laws replaced ancient mythology and cosmology. Darwin's Theory of Evolution, was opposed by some churchmen who sensed the dehumanizing and amoral implications of this new science. Tillich himself was strongly opposed to the depersonalizing forces of our technological society, which deprive the creative self of its selfhood. Rather than demonizing technological societies and deifying pretechnological ones, however, Tillich wanted to hold them in creative dialectical tension, as is evident in his following encounter with Albert Einstein.

In his essay, *Science and Religion*,[22] Einstein enjoined religion to do away with the kind of Personal God who would break the laws of nature to perform miracles. Tillich in response said that he agreed with Einstein in the sense that "God is supra-personal."[23] Tillich believed today we know what the New Testament always knew—that miracles are signs pointing to the presence of a divine power in nature and history and that they are in no way negations of natural law.

Mathematical physicist Paul Davies[24] is in basic agreement with Tillich. Davies wrote: "I do not cling to the notion of God as a miracle-working cosmic magician, who makes a big bang and then intervenes as a cosmic repairman (intelligent design). A God who can create a self-creating universe with laws is much more majestic. As an emergentist, I believe in a hierarchy of principles, with the laws of physics at the bottom level and emergent laws operating at higher levels. Thus, we have laws of complexity, such as self-organizing chemical cycles. There are Mendel's laws of genetics when life appears. The high-level laws do not violate the lower level laws, nor are they reducible to them. They supervene on them."

Paul Davies's book, *The Mind of God: The Scientific Basis for a Rational World*,[25] is a follow-up to his *God and the New Physics*.[26] He argues that the existence of consciousness in the universe cannot be a byproduct of mindless, purposeless forces. We are truly meant to be here. Though he is not religious in a conventional sense, Davies believes that the rationality of the universe, the fact that humans can understand how the universe works, is evidence of purpose and meaning. Davies points out that the fact that the universe's deepest laws can be expressed mathematically strongly suggests that there is more to our world than meets the eye. By the means of science, we can truly see into the mind of God.

It is interesting that Dr. Francis Collins, who led the international team that sequenced the human DNA genome, entitled his book, *The Language of God: A Scientist Presents Evidence for Belief*.[27] The "language of God" is wonderful and fitting metaphor for the molecular sequence by which genetic information is transmitted from one generation to the next via the DNA double helix. This stunning scientific achievement was also an occasion of worship for Collins. His book proposes the name "BioLogos" as a new term for theistic evolution.

"Bios" is the Greek word for "life." Logos is Greek for "word," with a broader meaning in Heracleitean Philosophy and Stoicism—namely, the rational principle ordering the universe. In Christian theology, "word" includes the Hebrew idea of a creative agent for all that exists, in addition to being an ordering principle. "BioLogos" expresses the belief that God is the source of all life and that life expresses the will of God. BioLogos represents the view that science and faith coexist in harmony and supports such scientific findings as (1) the universe is 14 billion years old, and (2) life evolves in accordance with Darwinian evolution. The spiritual and moral natures of humans are unique however as they were created in the "image of God."

Dr. Francis Collins had a spirited debate with his fellow biologist, atheist Dr. Richard Dawkins, author of *The God Delusion*.[28] The front cover of *Time* magazine on November 13, 2006 entitled the debate "God vs. Science." During the debate, Dawkins criticized the Biblical literalists who oppose Darwinian evolution. Collins defense was that of St. Augustine, Bishop of Hippo, 354–430 AD, who believed that the Biblical text should not be interpreted literally if it contradicts what we know from science and our God-given reason. At the end of the debate Dawkins noted that if there is a God, He has to be a lot bigger than how present religions represent Him.

Dr. Francis Collins's BioLogos worldview is supported by evolutionary evangelist Rev. Michael Dowd, author of *Thank God for Evolution: How the Marriage of Science and Religion will Transform Your Life and Our World*.[29] When Dowd was attending an evangelical college, he was greatly disturbed when he learned that the biology department was teaching Darwinian evolution. He was against it because its naturalistic explanations of the origin of the species did not involve God as described in the Bible. While at college, he became friends with other students who believed in Darwinian evolution. A few years later during a presentation of the scientific worldview, Dowd had an epiphany. He sought out science writer, Connie Barlow, and married her. They now travel around the United States giving talks supporting Darwinian evolution.

The TV Science Channel[30] recently aired the program, "Did we invent God? Did God invent humanity?" Dr. Andrew Newberg, author of *How God Changes Your Brain*[31] has used brain activity imaging to answer these questions. He discovered that when believers meditate on God, their brain activity is the same as having a conversation with another person. This is not the case for atheists. This is neurological evidence that God is real for believers. This does not mean that God does not exist. Belief in a loving not punitive God and the practice of meditation and prayer are beneficial for mental and physical health.

Conclusion

During his NDE, Eben Alexander, M.D., experienced God as neither a "he" nor a "she," but infinitely powerful, all-knowing, infinite love, transcending time and space, symbolized by a brilliant orb of light and expressed by the sound "Om." God did not have a face.

The lasting life-transforming effects of NDEs can hardly be explained as neurophysiological artifacts. No neurophysiological finding can explain the full range of near-death phenomena. NDEs' transcendent experiences are difficult to express in words. Artistic images can help.

Modern art, particularly abstract art, is depicting God and the Divine symbolically in contrast to Michelangelo's anthropomorphic God. The neglect of artistic expressions of beauty in many Protestant churches and our neglect of nature's divinely created beauty contributes to the declining main-line church membership. People fill this vacuum by expressions of God in the popular media.

Many scientists use God in their books as a symbol of their faith, which is not always that of traditional religions. However, physicist Lederman and neurologist Sacks have used God as way of gaining support for their point of view. Leon Lederman's labeled the Higgs boson the *God Particle* to gain support for the national expenditure of the billions of dollars required to construct the super particle collider needed to prove its existence. It is ironic that neurologist Oliver Sacks, M.D., who considers himself to be a nonmilitant atheist, chose the title "Seeing God In the Third Millennium," for his article offering a naturalistic, scientific explanation of Alexander's NDE.

The beauty of nature and of science, with their underlying mathematical order, point beyond themselves to a transcendent and immanent God. God is in nature and nature in God. Science emerged from myth to math.[32] God is in our beginning and in our earthly end. "I am the Alpha and the Omega" (Revelation 22:13). God as Ultimate Reality transcends time: the eternal from which we emerge and to which we return at death.[33]

Acknowledgment

I wish to thank artist Carol Berry for her helpful suggestions.

Notes

1. Paul Tillich, *Systematic Theology,* vol. 3 (Chicago: University of Chicago Press, 1963).

2. Raymond Moody, *Life After Life: The Investigation of a Phenomenon* (Fairhope, AL: Mockingbird Books, 1975).

3. Cassandra Musgrave, "The Near-Death Experience: A Study of Spiritual Transformation," *Journal of Near-Death Studies* 15, no. 3 (Spring 1997): 187–201.

4. Eben Alexander, *Proof of Heaven: A Neurosurgeon's Journey to the Afterlife* (New York: Simon and Schuster, 2012).

5. Ibid.

6. Oprah Winfrey, "Dr. Eben Alexander Shares What God Looks Like," 2012, https://www.youtube.com/watch?v=qQH_X1JByks.

7. Alexander, *Proof of Heaven*, 72.

8. Oliver Sacks, "Seeing God in the Third Millennium," *The Atlantic,* December 12, 2012.

9. William Blake, *Auguries of Innocence* (1863).

10. Pim Van Lommel, *Consciousness Beyond Life: The Science of the Near-Death Experience* (New York: Harper One, 2010).

11. Paul Tillich, "One Moment of Beauty," *Parade Magazine*, September 1955.

12. Wassily V. Kandinsky, *Concerning the Spiritual in Art*, trans. Michael T. H. Sadler (Whitefish, MT: Kessinger Publishing, 2004).

13. Rob Bell, "Everything Is Spiritual," 2012, http://www.youtube.com/watch?v=i2rklwkm_dQ\.

14. Rob Bell, *Love Wins: A Book about Heaven, Hell, and the Fate of Every Person Who Ever Lived* (New York: HarperOne, 2011).

15. Rob Bell, *What We Talk about When We Talk about God* (New York: HarperOne, 2013).

16. Paul Tillich, *The Courage to Be* (New Haven, CT: Yale University Press, 1952).

17. Leon Lederman, *The God Particle: If the Universe Is the Answer, What Is the Question?* (Boston: Houghton Mifflin, 1993).

18. Elaine Pagels, "What's So Heavenly about the God Particle?" *Newsweek,* December 26, 2011, vol. 158, Issue 26/1, p. 50.

19. Albert Einstein, From E. Salaman, "A Talk with Einstein," *The Listener* 55 (1955): 370–71.

20. Albert Einstein, Letter to S. Flesch, Einstein Archive. 30-1154, April 16, 1954.

21. Paul H. Carr, *Beauty in Science and Spirit* (Center Ossipee, NH: Beech River Books, 2006), 143–47.

22. Albert Einstein, "On Religion and Science," *New York Times Magazine,* 1–4, November 9, 1930. Also in Jammer, *Einstein and Religion,* p. 73, 1930.

23. Paul Tillich, "Science and Theology: A Discussion with Einstein," *The Union Review* 2, no. 1 (November 1940). Reprinted in *Theology of Culture*, ed. R. C. Kimball (Oxford: Oxford University Press, 1959), 127–32.

24. Paul Davies, "A Cosmic Religions Feeling," paper presented at Science and the Spiritual Quest Conference, Harvard University, Cambridge, MA, October 21, 2001.

25. Paul Davies, *The Mind of God: The Scientific Basis for a Rational World* (New York: Simon and Schuster, 1992).

26. Paul Davies, *God and the New Physics* (New York: Simon and Schuster, 1983).

27. Francis S. Collins, *The Language of God: A Scientist Presents Evidence for Belief* (New York: Free Press, 2006).

28. Richard Dawkins, *The God Delusion* (Boston: Houghton Mifflin Harcourt, 2006).

29. Michael Dowd, *Thank God for Evolution: How the Marriage of Science and Religion Will Transform Your Life and Our World* (New York: Viking Adult, 2008).

30. TV Science Channel, "Did We Invent God?" Through the Wormhole Series, http://www.sciencechannel.com/tv-shows/through-the-wormhole/videos/did -we-invent-god.htm.

31. Andrew Newburg and Mark R. Waldman, *How God Changes Your Brain: Breakthrough Findings from a Leading Neuroscientist* (New York: Ballantine Books, 2008).

32. Carr, *Beauty in Science and Spirit*, 12.

33. Tillich, *The Eternal Now* (New York: Scribners, 1963). http://www.religion -online.org/showchapter.asp?title=1630&C=1607.

CHAPTER FOURTEEN

Gods in Indian Popular Jokes

Amitabh Vikram Dwivedi

India has been progressing, and her rapid rise from the colonial past to a globalized nation reflects changes and transformation occurred during the past few decades. The modern India birthed; and the cultural, traditional, and religious forms started generating new meanings. This chapter provides accounts of Indian gods[1] (largely Hindu) in jokes with respect to popular culture. The "official culture" of the historical India documented the story of gods and goddesses in texts; the believers carved them into statues in temples and started worshipping them either in the form of reading the sacred texts or chanting prayers in front of them. But the popular culture adds a new medium to this traditional approach by realizing the existence of gods in the daily humor around us. It was started by employing the language of humor to gods. This chapter studies how the jokes depict gods in its popular form, and it will also discuss what god has become for the present generation.

The study is informed by the ethnographic approach, and the information is analyzed by the content analysis. This study describes the process of changes, and it gives an insight into this process where language is generating and influencing complex social norms. Jokes have transformed the way of experiencing gods and humor has added one more dimension to experience the divine in the way that suits best in a particular time, and this chapter seeks to explore how this change in religious understanding generates new meaning. It recounts how knowledge of the context multiplies the creative narratives and creates daily humor for everyone, and no one takes offense.

Indian Gods

For Hindus, *Brahma* is the creator; *Vishnu* is the preserver; and *Shiva* is the destroyer. All these chief Gods have wives. *Brahma* has *Saraswati* (the Goddess of knowledge), *Vishnu* and *Shiva* consort with *Lakshmi* (the Goddess of wealth) and *Parvati* (the Goddess of power), respectively. Besides these chief deities there are 330 million Gods: "male gods, female gods, personal gods, family gods, household gods, village gods, gods of space and time, gods of specific castes and particular professions, gods who reside in trees, in animals, in minerals, in geometrical patterns and in man-made objects. Then there are a whole host of demons."[2] Hindu religion is evolutionary by nature; *deva* or *demons* (supernatural powers) changes their characters and names according to the context (e.g., *angi* [fire] is not only a chemical process but also "the manifestation of transcendental power").[3] There are hundreds of references for the same Gods in different names in the Vedic hymns.

Most of the Hindu Gods are great warriors. Their weapons are: three-pronged spear, revolving discus, bow and arrow, rattle-drum, sword, fire, and so on, and they have divine powers to do anything. They wear bracelets, rings, armpits, bangles, crowns, necklaces, and other jewelry. Their clothes are dhoti, sari, and loose shirt without collar; a few Gods wrap only animals' skin. They live in different worlds and only visit earth in person occasionally—when there is a danger or their worshippers force them by their prayers to come. They are omnipotent, omnipresent, and omniscient, and their power resides in every particle of this earth. They are kind and compassionate, and they love human beings and other animates of this world but they also punish the evildoers.

Joking about Gods

Hindu religious literature is based on myths. These myths are not a synonym of falsehood but they tell many types of truths: subjective, objective, cultural, intuitive, logical, pertaining evidence, and grounded in beliefs. Each god has many myths, so there are innumerable narratives. The narratives of birth, death, reincarnation, body, soul, mind, consciousness, desire, conjugal relations, incest and adultery, values and judgment, ignorance and knowledge, carnal, divine, and so on. The official culture records these stories and myths in various languages and dialects on the basis of a commonly shared currency of belief. But the creative aspect of language allows the native speakers to coin new registers to capture the essence of gods and goddesses in their day-to-day lives, and therefore they start using the register of jokes.

The jokes about Gods are hyperbolic and fantastic in nature like many myths and folklores. The main difference between a myth and joke is of longevity. Myths have been in Indian society for ages and people take them as true. "Any attempt to edit them is frowned upon."[4] Moreover, many myths or oral folklores, unlike jokes, have been recorded in one form or another. The joke is a recent phenomenon, originating and developing in the mind of the language users or found in SMS and Internet texts. The unrealistic content of the jokes draws the attention of the listeners, and they actively engage to compare the new information with the already registered one in their minds and consequently engage in jokes and enjoy them. The irrational and creative narrative attracts the listeners, and they find jokes meaningful.

Gods are sacred and jokes are funny, but this analogy does not make the proposition that Hindu Gods are funny. Jokes about Gods create serious laughter. There is nothing degrading about it in present generation. It is a way to bring the Gods to mind. The history of the Hindu religion tells us that language of worship for hymns since the Vedic period was Sanskrit, and the "Vedic commentators have observed that women and low-caste members of society would not have understood the meaning of the words of the Veda."[5] Then Khariboli (a dialect of Avadhi and Braj) developed in 900–1200 CE, which later paved the path for Hindi, which is now an official language of Indians, and men and women of every caste and religion communicate in it. Presently, the use of Sanskrit is restricted to a formal religious function with Hindi or other regional languages where professional pundits perform the rituals for the people. Hindu at home has gradually replaced Sanskrit with native vernaculars and dialects for their convenience and meaningfulness. Survey on *Ethnologue* in 2001 indicates 2,950 native speakers of Sanskrit.[6]

Changes in Indian society have occurred at many levels. The language of worship has changed from Sanskrit to Hindi, the condition of schedule castes and tribes has been reformed, women have achieved an equal status to men in society, and Hindu Gods have been filmed in cartoons, soap operas, and movies. CD/DVDs have taken over the market of cassettes; piracy, plagiarism, and criminal support of the film industry have increased; and print media has gone online. Through this change in the register of popular culture, it is possible to recognize gods from the high seriousness of Sanskritized hymns to the highly informal medium of jokes.

The use of jokes for Gods by the Hindus also reflects that pop culture has impacted the psyche of the practitioners deeply as they find it a part of their culture. It has been customary among Hindus to complain to Gods about injustice, to bribe Gods for a favor, to chide Gods when something untoward happens, and to entice and persuade them at times. One thing is obvious from this record: People know that Gods listen to them in various registers, so why not experiment with one more to remember them? Jokes add a new dimension to this religious Indian-ness when they laugh by using jokes about Gods.

Theoretical Foundation

The turn of the 20th century saw some original theories on laughter by Bergson and Freud. Bergson's *Laughter* represents the first real social theory of laughter. He says that it is a human attribute, and any object or animal produces laughter "because of some resemblance to man."[7] He recounts that the comic "demands something like a momentary anesthesia of the heart."[8] In the similar vein, Mead believes that comic gives us a temporary relief from the customary restrictions of social empathy.[9] Smith suggests that it is "a beautiful thing" that nature has put boundaries to the ridiculous so that we may not laugh on a serious misfortune.[10] Bergson further shows that laughter is a social practice unlike what Spencer believes, that it is a psychological one. "Laughter appears to stand in need of an echo."[11] Modern sociologists agree that the laughter and all other humors produce solidarity.[12] It softens orders and provides chances to question authority.[13] Freud sees the psychological aspect of jokes that the unconscious rebels against the social restrictions in dreams, slips of the tongue, and jokes.[14] In jokes we play with words; we compare, contrast, and use puns. We exaggerate things, bring grotesque elements into communication, and we laugh louder in the company.

Generating laughter from jokes about Gods might be understood as craziness and fundamentalist Hindus might disapprove and condemn this activity. Kannabiran says that "fundamentalisms are reactionary; they engage in selective retrieval of the essences of the faith. They are exclusive and separatist; they are absolutists in determining who the enemies are, and in this regard they are authoritarian."[15] The present study does not claim that people who are joking about Gods are secular but it suggests that how people are devising new methods to make the official culture of remembering Gods popular among youths by using these jokes, and they laugh (or rather say they laugh) with Gods in their minds.

There is a thin line between the understanding of laughter (jokes about Gods) and misunderstanding of fun-making (making fun of Gods) as the two phases give different denotations. To state it simply, the religious Hindus are employing these jokes in their daily conversation, and when they crack a joke they positively believe that they are no way degrading Gods or using a foul language for their beloved and gracious Gods. Moreover, the listeners also do not take an offence, because the person who tells a joke is also from the same religion and he/she is aware of the intention and context of the usage. Few jokes are popular among kids and teenagers also who are too innocent to make a serious difference between fundamentalism and secularism.

Data and Discussion

Data for this study have been selected from the popular jokes about Gods in the contemporary India. Every year, the students of Shri Mata Vaishno Devi University (SMVDU),[16] India organize a fest named *Resurgence,* in which they invite other colleges and universities to participate. The audience includes the students of different religions, namely Muslims, Sikhs, Christians, and Hindus.

These jokes were told by the students of engineering in this cultural fest[17] in 2013. The themes of the fest included mock parliament, *Mea Culpa,* various sports events, cultural dance, poetry, and stand-up comedy. There was no direction from the university administration provided to the participants for the selection of jokes. All performances were *extempore,* and the participants were not supposed to prepare jokes on a specific theme in advance. However, it was assumed that they must have known hundreds of jokes. The audiences were mainly students, except for a few faculty members who assisted them in the fest. The performers were allowed to do a lot of code-mixing and switching during their performances. They mixed Hindi with English, Hindi with Punjabi, Hindi with Dogri, and so. There was a huge variation in the themes of these jokes. It could be anything from love to pregnancy, from noodles to flood, and from guitar to girlfriend.

The ethnographic approach has been employed to the data. This approach makes use of participant-observation method in the study, and the focus remains on the context and pattern of the field. The goal of "ethnographic research is to formulate a pattern of analysis that makes reasonable sense out of human actions within the given context of a specific time and place."[18] The ethnographic approach is employed here to study and interpret how the use of jokes depends on the interaction between the user and organizational environment. The jokes selected for the study are translated in English. Only shortcoming of the ethnographic research is that it is often blamed for the reliability of data.

The objectivity of this study is well balanced, as all the real participants were not able to observe and influence the author. The investigation studies the data from feedback and content analysis. Feedback includes the real-life practices, which are used to evaluate and analyze the various aspects of events. The content analysis enables the author to identify and examine themes and trends. A participant tells a joke:

Shiv ji (God, husband):	Where is my trident?
Parvati (Goddess, wife):	*Ganesh* (God, son) has taken it.
Shiv ji:	Why?
Parvati:	He was saying, "I am taking Dad's fork to eat noodles with my girlfriend."

This is a joke about Lord *Shiva's* family. *Shiva* is popularly known as a destroyer God, and *Parvati*, His wife, is a Goddess of power. Their son, Lord *Ganesha*, is also known as an elephant God among Westerners because His head is of an elephant and the rest of the body is of a human being. He is a chief deity in Hinduism. He is a God of intellect and wisdom. This joke tells that *Ganesha* has quick wit and humor, and youth connect with Him.

The jokes are notorious for their concern with the blending of the sublime with the trivial. It is interesting to see that this joke is coherent in itself. The context is a family: father, mother, and son. The trivial event of noodle-eating corresponds with developments in the previous events of a student's life, where noodles are the best substitute for mess food, and having a girlfriend becomes a big achievement. The consistency and reasonable explanation for the narrative lends itself to religious, cultural, and historical thinking. The participant engages the audience in the commemorative process that taught younger generation the values of family, noodles, and girlfriend that makes it a Generation-X.[19] This joke is illogical for a grand narrative as it replaces the grand cultural narrative with the small and local narrative. It brings into focus the singular event. But it is logical in its meta-narrative: "the new part of a joke has to have its own logic and, since the vast majority of jokes involve human characters, the new logic is often that of human desire and planning—frequently a personal, individual and context-dependent one as opposed to the generality expressed in the original script."[20] Here, the personal is too trivial to compare it with the sublime Gods, but the association is formed and thus the whole thing becomes humorous. The language generates meaning when we compare and contrast it with the other narratives similarly, "as 'dog' or 'god' do not acquire their meaning from their equivalents in the world outside language but from the way language contrasts them through its ordering of the letters."[21]

Another participant says:

"*Radha* (girlfriend of God Krishna):	sometimes in the guise of Lord *Ram* (a virtuous God) . . . sometimes in the guise of *Shyam* (a naughty God) . . . come to me."
Krishna (a God of love):	But why?
Radha:	If you come in same getup papa will recognize.

This joke is about Lord *Ram*, God *Krishna,* and His girlfriend, *Radha*. *Krishna,* a narrator of *Bhagavad-Gita,* is also famous for His love for *Radha*. This joke says something about the popularity of the topic "love" that despite the lack of new content attracts the attention of the audience. The concept of love is as an oasis for the youths who are home-sick, and they long for the emotional support of their families. We laugh here because "we pretend to take literally an expression which was used figuratively."[22]

And the one narrates:

When does God become angry?
When a girl becomes pregnant out of a wedlock and her mother says:
"O God! What have you done?"

Sex and sexuality is very important for human beings. "We know that a highly popular—to say the least—goal of human behavior is sex, and since we know enough about the joke discourse conventions to know that characters in them are very frequently involved in the search for sex."[23] Using one's own point of view, the participants always place their jokes under the seal of intimacy; no one God is specified this time and a generic God is meant. The pun is intended to state the victimization of a girl, the status of the society, the fears of the girl's mother, and the opinion of the general public. However, this joke is indeed ambiguous and two readings are available; the second meaning indicates sexual innuendo.

Another joke compares Hindu Gods with computer terminologies: *Brahma* (creator) is System installer, *Vishnu* (preserver) is System operator, *Shiva* (destroyer) is System programmer, *Narad* is Data transmitter, *Yama* (death God) is Delete(r), Apsara (Hindu nymph) is Virus, *Saraswati* (Goddess of knowledge) is Internet explorer, *Parvati* (Goddess of power) is Mother board, and *Lakshmi* (Goddess of money) is an Automated Teller

Machine (ATM). It is interesting here to see that how social construction of technology has adopted and appropriated the complex social construct. Barker suggests that comic is understood in terms of a "contract" between the reader and the text, which is based on a dialogue between them. The meaning of the text arises from this social relationship.[24]

Table 14.1   Comparing Methods of Remembering Gods

Method One	Method Two
Religion is divine, sublime. learned, and esoteric (use of Sanskrit)	Religion is human, trivial, acquired, and lucid (use of Hindi and other vernaculars)
Visiting temples to see Gods	Watching soup opera, cartoons, and movies to see Gods
Fixed and ritualistic actions and performance	Flexible and individualistic actions and performance
Promotion of classical literature	Promotion of folk and popular literature
Fewer meetings and availability of Gods	More meetings and Gods are always available
Reading text	Watching screen
Gods are stranger	Gods are familiar
Less knowledge about the actual text	More knowledge about the actual text
No question on Gods' action	Gods is also questionable
Promotion of fundamentalist activities	Promotion of secular activities

Conclusion

It is possible to read this chapter without worrying about this conclusion. But if readers are rather concerned about the question what has happened to Hindu culture, then the answer is that it has been evolving ever since. And those who want to draw a line to restrict these activities then the flexibility of Hindu religion does not fit in any fundamentalist scheme to ban such activities. Hinduism is a prescription to live a happy life, and it is happening to all religions and societies that are liberal, tolerant, and alive. The need is to do some more exploration in each religion and societies by the users.

Even though the themes of sexuality, pregnancy, noodles, extra-marital relationships, and girlfriend are involved, it is not offensive and libelous. The language is employed only in a figurative sense. The context is humor, the text is jokes about Gods, and the participants are the believers of the same religion.

Notes

1. "Gods" is an umbrella term in this paper, which covers both gods and goddesses.
2. Devdutt Pattanaik, *Myth = mithya: A Handbook of Hindu Mythology* (New Delhi: Penguin Books India Pvt. Ltd., 2006), 5.
3. Klaus K. Klostermaier, *A Survey of Hinduism* (Albany: SUNY Press, 2007), 102.
4. Pattanaik, *Myth = mithya*, xv.
5. Laurie L. Patton, *Bringing the Gods to Mind: Mantra and Ritual in Early Indian Sacrifice* (Berkeley, CA: University of California Press, 2005), 19.
6. Svarsa.com. *Fluent Sanskrit Speakers in India,* 2014, accessed March 3, 2014, http://www.svarasa.com/m-w/sanskrit.html.
7. Henri Bergson, *Laughter: An Essay on the Meaning of the Comic* (London: Macmillan, 1911), 4.
8. Ibid., 5.
9. George H. Mead, *Mind, Self and Society* (Chicago: University of Chicago Press, 1962), 206.
10. Sydney Smith, *Elementary Sketches of Moral Philosophy, Delivered at the Royal Institution in the Years 1804, 1805 and 1806* (New York: Harper and Brothers, 1864), 134.
11. Ibid., 5.
12. Elizabeth Graham, Michael Papa, and Gordon Brooks, "Functions of Humor in Conversation: Conceptualization and Measurement." *Western Journal of Communication* 56 (Spring 1992): 161–83.
13. Janet Holmes, "Politeness, Power and Provocation: How Humour Functions in the Workplace," *Discourse Studies* 2, no. 2 (May 2000): 159–85.
14. Sigmund Freud, *Jokes and Their Relation to the Unconscious* (Pelican Freud Library, 6; Harmondsworth, UK: Penguin Books, 1975[1901]).
15. Robert J. Stephens, "Hinduism in Independent India: Fandamentalism and Secularism," in Robin Rinehart, *Contemporary Hinduism: Ritual, Culture, and Practice* (Santa Barbara, CA: ABC-CLIO, 2004), 309–40.
16. SMVD University is a Hindu university named after Goddess Vaishno Devi, located in Jammu, India.
17. The author has been judging these events on many occasions as a faculty member of this university.
18. Wayne Fife, *Doing Fieldwork: Ethnographic Methods for Research in Developing Countries and Beyond* (New York: Palgrave Macmillan, 2005).
19. A connotation used for the present generation.
20. Alan Partington, *The Linguistics of Laughter: A Corpus-Assisted Study of Laughter-Talk* (New York: Routledge, 2006), 40.

21. Dominic Strinati, *An Introduction to Theories of Popular Culture* (London: Routledge, 1995), 83.

22. Bergson, *Laughter*, 36.

23. Partington, *The Linguistics of Laughter*, 40.

24. Strinati, *An Introduction to Therories of Popular Culture*, 238.

CHAPTER FIFTEEN

The Presence of the Cross in Popular Culture: A Womanist Perspective

Andriette Jordan-Fields

"At the Cross, At the Cross where I first saw the light and the burden of my heart rolled away," is a hymn sung fervently in many African American Baptist churches Sunday after Sunday. The lyrics of "At the Cross," specifically the refrain, situate this hymn with non-sequitur status, leaving one with the question of what light does one see when gazing upon the cross. The presence of the cross in the songs and lives of African Americans might suggest that despite the circumstances of the time, this soteriological symbol appears to stand the test of time and remain a ubiquitous symbol, not vitiating with time.

I will argue two points. First, I will show that the lyrics of this particular hymn are a non-sequitur phenomena, attempting to pronounce the salvific power and presence of the cross, sung by my grandmother. Second, I will entertain the notion of the commodification of the cross, questioning whether there is any salvific power, utilizing my grandmother, Delores Williams, James Cone, and popular culture artists to establish my point. I will venture to take a "deconstructive" approach that implies an analysis, which questions presuppositions, ideological underpinnings, hierarchical values, and frames of reference in this short segment. My goal is to address this soteriological quandary the cross creates. I propose to discuss the eerie adulation of the cross, irrespective of what it signifies and its apparent commodification and secularization in this present age. There are several possible connotations for the cross; I will propose four potential meanings of the cross in popular culture: first, the symbol of the cross could represent spirituality; second, the cross could represent religion/religiosity; third, the cross can represent a new fashion trend as jewelry; and finally, the cross can represent a theological interpretation about God. Navigating this quandary through the idyllic lyrics of the hymn, "At the Cross," should lead to an understanding of the need for a closer rereading and rethinking of the meaning and the relevance of the cross in popular culture.

I will make four paradigmatic moves, exploring the incongruent uses and understandings of the cross, each developing a truth(s) in their own manner. Starting with my grandmother's experience in the black church, connecting the spirituality located in the cross, found in the hymns she sang, specifically focusing on the hymn, "At the Cross." The next move is to investigate the religiosity of the cross, employing the thoughts of Delores Williams, which assist with understanding this notion of the cross's religious representation. In the final two shifts, one is located within the hip hop popular culture, where the cross is displayed as fashion/jewelry; questions are introduced in an effort to comprehend the increase influx of the cross. Finally, a glance toward a theological perspective of the cross, offered by James Cone's ideas about the cross, found in his latest book, *The Cross and the Lynching Tree* might prove insightful. These four moves or meaning of the cross are an effort to situate the cross and the power it holds or no longer holds in popular culture. This thought-provoking exercise will at least open the readers' consciousness to the proliferation of the cross, be it on clothing, jewelry, or persons' bodies (i.e., tattoos), sermons, and so on.

> At the cross, at the cross where I first saw the light,
> And the burden of my heart rolled away,
> It was there by faith I received my sight,
> And now I am happy all the day!

As a child, I can recall hearing my grandmother sing this song with pride and enthusiasm despite the fact that she was a young woman growing up during the time of Jim and Jane Crow, Civil Rights Movement, and participating in boycotts. She was keenly aware of the Ku Klux Klan (KKK) and their practices of violence and hatred. In spite of the lynching and intimidation tactics of burning crosses on lawns, hillsides, and in woody clearings—as an announcement that trouble or hard times were coming—she continued to sing. My grandmother, Hazel T. Jordan, was born in Augusta, Georgia in 1923 during perilous times—a beautiful black young lady whose mother died when Hazel was only three years old.

My grandmother was truly a survivor, born in the same year the Ku Klux Klan made a surprise attack on black residential area Rosewood, Florida,

Garret Morgan, an African American man, invented and patented the traffic light; President Harding died, and Vice President Calvin Coolidge was sworn into office; the stock market crashed; and the Great Depression began. These are just a few events that occurred in the early years of her life. As my grandmother matured and started her family in 1939, one of the world events occurring was the Nazi Holocaust, World War II was in full swing, and racism was strong as ever in Southern states. The great migration(s)[1] were in progress at the time, which was an additional misfortune, during that particular stage of her life.

Notwithstanding those events of the time, my grandmother and the senior choir members at Liberty Baptist Church, a small church in Georgia, would faithfully sing the hymn, "At the Cross"—which in retrospect was often sung like a battle cry of diligent soldiers, believing that some euphoric light would be seen and assist in the burdens of the singers' hearts receding. These blind soldiers will regain their sight by faith; and despite the circumstances and situations they will be happy all the days of their life. The plight of a young African American woman raised in the South can appear bleak and often hopeless, yet the tenacity and survival instincts prevail; often the source of refuge was found in the African American church in song. My grandmother was the treasurer for the missionary (benevolent) offering, she never missed a Sunday and appeared to find her strength in the rituals of the church. The songs appeared to provide a sense of security or connection with the sacred (God), which created an existential steadfastness that allowed her to tackle any task or situation as if it was easy. I would dare to say that my grandmother gained her strength by taking on the persona of Christ when she sang those songs. This symbol stood as a spiritual well despite the evil and mortification it represented during her era.

Alas! And did my Saviors bleed
And did my Sov'reign die?
Would He devote that sacred head
For such a worm as I?

Thy body slain, sweet Jesus, Thine –
And bathed in its own blood –
While the firm mark of wrath divine,
His soul in anguish stood.[2]

The first and second verses of the this hymn speaks to the pain and suffering endured, declaring how the Savior took on the bloody task of anguish and despair for the lowly souls of the oppressed, specifically these oppressed church women. These women, who sang especially on the first Sunday (communion Sunday), were seeking a cathartic fix with the melody of "At the Cross." My grandmother knew this song and many others from memory like the back of her hand, and she appeared to find some type of salvific power in singing them. Ironically, in 2013, as my grandmother prepared for her 90th birthday, living with Alzheimer's disease and the loss of pertinent segments of her life, the lyrics of the old Baptist hymns resided within her. If I begin to sing one of those hymns such as "At the Cross," somewhere in the deep crevasses of her mind she can recall and began to sing with me. "At the Cross, at the Cross, where I first saw the light and the burden of my hearts rolled away . . ."—for my grandmother, Hazel T. Jordan, there appears to be a peculiar salvific power in the hymn that speaks of the cross, a deep-seeded understanding that transcends problems with memory, thinking, and behavior issues. This appearance of blind allegiance toward a symbolic artifact known as the cross no longer emerges as blind, as a result of uncovering the strong spiritual significance, despite the historical atrocious it represents.

The Spirituality Found in the Cross

Emilie Townes describes the spirituality of African American women's prophetic presence.[3] She says; "Womanist spirituality is not grounded in the notion that spirituality is a force, a practice separate from who we are moment by moment. It is the deep kneading of humanity and divinity into one breath, one hope, and one vision. Womanist spirituality is not only a way of living, it is a style of witness that seeks to cross the yawning chasm of hatreds, prejudices and oppressions into a deeper and richer love of God as we experience Jesus in our lives."[4] Townes tapped into this strong resilient power found in the African American females, that *jena se qua*, that makes them press on when there appears to be no reason to fight or move forward. Townes states, "out of our particularity as African American women, we strive for dialogue and engagement with others in their particularity. This relationship is premised upon mutual respect, accountability, and responsibility as keys to dismantling the oppressive systems that divide us."[5] I would assert that my grandmother's spirituality was grounded in her being, an ontological fortitude that made her that prophetic presence in the church, affording her the designation as one of the "Mothers of the church."[6] This strength enabled her to negotiate the patriarchy inside and outside the church, with confidence; she navigated the church politics for years, powerfully and unapologetically.

Was it for crimes that I had done
He groaned upon the tree?
Amazing pity! Grace unknown
And love beyond degree!

Well might the sun in darkness hide
And shut his glories in,
When Christ, the mighty Maker died,
For man the creature's sin.

The Religiosity of the Cross

In the third and fourth verses of "At the Cross," we find the question being asked, why was such a deed being done on the cross; and why did someone who was not guilty pay that price? Was the offence taken and paid on another's behalf? In order to make sense of the cross in popular culture we must first understand what progenitors have to say about the cross. James Cone and Delores Williams argue that the oppressed community is the place where we are called "to hammer out the meaning of Jesus's presence for Christian behavior." Williams posits we must do so by a process of revaluing from invisibility, the life-world of African American women.[7] Cone states, "African Americans embraced the story of Jesus, the crucified Christ, whose death they claimed paradoxically gave them life, just as God resurrected him in the life of the earliest Christian community. While the lynching tree symbolized white power and 'black death,' the cross symbolized divine power and 'black life'—God overcoming the power of sin and death."[8]

Cone prudently recognizes the paradox of the cross, especially in the African American community; yet he still finds some strength and power in the cross. Cone quotes Kierkegaard when describing the "dread and powerlessness faced by the threat of death on the modern day cross the lynching tree." He states that it creates a pit of despair and nothingness, what Kierkegaard calls "sickness unto death," a "sickness in the self"—a loss of hope that life could have meaning in a world full of trouble.

Cone calls on Job, a biblical character, who also faced a difficult life contradiction. Cone claims that African Americans refused to go down into the "loathsome void," regardless of the troubles they encountered, they kept on believing and hoping that a "change is gonna come."[9] This community, Cone declares, faced "hard living" and refused to give in to adversity. In fact, he asked, "how could you be black in America during the lynching era and not know about the existential agony that trouble created for black people?"[10] Cone recalls that hope is carved out in the mist of "trouble" and "sorrow," expressed in our singing, and evident in the source of hope Jesus, who is considered a friend, who knows all about our troubles. It is this Jesus, whose divine presence is the most important message about black existence, according to Cone.[11] He recalls the salvific songs, sermons, prayers, and testimonies about the cross were the most spoken theme, focusing on how Jesus achieved salvation for the least unto death. The cross was the foundation on which their faith was built.[12]

Cone suggests, "the more black people struggle against white supremacy, the more they found in the cross the spiritual power to resist the violence they so often suffered." He emphatically stresses that other songs, such as "Jesus Keep Me near the Cross," "Must Jesus Bear the Cross Alone?" and "At the Cross," sung by white Protestants just do not have the same feel or sound because the life experiences are different.[13] There is just something about the ability to express oneself when you live what you talk and sing about, according to Cone. Finally, Cone proclaims that the coup d'état about black life and for black people is not the death on a lynching tree but the redemption in the cross—a miraculously transformed life found in the God of the gallows. I agree with Delores Williams's statement that the cross epitomizes the image of defilement. Williams reminds us that this execution on the cross was accompanied with mockery, dehumanization, and destruction; therefore, the cross becomes an image of defilement:

> Cultures and peoples (Native Americans, African, Jews) have been defiled and destroyed by the onslaught of Western, Christian, patriarchal imperialism in some of the ugliest forms. The oceans are defiled by oil spills, and industrial waste destroys marine life, logging and mining processes are destroying rainforest. The cross is a reminder of how humans have tried throughout history to destroy visions of righting relationships that involve transformation of tradition and transformation of social relations and arrangements sanctioned by status quo.[14]

Ironically, Cone proposes that the pain, agony, and fear are all wrapped in joy, peace, and freedom, for the female body that has been tested and tried through experiences. Williams reminds us that as Christians and as black women, particularly, we cannot forget the cross but neither can we glorify it.[15]

The Theological Interpretation of the Cross

W. E. B. Du Bois called black faith "a pythian madness" and "a demoniac possession"—"sprung from the African forest," "mad with supernatural joy."[16] He also stated one has to be a little mad, kind of crazy, to find salvation in the cross, victory in defeat, and life in death. Cone acknowledges Du Bois sentiment, yet he maintains that yes, there might be some madness. In fact madness and crazy might be prerequisites "to find salvation in the cross, victory in defeat, and life in death."[17] The debate about the significance and power of the cross continues in both secular and theological settings.

Delores Williams poignantly states in *Sisters in the Wilderness*, "there is no redemptive suffering; the encounter with suffering is always encountered with sin, not holiness, or God's will."[18] Interestingly enough, for at least a paragraph and a half (equivalent to less than a minute), Cone agrees with Williams's rejection of theories of atonement and uncritical proclamation of the cross in many black churches. Conversely, Williams addresses the atonement by postulating, "if Jesus were a surrogate, then his gospel encourages black women to accept their surrogacy roles as well—suffering for others as Jesus did on the cross. But if the salvation that Jesus brought could be separated from surrogacy, then black women were free to reject it too."[19] Williams offers the point of view that whether Jesus was a coerced surrogate or a voluntary surrogate, either constructs suffering as a "divine experience, and makes Christianity a holy sedative for a segment of society who has no choice in suffering."[20] Instead she offers an alternative view. Williams stresses that Jesus can be best understood as promoting a "'ministerial vision' that placed people in right relationship to one another and to God."[21]

Ironically, Cone agrees with Williams's rejection; he too stated, on the one hand, that "he finds nothing redemptive about suffering in itself"; moreover, "the gospel of Jesus is not a rational concept to be explained in a theory of salvation, but a story of God's presence in Jesus's solidarity with the oppressed, which led to his death on the cross. On the other hand, what Cone finds redemptive is the faith that God snatches victory out of defeat, life out of death, and hope out of despair."[22] Cone's statement sounds uncannily like a black male Baptist whooping preacher, the recapitulation of identical messages that my grandmother heard and reveled. Unfortunately, like many others, she failed to question the contradictory messages that the cross created. This theological conundrum left countless parishioners with the only option being a salvific power in the cross.

After the minute-or-less agreement with Williams, Cone unexpectedly sides with the more conservative liberal womanist theologians Shawn Copeland, JoAnne Terrell, and Jacquelyn Grant, who all view the cross as central to the Christian faith.[23] It appears that Cone shifts again, when he acknowledges Nietzsche, by suggesting that Nietzsche was right when he said that Christianity is a religion of slaves. Cone validates this statement by offering, "God became a slave in Jesus and thereby liberated slaves from being determined by their social condition."[24] Cone closes with two poignant questions, which his book is based on: Can the cross redeem the lynching tree? Can the lynching tree liberate the cross and make it real in American history? These are two questions that must be asked of the cross in the 21st century. Cone appears to straddle the fence, standing on the side of the cross not being redemptive at one point and the cross being redemptive at other times. Cone identifies the lynching tree as freeing the cross from the false pieties of well-meaning Christians.[25] There might be some freeing in the acknowledgment of the tragedies of the cross, it might even be cathartic, but I cannot agree with Brother Cone when he concludes his book in a sermonic fashion by proclaiming; "the lynching tree is a metaphor for white America's crucifixion of black people, and just as Jesus had no choice in his journey to Calvary, so black people had no choice. Given God took the evil, the cross and lynching tree and transformed them both into the triumphant beauty of divine." Cone leaves the salvific power, I believe, in the hands of white America, hope in the hand of the oppressor. His last sentence is, "If America has the courage to confront the great sin and ongoing legacy of white supremacy with the repentance and reparation there is hope 'beyond tragedy.'" If that is the case, Cone should realize that there is no hope. I think our foremothers and fathers are still waiting for their 40 mules and an acre, the 400 black men in the Tuskegee experiment of 1932[26] did not survive their tragedy without reparations. Finally, there are those strange fruits that Billie Holiday sang about, which were never allowed to blossom. So before there is a rush to the hope in the cross, there is a need for a critical reassessment of the cross and its significance for this generation.

The Fashioning of the Cross—by Hip Hop Culture

In the 21st century, where fashion trends are determine by magazines, reality television, red carpet events, and social media, the ubiquity of the cross is prevalent. There is an interesting phenomenon taking place in modern society: an appropriation of the cross, without critically thinking through the problems that this symbol creates. Christian theologians find that they are attached to the cross, hanging onto the portions, which promise salvation while ignoring the violence it portrays, also failing to problematize the glorification of the cross. This uncritical embracing of the cross can also result in an unconscious embracing of victimhood. In popular culture there is an ad that states, "Do you want to look like a real baller?

Then get your self an icy chain! Get the look and feel of real diamond chain and look like a real time baller . . . get iced out today at hiphopbling. com." The hip hop and religion concept alone is an entirely different conversation in and of itself and beyond the scope of this work. However, I would like to briefly focus on the commodification of the cross. Before I go any further, a brief engagement of one genre of this generation's music, called RAP, might be helpful. "RAP" refers to "rhythmic-applied poetry" or "rhythmic-associated poetry," simply the use of word to describe quick and slangy speech, a billion-dollar industry, which is pervasive internationally. Modern hip hop stems from the use of anticolonialism and "Ganja" references, which Rastafarians believe bring them closer God.[27] Religion and spirituality is found in all forms of music of many successful artists: Kanye West; Muslim rapper Snoop Dog, Mos Def, and Ice Cube; the Beastie Boys are the successful Jewish group; Eminem; and Toby Mac, to name a few. Several of these artists at some point in their careers have been photographed wearing a cross. Among this eclectic group of artist are pagans, Sikhs, Baha'i faiths, along with Muslims and Christians, all who expressed their beliefs and spirituality in various ways. Often this generation is considered lost; yet when you speak to them individually they profess strong spiritual grounding, which they express in various manners.

Hip hop originated in the Bronx in the 1970s around a culture of protest and freedom of expression, in the wake of oppression. The present-day hip hop is being questioned as to whether or not that original spirit is embodied in protest or has it integrated into a marketable moneymaking industry.[28]

Analysis of the Fashion Statement Made by the Wearing of the Cross

I would like to suggest that this moneymaking industry is cognizant of the fact that whatever is worn on the music videos, award shows and concerts, and so on, becomes the next fashion trend, making a statement for the duration of that particular rage. After any major event that has a red-carpet occasion, photos are posted on social media, appear in magazines, and on television, suggesting who and what is or is not fashionable. Several of these artists appear with the cross tatted on their bodies; embroidered/painted on clothing; or wearing necklaces, bracelets, earrings, and rings—as an expression of what? This idea makes me question the meaning behind the blinging of crosses worn by many artists of several genre, be it music, movies, or television. After tersely researching the hip hop industry, I can only stand on the fact that the commodification of the cross has created an attention-grabbing fashion trend. I have located several websites where you can purchase what they call a "blinged-up cross" with faux and actual diamonds. The accessibility of such jewelry speaks to my point of the commodification of the cross; intriguingly, the cross appears to have lost its old meaning or has it gained new meaning, which proves to be clear evidence. My research revealed that a few of the rappers are ordained and, at the very least, some clearly consider themselves spiritual versus religious. I cannot unequivocally state where all performers stand in their spiritual life or what they believe about the crosses they wear. For those who wear a cross in some form or another, we can surmise that there is some type of power it bears for the wearer, but without personal interviews or some autobiographical book about the wearing of religious jewelry, it would not be good scholarship to make such a pervasive leap. Until we conduct such research, pertinent questions must be asked of the artist: Is salvific power found in the cross, or is it simply a piece of wearable art?

Regardless of age or generational gaps, we must remember that the cross embodies a history of colonialism, work reaching as far back as the Roman Imperialism. Notwithstanding the fact that the cross represents for some the crucified God, it could also represent theories of atonement and for others a critique of power and liberation. The cross has existential significance, whether it is redemptive or provides people with the psychological material needed to negotiate their pain. We must consider that the one of the functions of the cross is not always to point in the direction of a saving God, but possibly in a God that can be called into question; remember even Jesus questioned God while hanging on the cross.

Conclusion

In summary, it can be inferred that the womanist idea is an important matrix for interdisciplinary dialogue and multidisciplinary investigation. It is a way of seeing, a medium for a holistic approach that centers African American women in the consideration of the cross and its relevance in popular culture. Williams warns us to keep in mind that African American women "should never be encouraged to believe that they can be united with God through suffering, like that suffering on the cross. There are quite enough black women bearing the cross by rearing children alone, struggling on welfare, suffering through poverty, experiencing inadequate health care, domestic violence and various forms of sexism and racism."[29]

Reflecting on the paradigmatic moves made previously. First, with my grandmother's experiences of spirituality, located at the cross, and centered in the black church. Second, the religiosity of the cross, which provides an understanding of this notion of the religious representation of the cross rooted in defilement, dehumanization, and pain. Third, the hip hop/modern popular culture displaying the cross as fashion/jewelry leaves us with the questions of the cross's existential significance. And fourth, a theological perspective of the cross provides for some atonement with a salvific resolved. In appears in every move there was a sense of strength and power through hymns, fashion, religion, and a theological epistemology that enabled different understanding of the cross without the critical reassessment of the its meaning in the 21st-century sociopolitical conundrum of everyday life.

Emilie Townes states in her article "To Be Called Beloved," "the task of womanist ontology is to illuminate question and begin the eradication of radical oppression and devaluation of the self and the community in the context of structural evil."[30] I agree wholeheartedly with Townes and would like to suggest that if we rush too quickly back to the cross or perceived space of safety before looking circumspectly at the lay of the land, societal norms, and cultural ideologies, we must continue to question the power and knowledge that the cross holds, questioning whether that keeps some at the center and others on the peripheral gazing in but years later still searching for salvation. Consequently, if for more than 200 years the cross has failed to save all from carnage, maybe, just maybe it is time to put it down and imagine anew, because the once-longed-for salvific power has not and is not working. We are failing to see the light and there are no burdens rolling away.

An examination of a meta-narrative of the cross can be the next exciting endeavor to consider additional paradigms, moving beyond the parameters of this work. This ephemeral attempt to comprehend the soteriological symbolism and power of the cross has proven to be fundamentally larger task than anticipated.

Notes

1. Some historians differentiate between the first Great Migration (1910–1930), numbering about 1.6 million migrants who left mostly rural areas to migrate to northern and midwestern industrial cities, and, after a lull during the Great Depression, a Second Great Migration (1940–1970), in which 5 million or more people moved, including many to California and other western cities.

2. Isaac Watts, refrain, Ralph E. Hudson, "At the Cross" (1707).

3. Marcia Y. Riggs, ed., *Can I Get A Witness? Prophetic Religious Voices of African American Women: An Anthology* (Maryknoll, NY: Orbis Books, 1997), 189–96. The term prophetic presence is derived from Walter Brueggemann's discussion of the prophetic task as that of maintaining " a destablizing presence." It refers to the moral agency of African American women who engage in a process of mediating

the tensions between what is and what should be as they discern ceative reponses to lived reality.

4. Emile Townes, *In a Blaze of Glory: Womanist Spirtuality as Social Witness* (Nashville, TN: Abington Press, 1995).

5. Ibid., 11.

6. The term "Mother of the Church" in the African American church referred to older women that fervently prayed and were often sought out for their wisdom, which was bestowed on the younger generations.

7. Delores Williams, *Sisters in the Wilderness* (Maryknoll, NY: Orbis Books, 1994), 174–75.

8. James H. Cone, *The Cross and the Lynching Tree* (Maryknoll, NY: Orbis Books, 2011).

9. Ibid., 20.

10. Ibid.

11. Ibid., 21.

12. Ibid.

13. Ibid., 23.

14. Williams, 166–67.

15. Ibid.

16. W. E. B. Du Bois, *The Souls of Black Folk* (New York: Dover, 1994), 105.

17. Ibid.

18. Williams, *Sisters in the Wilderness*.

19. Cone, *The Cross and the Lynching Tree*, 150.

20. Williams, *Sisters in the Wilderness*, 174.

21. Ibid., 174–75.

22. Cone, *The Cross and the Lynching Tree*, 150.

23. Ibid., 151–52.

24. Ibid., 160.

25. Ibid., 161.

26. Although in 1973 the NAACP filed a class-action lawsuit, many of the men infected had died; they also carried this plague to their wives and children, $9 million was divided among the remaining families, along with free health care for the men still living and their wives, widows, and children. President Clinton in 1997 formally apologized for the unethical study, stating what the government had done was deeply, profoundly, and morally wrong. "And I am sorry," although it might be a panacea, it does not truly cure all or bring back those who died and were senselessly infected all in the name of science.

27. "Hip Hop Culture," http://rap.wikia.com/wiki/Hip_hop_culture#cite_note-11.

28. Ibid.

29. Williams, *Sisters in the Wilderness*, 169.

30. Katie G. Cannon, Emilie M. Townes, and Angela D. Sims, eds., *Womanist Theological Ethics: A Reader* (Louisville, KY: Westminster John Knox Press, 2011).

CHAPTER SIXTEEN

African Language, Drum, and Dance: Powerful Symbols of God's Saving Mystery

Guido Oliana

Premises

I have eagerly welcomed the possibility to contribute to the present publication, which looks at how God is represented in "popular culture," interpreted widely across television, film, music, visual and performance media, and sports. I need, however, to make two basic remarks in order to introduce my particular perspective.

First, my concern has a peculiar viewpoint. It focuses on "African culture," whereby one can hardly distinguish between "culture" and "popular culture" as such. Of course, there are many definitions of "popular culture" because the term is equivocal. I consider "popular culture" according to the simplest definition: "Popular culture is the culture which originates from 'the people' . . . , an 'authentic' culture of 'the people.'"[1] What in Africa deals with television, film, music, visual and performance media, and sports cannot be properly defined "popular culture" but a culture of elite, which is so much influenced by the phenomenon of globalization, while "popular culture" is what could be simply called "African culture." I will use the expression "African culture" in this general perspective.

Second, the term "representation" needs clarification. In general terms, "representation" is defined by the *Free Dictionary* as "the act of representing or the state of being represented; something that represents; an image or likeness of something."[2] In theological terms, "representation" can refer to the redeeming action of Jesus Christ who became man in order to identify himself with the human race and represent it, so that by dying on our behalf he could vicariously atone for our sins.[3] In a more specific manner, "representation" can assume the liturgical meaning of "making present and operative" (symbolically or sacramentally), in reference in particular to the saving power of the sacrifice of Christ of the cross through the Eucharistic celebration.[4] I will use this term in a liturgical perspective.

In the present essay I would like to express impressions and reflections that I have gathered in my 25 years of missionary service in Uganda, Kenya, and now South Sudan. During these years I have been touched in particular by three vital expressions of African culture: (1) the communicating power of African languages, (2) the rhythmic musicality of African drums, and (3) the corporative engagement of African dances.

As a general premise, I like to state a fundamental theological principle: The transcendent God, who is the creator of all that exists, becomes mysteriously present or "paradoxically immanent"[5] in human history through his own creation. Taking into account the transcendent nature of God, by "paradoxical immanence" I refer to the fact that no material or personal symbol can capture, control, or manipulate the unfathomable power of God through forms that would then become idolatric or superstitious. Hence all these forms must be subjected to a serious critical assessment.

Applying this general principle to our three topics, we can say that African languages (not only Hebrew, Greek, or Latin), drumming (not only the sound of organ or piano), and dancing (not only composed postures) can become poignant expressions of this "paradoxical immanence" of God's mystery in the life of African people.

No cultural system is foreign to the Holy Spirit. Nor is there any reason to believe that the Spirit speaks more efficaciously in Judaic, Greco-Roman, or Teutonic cultural terms than in African, Indian, Chinese, or any other people's terms. The cultural patterns of the people being evangelized are all under the same universal redeemer and lord of history; hence, they are all inundated by the same recreating and superabounding grace of God; *all cultures are, therefore, presumed to be compatible with Christianity.* This compatibility needs not to be proven beforehand, because the local ways of being human enjoy the privilege of *melior conditio possidentis* (the better condition of the owner).[6]

This calls for a more daring appreciation of the symbolic import of African language, drumming, and dancing in the process of evangelizing African culture.

The African Language

I had the joy to learn and speak Luganda, the language of the Baganda, the population living in Southern Uganda in the regions surrounding the capital, Kampala, where I lived for 12 years. I enjoyed the powerful feeling of communicating with people through their own rich and expressive language. The experience of this African language moves me to deal with the issue of African language according to two perspectives: (a) African liturgical preaching as an inculturated way of communicating a Christian interpretation of life and (b) African ritual language as an inculturated way of participating in Christ's saving events.

African Liturgical Preaching

When I began to preach in Luganda, I immediately realized that it is not enough to know well the language as far as vocabulary, grammar, and syntax are concerned. One needs to perceive and assimilate also the way people view and judge the world around them. Homilies can be literarily correct but may still carry a foreign way of thinking and judging.

I give an example of foreign preaching. This experience took place in Karamoja (northeastern part of Uganda) among pastoralist people. On the occasion of an important celebration, I was shocked by the awkward situation created by a homily of an elderly colleague of mine. This person had spent almost 50 years among the Karimojong. He was an expert in the language that he was teaching to the incoming missionaries. He was very friendly with the people. In his preaching he could raise his voice enthusiastically about what he felt important. However, people did not seem concerned or existentially engaged in his talk. They seemed rather absentminded. The preacher was talking very passionately about some religious devotions, but people could not have cared less. On that occasion, I understood that in order to create an "impression" or to have an impact on people as Jesus did (cf. Mark 1:22), one needs to touch people's life and show practically how the Gospel is addressing their concrete existential problems.

If the idea of God that a missionary tries to convey does not reflect people's worldview, it sounds foreign, ideological, and therefore dangerous, because it may create a dichotomy between what they feel existentially according to their traditional way and the new contents that the missionary tries to convey. This kind of dichotomy created by the presentation of a foreign worldview can also be fostered by a native minister, who just repeats traditional Church doctrines without attempting to actualize and reinterpret them in the light of people's life experiences.

In this regard, I would like to share an interesting episode. It happened during my first years of priestly ministry in Uganda. A lady came to me for the sacrament of penance. She started saying that Satan had tempted her. Sympathetically, I asked her whether she had any child sick and had gone to the local doctor in search of a cure. Feeling understood in her problem, presumably, she started telling her story again, but in a positive way. At a certain moment of our conversation, I asked, "Do you still believe in those things?" (*Okyakkiriza mu bintu ebyo?*). Immediately, this lady started retelling me the story in a negative way as she had started, speaking about her having fallen into Satan's temptation. This experience shocked me, because I could perceive in her a profound dichotomy. This makes me question our way of evangelizing, at times insensitive to, or unaware of, African Traditional Religions and their enduring existential symbolic impact in the concrete life of African people.[7]

The exercise of preaching has made me sensitive to the way we correlate the "existential questions" of African people to the "theological answers" implied in the Word of God.[8]

In this regard, once I had a moving experience. It took place among the Acholi population (northern part of Uganda), who were harassed and terrorized by the rebels of the so-called Lord Resistance Army (LRA). I was asked to preach during a Eucharistic celebration. I was worried about what to say and how to become relevant to the people's painful situation. The church was crowded. I thought to bring the experience of Christ, who on the cross shouted, "My God, my God, why have you abandoned me?" (Mark 15:34). I told the people, "Let us identify ourselves with Christ on the cross. Let us shout to God the Father the same words of Jesus. Certainly he will hear us through the words of his Son." I asked the congregation to repeat with me Jesus's words three times raising their voice each time. It was a tremendous experience! People were truly involved and personally touched. I felt that Christ was shouting through us to the Father and God could listen to our cry. I had a clear impression that that liturgical celebration was very meaningful to the people and gave them great hope. This event convinced me that the language we use in preaching has to bridge between the existential situation of people and the transforming truth of the Word of God, which continually finds its way to become flesh among the people also through our preaching. As Jesus said, "The truth will make you free" (John 8:32).

The "Odd Language" of Rituals

Another important question pertains to ritual language. I feel always impressed when Africans sing traditional songs accompanied by drums. The engaging power of their linguistic style, tunes, and rhythms, though apparently repetitive, is amazing. When people sing at particular events (marriage or funeral), they show the engaging power of the responsorial interaction between the solo and the assembly. One singer passionately narrates the story, and all present promptly answer with a simple and short refrain. I admire the vivid participation of people in this form of singing.

Yet, when we celebrate the Eucharist, I often perceive in the congregation passivity and lack of vitality and personal engagement. The Eucharistic prayer, objectively speaking, is the highest and most significant moment of the celebration. We can see that the text in question in general is conceptually well translated in the local language, but the event, which the text intends to "represent," is not effectively represented or communicated. I feel that here we have a linguistic problem. Our official Catholic Eucharistic Prayers are optimal doctrinal texts, yet the language used is not able to communicate the richness of the saving event that the texts intend to proclaim.

One perceives a certain distance of the people, who become more spectators of something that they are told about than participants in, or makers of, the memorial by feeling and being essential part of it, as they are when they sing their traditional songs. I think that we have not yet found a totally adequate African-Christian ritual style that would awake the religious receptive faculties of people.[9] Faith needs a way of being enacted that is correlative to the symbolic way of perceiving and expressing authentic cultural values. Hence the ritual dimension of a faith that generates, enhances, and expresses itself has to be fully incarnational and corporeal, culturally inherent to the way of feeling and expressing of people, of course enlightened, transformed, and empowered by the Gospel of Christ.

We need to verify whether the ritual language adopted by the liturgy in Africa is a mere translation of a Western Christian worldview in an African "ordinary language," which exerts poor impact in people's life, or whether it is a creative adoption of an African "odd" or "extraordinary language" or "metaphorical language," which leads the participants into a vivid experience of the transcendent that becomes transformative.[10] This is possible thanks to the intrinsic power of a ritual language that is: (a) *descriptive* (interprets and communicates to the participants the meaning of the ritual action while they perform it); (b) *heuristic* (arouses existential interests and evokes the discovery of transforming meanings in the process of the celebration); (c) *prescriptive* (motivates a praxis coherent with the meanings discovered and experienced); (d) *promissory* (guarantees the stability of the community by celebrating its identity); and (e) *performative* (motivates a concrete existential commitment to live what is celebrated).[11] In this way, the traditional correlation between *lex orandi* (prayer), *lex credendi* (faith), and *lex vivendi* (life) is vitally guaranteed, in the sense that the experience of God in prayer motivates and enhances faith by transforming and energizing life in the community context of liturgical prayer.[12]

The liturgical texts that the Church has received from its long tradition must be adapted to the mentality of the African people. The Philippino Benedictine theologian of liturgical inculturation, Anscar J. Chupungco, discusses the issue of the threefold stage translation-adaptation-creation of liturgical texts. He states:

> The message of the original text will have to be expressed according to the thought and language patterns of the liturgical assembly. Anything less than this may lead to a misunderstanding of the message, since a message is communicated to a person normally through expression of his or her own culture. Faithful translation is the communication of the message in the linguistic expressions of the people for whom the text is prepared.[13]

Translation and adaptation are not enough. The process has to go further. New texts must be created that correspond to the particular sensitivity of the people. In the words of Chupungco, "composition of new liturgical texts, assumption and assimilation of the best elements a language can offer, development of a liturgical language that suits perfectly the culture of the people and bears faithfully the message of the liturgy: all this is called for by the liturgy of Vatican II."[14]

I have a dream: to be able, one day, to experience a Eucharistic Prayer constructed in a true African linguistic style, where, in a dynamic responsorial manner, the main celebrant passionately and imaginatively narrates the story of God's love in Jesus Christ and people intervene with vibrant acclamations, accompanied by thunderous drums and captivating dances, creating a compelling desire to live existentially what they celebrate.

The African Drum

The drum can be considered the most emblematic symbol of African culture. I have experienced the beautiful and efficacious power of African drums, especially among the Baganda. During their liturgical celebrations I have always been intrigued by the great effectiveness of drums in creating an atmosphere of sacredness, joy, sadness, meditation, or contemplation according to the different styles of drumbeat. When the full set of drums are used (corresponding to the pitch of the bass, the baritone, the alto, and soprano) and when competent people beat them, one has the feeling of a full symphonic orchestra. All the range of harmonics is perceived in a dramatic marvelous and moving way.

Symbol of Divine Power

The African drum has a strong symbolic meaning connected with all dimensions of life including religion. People have handed over from one generation to the next information and knowledge on the drum usually in connection with some myths in reference to the origin and identity of the tribe or the clan and their vital relationship with the supreme creator, the spirits, and ancestors.[15]

The Baganda have about 52 clans. Every clan has its own name and its own geographical location where the clan headquarter is. Each clan identifies itself with a particular drumbeat, which has its own unique drum rhythm. Clan rhythms vary. Drum rhythms ask the members of a particular clan to safeguard cultural values, such as working, conserving nature, giving mutual respect, keeping moral standards, saving the environment, getting married, caring of the family, and begetting children.

The drum is also used as an instrument for calling the community to participate in ritual ceremonies, healings, and dances. The drum communicates information within a society in the case of insecurity, crimes, death, accidents, loots, and so on. Drumbeats even send messages from far. In the past the drum took the place of our modern telegraphic services or mobile phones.

The drum is an important instrument in the ancestor worship of the Baganda. There is no celebration of a shrine ritual without drum accompaniment. The drum serves a medium between the visible and the invisible world in the course of invocations and prayers. In worshipping ceremonies all drum rhythms are played in order to call ancestors, deities, and spirits identified with a particular drumbeat.

Drums are also used for therapeutic purposes. People having emotional, psychological, or mental disorders enter the healing process at the beat of the drum. Spirits and ancestors are invoked to participate in the healing process. The patient often goes into a trance. This helps heal people that have psychological disorders, suffer from stress, or have problems of infertility. "For this reason, the drum is considered a mediator of these persons, trying to bring them back into life, into a daily routine, to free them of their problems and their aches and pains, and to bring them back into community life."[16]

The African theologian Laurence Magesa states that "the use of the drum as symbolic of (thunderous) divine power and its effects on the African psyche and emotions have as a whole not been superseded. In fact, in the African context, the drum reveals divine power."[17]

Memorial of the Foundational Event of Jesus Christ

Elochukwu E. Uzukwu, relying on the research of Georges Niangoran-Bouah,[18] writes that the drum is "comparable to the Bible or the Koran. It both carries the primordial word and is identified with the primordial word."[19] Magesa comments, "More than in the Bible and Koran, playing the ritual drum in Africa elicited bodily movements and gestures as well as mental states that made the cosmic unity immediately palpable to the hearts and minds of worshippers. It connects people to the earth and to the spiritual beings."[20]

In the past the missionaries in general did not understand the great importance of African drums. Being drums used in indigenous music and dances, which were considered pagan and satanic practices, the use of drums was forbidden in church services by almost all Christian denominations. "The drum was regarded as an instrument of the devil. . . . African dances and songs were condemned, as being too sexy. Institutions, like puberty and funeral rites, enstoolment of chiefs, and such-like were forbidden, as being idolatrous. This was the situation until quite recently."[21]

The African drum has a strong memorial power. According to Magesa, particularly in rural African contexts, the drum remains the best instrument for recalling the foundational story of the Christ-event—the birth, ministry, death, and resurrection of Jesus. It must also be given a prominent place in the celebration of the sacraments, especially of the Eucharist, as the central sign of the remembrance (*memoria*) of the creation and ongoing recreation of the Christian community. Hence dance, which the paying of the drum oftentimes urges, comes into play.[22]

The consideration of the African drum as the best "instrument for recalling the foundational story of the Christ-event" is quite intriguing. In sum, this statement is based on five liturgical potentials of African drums: (1) The African drum is symbolic of divine power. (2) The African drum can convey an emotional and intellectual mode of participation in the history of salvation that continues in the present liturgical "representation" of

God's saving mystery. (3) The African drum can bridge the time of preparation and expectation (African Traditional Religion) with the time of Christian fulfillment (Christian faith). (4) The African drum can unify creation (cultural values) with the new creation fulfilled in the paschal mystery (Christian values). (5) The efficacious musicality and rhythmic properties of the African drum can efficaciously serve people's conscious, active, and full participation in the cosmic memorial of salvation history in a way that other musical instruments do not have in the African context.

The African Dance

In my long stay in Africa I have been fascinated by some forms of African dances. I like to mention at least four: two Acholi dances (northern Uganda): the royal dance (*bwola*) and the *dingding* dance; the "jumping dances" of the Karimojong (northeastern Uganda); and the gentle dance of the Banyankole (southwestern Uganda).

The *bwola* dance is a circular dance composed of men putting on their heads crowns of erected white feathers and wearing leopard skins. They move forward with a beautiful and dynamic synchronic pace while beating their drums. They show a majestic sense of order and control of the environment and people. The *dingding* dance is performed by young girls colorfully dressed. Their movements try to imitate birds. They radiate a charming feeling of joy and beauty. In Karimojong "jumping dances" men make solemn high jumps. Their synchronic movements seem to show a desire to bridge heaven and earth. I admired the Banyankole dance in a liturgical adaptation being performed during a Eucharistic celebration after Holy Communion. It touched me for its gentle and graceful movements radiating an affective and intimate sense of joy and gratitude to the Lord.

Symbol of a Holistic Interpretation of Life

The African dance has an essential cultural role in the life of the African tribes. "Much more than entertainment, dances communicate emotions, celebrate rites of passage, and help strengthen the bonds between members of the tribe as a whole."[23]. According to Wanjiru Gichigi, "dance is almost without doubt the most ancient art form known to man."[24] Gichigi reports the statement of the danceologist Alphonse Tierou from Ivory Cost on the essential meaning of dancing as a "complete and self-sufficient language" that expresses the deepest human experiences with the whole range of emotions.

Because it has more power than gesture, more eloquence than word, more richness than writing, and because it expresses the most profound experiences of human beings, dance is a complete and self-sufficient language. It is the expression of life and of its permanent emotions of joy, love, sadness, and hope, and without emotion there is no African dance.[25]

Various characteristic can be attributed to the African dance. Richard Djiropo gives four basic functions.[26] First, African dance is a *cultural vector*. It expresses African uniqueness. It plays "an imperceptible role as Africa's spokesman." It has become "Africa's best ambassador," mainly "because it permits both the dialogue between peoples and the purest expression of the African being." Second, African dance represents the *source of meeting between peoples* by favoring cultural dialogue and expressing "at once the 'same' and the 'different,' the self and the other, particularities and commonalities, better than other forms." Third, African dance is *an expression of African genius*. This is so especially for its "capacity to reveal the unity of the body and the spirit, and to suggest a vision of the world that escapes the temptations of monism and dualism which characterize, respectively, Eastern and Western thought."

Finally, and in sum, African dance is defined as a *"somalogie"* (in English we could say "somalogy"), namely, a discourse (*logos*) of the body (*soma*), or, better, a discourse by the body. Dance is the liberation of the spirit, a spirit in movement. African dance is a form of language. It expresses not only emotions but also ideas. It is not only a way of feeling but also a way of thinking. It expresses the unity of being by overcoming the distance between the body and the spirit. African dance is the clearest corporeal-spiritual language that communicates people's interpretation of their life, history, culture, and society in relation to the environment and other people. The movements of the dance, however bizarre they might appear, are poignant signs or symbols of such a profound interpretation and communication of life.

Effective Memorial of the Paschal Mystery

An official document of the Catholic Church, considered as "an authoritative point of reference for every discussion on the matter," was issued by the Vatican Congregation of Divine Worship in 1975.[27] The document discusses the meaning of dance. Dance is defined as an art, "a synthesis of the measured arts (music and poetry) and the spatial arts (architecture, sculpture, painting)." It can become a form of prayer that "expresses itself with a movement which engages the whole being, soul and body."

The document recognizes that a long tradition since the time of the Old Testament has always considered dance as a meaningful symbol of spiritual life. Spiritual authors and some liturgies (Byzantine, Ethiopian, and Syriac) have accepted dance as "an expression of the fullness of their love of God." St. Thomas Aquinas describes heaven in terms of dancing angels and saints.

The document recalls the Constitution on the Sacred Liturgy of the Second Vatican Council No. 47, which seems to allow the theoretical possibility of liturgical dances by adopting cultural forms that are not contrary to the faith.[28] Two conditions for this possibility are underlined at least in non-Western cultures: (1) The dance should express "sentiments of faith and adoration in order to become a prayer," and (2) the liturgical dance should be "regulated by the competent ecclesiastical authority."

Analyzing the understanding of dance in the Western culture, the document states that religious criteria do not apply to it because "here dancing is tied with love, with diversion, with profaneness, with unbridling of the senses: such dancing, in general, is not pure." The conclusion is clear: For that reason it cannot be introduced into liturgical celebrations of any kind whatever; that it would inject into the liturgy one of the most desacralized and desacralizing elements; and so it would be equivalent to creating an atmosphere of profaneness that would easily recall to those present and to the participants in the celebration worldly places and situations.

If at all that some forms of dance are to be allowed in the Western world, it should be in "a place found outside of the liturgy, in assembly areas which are not strictly liturgical."

The main worry of the document is that dances performed in a liturgical context may degenerate in folkloristic shows that lose the sense of sacred, whereby people are not helped to enter into spiritual communion with God. Thus the liturgy may degenerate into a situation where the saving mystery of God in the Spirit through Christ is suffocated by a self-centered immanent expression of human emotions. Consequently, the liturgy would lose its meaning as participation in the saving paschal mystery of Jesus's death and resurrection.

The then-cardinal Joseph Ratzinger was in the same vein when he wrote severe, critical remarks about the possibility of liturgical dances:

> The cultic dances of the different religions have different purposes—
> incantation, imitative magic, mystical ecstasy—none of which is com-
> patible with the essential purpose of the liturgy of the "reasonable
> sacrifice." It is totally absurd to try to make the liturgy "attractive" by
> introducing dancing pantomimes (wherever possible performed by

professional dance troupes), which frequently (and rightly, from the professionals' point of view) end with applause. Wherever applause breaks out in the liturgy because of some human achievement, it is a sure sign that the essence of liturgy has totally disappeared and been replaced by a kind of religious entertainment. Such attractiveness fades quickly—it cannot compete in the market of leisure pursuits, incorporating as it increasingly does various forms of religious titillation. I myself have experienced the replacing of the penitential rite by a dance performance, which, needless to say, received a round of applause. Could there be anything farther removed from true penitence? Liturgy can only attract people when it looks, not at itself, but at God, when it allows him to enter and act. Then something truly unique happens, beyond competition, and people have a sense that more has taken place than a recreational activity. None of the Christian rites includes dancing.[29]

The African theologian Laurence Magesa is critical of this negative approach. He says that to consider dancing just a way of making liturgy "attractive" to elicit applause is not to understand properly the meaning of African dance. He acknowledges that "few African worshippers would feel themselves fairly described in the cardinal's remarks." Then Magesa argues for the deep meaning that African culture find in dancing:

> Dancing in the context of authentic African worship is not a spectacle, a display, a show, an act of entertainment; it is an integral part of worship in which all worshippers participate. There is no "applause" after dancing has run its course because it is harmonious and consistent with the whole act of worship.

According to the Congolese theologian Bénézet Bujo, "dance is more than talent and folklore,"; it has a deeper symbolic and sacramental sense as memoria.[30] He states:

> Within the framework of the idea of memoria, dance is no mere choreography in which human beings reveal their ability and talent. Rather, it is a language that intends to communicate the deeper dimension of the total reality of life. To see a kind of a folkloristic beauty in African dance is to fail to grasp the depth of the transcendental experience which is expressed by the person dancing. This is because the human being in Africa dances his own life. In fact, all the existential events are danced: birth, marriage, and death, but also the new moon, political events, and so on. The various genres of dance express various hidden religious

dimensions. For example, the dance can tell about pain and suffering, about joy and sadness, about love and thankfulness. It is always a cantatory, narrative poiesis, which makes the message from beyond the grave a present reality in solidarity with the entire fellowship.[31]

In the quoted text, Bujo describes African dance as "a language that intends to communicate the deeper dimension of the total reality of life." African dance expresses "various hidden religious dimensions." It is defined as "narrative *poiesis*, which makes the message from beyond the grave a present reality in solidarity with the entire fellowship."

Poiesis indicates an action that transforms and continues the world; it reconciles thought with matter and time; it reunites the person with the world; it brings forth a new reality.[32] In the Bible *poiesis* refers both to the creative action of God both in creation and salvation history and to the human answer in faith and obedience through concrete actions (praxis). Our human answer to God's initiative is made possible only through the action of the Spirit. Without Christ the believers can do nothing (John 15:3). 1 John 2:29 highlights the imperative of right action (orthopraxis).[33] In one word, *poiesis* is the process that "produces or leads (a thing) into being."[34]

In the liturgical context *poiesis* could be considered the efficacious action of the Triune God that continues his creative and redeeming action through Christ in the Spirit through the celebration. It could also refer to the participation in faith, hope, and love of the community, thus becoming consciously, actively, and fully engaged in the celebration.[35] Hence the liturgical *poiesis* is made possible by the *anamnesis* (memorial of God's salvific deeds in Christ through the Spirit),[36] the *epiclesis* (invocation and intervention of the Spirit making possible the representation of Christ's saving deeds), and the *methexis* (participation of the assembly that enacts the celebration).[37]

These features of the liturgical celebration could be very well applied to the potentials of African dance. Bujo says that "when one dances death, the dead person is 'danced through' or danced into life. This means that the dead person is formed anew and fetched back into the fellowship."[38] This could be said of the liturgical memorial of Christ's death. When the African dances the death of Christ, Christ is "danced through" and danced into life creating a newly felt living presence of his saving death, thus experienced as transforming resurrection for the participants.

The liturgical memorial, according to Bujo, becomes a *poiesis* resulting in praxis. "In the case of the dance of death, this means new relationship with the dead, who are once again among us."[39] The crucified Jesus through the liturgical African dance is memorialized, "danced through" into life, thus becoming present and active here and now as the risen Lord in the midst of his followers. This has practical consequences in the life of the participants. The Eucharist memorial through the African dance becomes an impacting prophetic challenge of the "dancing Christ into life" that moves the participants to actualize their own message of love of God and neighbors in the concrete situations of the worshipping community.

Drumming and dancing become one act of *poiesis* (*anamnesis-epiclesis-methexis*) in order to "dance through" the crucified Lord into the risen Lord that brings transforming effects in the participants. In this way, African drumming and dancing as *poiesis* unify the threefold function of *anamnesis-epiclesis-methexis*, that is, the perpetuation of the life of the crucified and risen Lord Jesus Christ in the life of his followers here and now. In sum, *poiesis* would promote a *mimesis*, an imitation, or, better, an existential actualization of Christ's crucified and risen love.

In my presentation of a book written by an African student of mine, I summarized the cultural-anthropological and theological meaning of African dance as follows.

> For African people, *dance* is an efficacious way of expressing this holistic participation in a significant event. Cultural anthropology, expressed also in some iconography, considers dancing as the most complete way of influencing time and space, thus crossing time and space to reach and transmit the import of foundational events of the present community. While singing expresses and embodies time and painting or sculpture space, dancing expresses and embodies the two dimensions together in a supreme vital synthesis. Hence liturgical dancing, if properly studied, pastorally prepared and theologically, spiritually and aesthetically monitored, could really become an eminent way of making meaningful sense and effective experience of the mystery of Christ in an African context, where the corporal and corporative dimensions are essential for life. These have a powerful therapeutic dimension.[40]

African liturgical dancing has to be "properly studied, pastorally prepared, and theologically, spiritually, and aesthetically monitored." The concerns of those who are afraid that African dance may degenerate in a show searching for applause rather than being a deep religious experience of prayer are real. At times superficial and shallow adaptations attract criticisms that do a bad service to the powerful meaning and potentials of African dance.

In synthesis, we could apply to the liturgical African dance what Carla De Sola says about liturgical dance in general:

> Liturgical dance has a healing and prophetic role to play in the church and for the world. It is not "icing on the cake." It epitomizes our relation to our bodies and by extension our relation to the earth. Redeeming the body and redeeming the earth are connected. In today's world, our earth is in trouble. The earth is dancing a passion. The vibrations of the earth's dance resound in every one of our cells. Liturgical dance calls us to respond to the anguish around us with a reaffirmation of the spirit. The dance and the dancer may shake us from our lethargy to a positive re-engagement to help restore the earth's harmony.[41]

Pointers for a More Daring Liturgical Inculturation

The appreciation of the deep cultural-religious meaning of the African language, drum, and dance should lead efforts to fully integrate their potential power of ritual "representation" of the saving mystery of Jesus Christ in "making present and operative" the events of his death and resurrection with an actualizing power of existential transformation. This is in the light of the axiom of Leo the Great: "What was visible [conspicuous, as corporeally perceivable] in the Redeemer now [after his Ascension] is transferred to the sacraments [liturgical celebrations]."[42]

The traditional liturgical trilogy *anamnesis-epiclesis-methexis* is somehow one-dimensional (intellectual-spiritual participation through the mediation of a text). In an African setting, it would become more corporeal (conspicuous). It would be a three-dimensional expression of poetry, music, and dance (text-music-movement or language-drum-dance). The African dance would become a vital synthesis of painting-sculpture-architecture at the service of the ritual memorial. It would respect a holistic incarnational perspective, more in line with the mystery of Christ's incarnation, thus less "gnostic," as the Western doctrinal and abstract texts and their spiritual assimilation risk to become.

This more daring process of liturgical inculturation demands some conditions that somehow meet the concerns of those who are critical of liturgical dances, like the then-cardinal Joseph Ratzinger, for fear that they degenerate into merely aesthetic shows. There is need of a deep study and appreciation of our three elements of African culture. In his recent Exhortation *Commitment of Africa* (November 19, 2011), the pope emeritus deals with the topic of inculturation underlining three basic dimensions, which could serve as methodological guidelines to creatively inspire a true process of inculturation.[43] I try to reinterpret the three pointers in the light of our topic.

First, a deep study of African language, drum, and dance would revealed their great potentials to evoke, make present and effective in the life of the liturgical participants the foundational events of Jesus Christ (life, death, and resurrection), as the fulfillment of African cultural and religious longings and expectations. There is need of a rigorous discernment of the linguistic expressions and the drumming and dancing styles that would facilitate this liturgical representation-actualization of the event of Christ in view of an incarnation of the Christian value of unconditional love. Discernment always implies clarification, distinction, purification, and selection.

Second, there is need to highlight the fact that the Holy Spirit is the true agent of inculturation. This helps to understand that inculturation is not an artificial construct. Through trial and error, in the context of living Christian communities and in communion with their pastors, who should empower courageous experimentations, the Holy Spirit will lead to the assumption of cultural forms that will be both African and Christian in the true spirit of incarnation. This would lead to a creative pluralism of liturgical forms that overcomes preconceived formats of fixed and stifling uniformity and opens up a variety of options according to the creativity of the Spirit, who both enriches the Church and deepens the Christian roots of evangelized cultures. It is matter of conjugating properly the principle of incarnation with the principle of catholicity or universality.

Third, one needs to underline that the courageous and creative imagination of various forms of liturgical language, drumming, and dancing would help detect and appreciate the deep-rooted human longings of African culture in the dynamic perspective of their true and final fulfilment in Jesus Christ. In this way, the African participants in the process of liturgical *poiesis* through selected linguistic, drumming, and dancing styles will become truly more human, truly more African, and truly more Christian.

In conclusion, we can ask the question: Which picture of God do these three cultural African expressions "represent"? The threefold answer is simple but poignant: (1) the picture of a passionate God, who is in love with his people of whatever culture they belong; (2) the picture of a concerned God, who has been looking to meet personally people through their own cultural values and expressions; (3) the picture of an affective and compassionate God, who eventually assumes a human face in Jesus of Nazareth, who mixes and dines with sinners, who is crucified with criminals, who forgives his executioners and surrenders unconditionally to God his Father, drawing humanity in one hug of love. This hugging movement of surrender can be vitally interpreted by the various African languages, existentially experienced through the polyrhythmic musicality of African drums and beautifully expressed by the variegated engaging movements of African dances.

Notes

1. John Storey, *Cultural Theory and Popular Culture: An Introduction* (London: Pearson/Prentice Hall, 2000), 10. In the first chapter ("What Is Popular Culture") the book presents six definitions of "popular culture."

2. http://www.thefreedictionary.com/representation.

3. For an elaborate discussion on the meaning of "representation" from the biblical and theological point of view, see Lothar Ullrich, "Representation," in *Handbook of Catholic Theology*, ed. Wolfang Beinert and Francis Schüssler Fiorenza (New York: Crossroad, 2000), 583–86.

4. See Francis Clark, *Eucharistic Sacrifice and the Reformation* (Devon, UK: Augustine Publishing, 1981), 264–65, where it is said that the Latin verb *repraesentare* could be understood as "to represent" in the ordinary English sense, or "to portray," "to recall something past or absent by a likeness or token"; Salvatore Marsili, "Teologia della celebrazione dell'Eucaristia," in S. Marsili et al., *Anamnesis, 3/2: La Liturgia, eucaristia: eologia e storia della celebrazione* (Casale Monferrato, IT: Marietti, 1982), 119–20, n. 6, where the meaning of *repraesentare* is understood as "rendering or making present again" in the sense of "perpetuating."

5. See Paul Tillich, *What Is Religion?* ed. James Luther Adams (New York: Harper and Row, 1969), 15: "Tillich speaks of the relation between the Unconditional and the conditioned as the 'paradoxical immanence of the transcendent'."

6. Eugene Hillman, "Missionary Approach to African Cultures," in Teresa Okure et al., *Inculturation of Christianity in Africa*, Spearhead Numbers 112–14 (Eldoret, KE: AMECEA Gaba Publications, 1990), 155 (italics in original text).

7. I reported this experience in the following article: Guido Oliana, "The Theological Challenges of Religious Pluralism: Towards a Christian Theology of Other Faiths, 'To be Religious is to be Interreligious,'" *Tangaza Journal of Theology and Mission* 1 (2010): 13–14.

8. This relationship between questions and answers is systematically discussed in the method of correlation by Paul Tillich; see Paul Tillich, *Systematic Theology* (Chicago: University of Chicago Press, 1967), vol. 2, 8.30–31.34.59–60.6.64–66; vol. 2, 13–16; G. Oliana, *Gesù, la domanda, e Cristo, la risposta: Il metodo della correlazione nella teologia cristomorfica di Paul Tillich* (Tione di Trento, IT: Antolini Editore, 2011); *Il progetto teologico di Paul Tillich: La sfida del coraggio di essere e del realismo credente* (Tione di Trento, IT: Antolini Editore, 2012).

9. There have been several attempts to inculturate the liturgy in Africa, but still a lot is to be done. For a general survey of "emergent creative liturgies in Africa," see Elochukwu E. Uzukwu, *Worship as Body Language: Introduction to*

Christian Worship: An African Orientation (Collegeville, MN: The Liturgical Press, 1997), 265–321.

10. See George S. Worgul, *From Magic to Metaphor: A Validation of the Christian Sacraments* (Mahwah, NJ: Paulist Press, 1980), 73–74. The idea of "odd language" is derived from Ian Ramsey, *Religious Language: An Empirical Placing of Theological Phrases* (New York: Macmillan, 1967); *Models and Mystery* (New York: Oxford University Press), 1964.

11. See Worgul, *From Magic to Metaphor*, 75–77, where the author reports the insights of B. R. Brinkman, "On Sacramental Man: I Language Patterning," *Heythrop Journal* 13 (1972): 383–401.

12. The additional *lex vivendi* is also called *lex agendi* or *lex faciendi*. For the classical formulation *Lex orandi, lex credendi*, see Paul de Clerck, "'Lex orandi, lex credendi': The Original Sense and Historical Avatars of an Equivocal Adage," *Studia Liturgica* 24 (1994), 178–200. For the expression *lex faciendi*, see Worgul, *From Magic to Metaphor*, 77.

13. Anscar J. Chupungco, "The Translation, Adaptation and Creation of Liturgical Texts," in *Costituzione liturgica "Sacrosanctum Concilium,"* ed. Congregazione per il Culto Divino (Rome: Edizioni Liturgiche, 1986), 236.

14. Ibid.

15. In the following discussion on African drums, with particular reference to Baganda culture, I summarize or quote from the following informative article: "The Drum of the Black Africans," http://www.face-music.ch/instrum/uganda_drumen.html.

16. Ibid.

17. Laurence Magesa, *Anatomy of Inculturation. Transforming the Church in Africa* (Nairobi: Paulines Publications Africa, 2004), 227.

18. See George Niangoran-bouah, "La Drummologie et la Vision négro-africaine du sacré," in *Médiations Africaines du Sacré*, Actes du 3e Colloque International du CERA, February 16–22, 1986 (Kinshasa, CG: Faculté de Théologie Catholique, 1987), 281–293.

19. Uzukwu, *Worship as Body Language*, 12; see Magesa, *Anatomy of Inculturation*, 227.

20. Magesa, *Anatomy of Inculturation*, 227.

21. Peter K. Sarpong, "Emphasis on Africanizing Christianity," in T. Okure et al., *Inculturation of Christianity in Africa*, 107.

22. Magesa, *Anatomy of Inculturation*, 227.

23. Gray Miller, "African Dance," http://dance.lovetoknow.com/African_Dance.

24. Wanjiru Gichigi, "African Dance—Ancient to the Future," http://www.adad.org.uk/metadot/index.pl?iid=22794. See Alphonse Tierou, *Dooplé: The Eternal Law of African Dance* (Choreography and Dance Studies) (New York: Routledge, 1992).

25. Wanjiru Gichigi, "African Dance—Ancient to the Future." http://www.adad.org.uk/metadot/index.pl?iid=22794.

26. I summarize and quote from Richard Djiropo, "African Dance: A Pathway and a Voice for Africa?," *AFIAVI* (Magazine des cultures d'Afrique, des Caraïbes,

de l'Océan Indien, du Pacifique et de la Diaspora africaine). http://afiavi.free.fr/e_magazine/spip.php?article576.

27. *Notitiae* 11 (1975), 202–205.

28. See Austin Flannery, ed., *Vatican Council II: The Conciliar and Postconciliar Documents* (Northport, NY: Costello Publishing, 1975; Bandra, Mumbai: St. Paulus, 2004), 32: "Even in the liturgy the Church does not wish to impose a rigid uniformity in matters which do not involve the faith or the good of the whole community. Rather does she respect and foster the qualities and talents of the various races and nations. Anything in these people's way of life which is not indissolubly bound up with superstition and error she studies with sympathy, and, if possible, preserves intact. She sometimes even admits such things into the liturgy itself, provided they harmonize with its true and authentic spirit."

29. Joseph Ratzinger, *The Spirit of the Liturgy* (San Francisco: Ignatius Press, 2000), 198–99.

30. See Moses Alir Otii, *The Transforming Presence of the Mystery of Christ: Odo Casel's Mystery Theology and the Possibility of an African Liturgical Theology* (Tione di Trento, IT: Antolini Editore, 2012), 184.

31. Bénézet Bujo, *Foundations of an African Ethic: Beyond the Universal Claims of Western Morality* (Nairobi: Paulines Publications Africa, 2003), 61–62 (italics are mine).

32. The terms "poiesis" is etymologically derived from the term "poieo" meaning "to make." "This word, the root of our modern 'poetry', was first a verb, an action that transforms and continues the world. Neither technical production nor creation in the romantic sense, *poietic* work reconciles thought with matter and time, and person with the world. . . . Martin Heidegger refers to it as a 'bringing-forth', using this term in its widest sense. He explained *poiesis* as the blooming of the blossom, the coming-out of a butterfly from a cocoon, the plummeting of a waterfall when the snow begins to melt." http://en.wikipedia.org/wiki/Poiesis.

33. "Poieo," in Verlyn D. Verbrugge, *New International Dictionary of New Testament Theology*, abridged ed. (Grand Rapids, MI: Zondervan, 2000), 479–80.

34. Derek H. Whitehead, "Poiesis and Art-Making: A Way of Letting-Be," http://www.contempaesthetics.
org/newvolume/pages/article.php?articleID=216.

35. The traditional abstract scholastic terminology speaks of *ex opere operato* (performance of the ritual) and *ex opere operantis* (participation of people). We could explain these expressions as follows. *Ex opere operato* refers to the Trinitarian dimension of the liturgy. The efficacy of the rite depends on the fact that God the Father, Christ and the Spirit are at work in the performance of the ritual. *Ex opere operantis* refers to the quality of people's participation: conscious, active and full in vital correlation with their faith, hope and love. The intrinsic correlation between *ex opere operato* and *ex opere operantis* makes of the liturgical celebration an efficacious and effective spiritual experience.

36. *Anamnesis* (Greek: "remembrance) can be defined "the bringing to mind [to the body as synthesis of heart, mind and will] of God's saving interventions in history especially in Christ's passion, death, resurrection, and glorification. In the

Eucharist the Lord's command 'do this in memory of me' (1 Corinthians 11:24–25; Luke 22:19) invites the assembly to appropriate the salvation he has effected once and for all." Gerard O'Collins and Edward G. Farrugia, eds., *Concise Dictionary of Theology*, rev. and expanded ed. (Mahwah, NJ: Paulist Press, 2000), 9.

37. For the interaction between *anamnesis, epiclesis,* and *methexis,* cf. Achille Maria Triacca, "Spirito Santo: Linee metodologiche per un approfondimento," in Gerardo J. Békés and Giustino Farnedi, eds., *Lex orandi Lex credendi: Miscellanea in onore di P. Cipriano Vaggagini, OSB* (Rome: Editrice Anselmiana, 1980), 142, n. 35; G. Oliana, "Liturgia: 'fonte e culmine' della teologia e della spiritualità presbiterale," *Ephemerides Liturgicae* 102 (1988): 459, n. 8.

38. Bujo, *Foundations of an African Ethic,* 62.

39. Ibid.

40. G. Oliana, "Presentation," in M. Alir Otii, *The Transforming Presence of the Mystery of Christ,* 8.

41. Carla De Sola, "Liturgical Dance," in *The New Dictionary of Sacramental Worship,* ed. P. E. Fink (Collegeville, MN: The Liturgical Press, 1990), 318.

42. Leo the Great, *Sermo* 61 [74] *De Ascensione Domini* II, 2, in *Patrologia Latina* 54:398; *Sources Chrétiennes* 7.4 bis, 277 (my translation).

43. Benedict XVI, Post-synodal Apostolic Exhortation *Africa's Commitment (Africae Munus)* (Nairobi: Paulines Publications Africa, 2011), nos. 36–38.

CHAPTER SEVENTEEN

Puppetry and the Divine/Human Relationship

Carolyn D. Roark

Call a man a puppet, and like or not, he will respond very badly; if you do not end up with a black eye, you probably will not expect him to become your friend. And historically, puppetry is about as lowbrow as entertainment can get—fairgrounds, children's birthday parties, Broadway. Yet puppets emerge from sacred beginnings. The earliest puppets were totems: jointed figures intended for ritual use. In the hands of priests and shamans, they became gods and demons.

Kenneth Gross, in his book, *Puppet*, reminds us that the Latin root of the word, *pupa*, also forms the basis for *pupae*, the chrysalis phase of insect life. It is apt in the case of the performing object: they too undergo a transformation; they serve as a visible sign of the promise of life, albeit of a different kind. Movable models designed to perform/represent living things (or the "life impulse" it sometimes pleases us to imagine in the ordinary implements of our lives), they are by themselves empty vessels. They wait to be suffused with life by a source outside of themselves. Puppet practitioners and scholars have long commented on the existential paradox of the puppet—always imbued with the potential for life, convincingly animated for brief periods, yet never truly alive—but only recently has the discipline begun to work out a sound methodology for theorizing the puppet's uncanniness. Belgian avant-garde playwright Michel de Ghelderode once confessed:

[T]here is something rather disturbing about a puppet! I realize that these little actors are only so much dead matter; that they are only made of weed, cloth and paint. I know that their piercing eyes are but glass. But what these human figures in miniature produce, despite their silence, has such magical power that all sorts of images arise unbidden from me and I cannot prevent my imagination from running riot.[1]

Jane-Marie Law identifies a parallel between puppets, puppeteers, and gods. All must exist in some way beyond physical and social boundaries, because they share an innate ability to cross them. They hold an outcast status both abject and elevated, which gives them the power to create transformation. Having this in common, there is a kind of triangular reflection between them. Human parallels god, puppet parallels human, and god indwells (or is surrogated by) puppet.

Human as Puppet/Puppet as Person

Let us speak first of the parallel between human and puppet. To call someone a puppet is an insult or a condemnation; it suggests that they and their will do not belong to themselves. Nevertheless, the puppet is an apt metaphor for our own predicament: They move because an outside force first animates them; this force is a perfect mystery to them; when the story is over, that force deserts them. We (nor they) need not perceive that force as a distinct personality or discrete being—the spark of life could be Godsbreath or electrical impulse. We are ultimately reduced to conjecture in either case. Whether you believe in a divine puppeteer or a random firing of nerves, there is an essence without which you would not be, and which exerts more control over your life than you do yourself in some very important ways. Puppetry responds to the deep-seated existential anxieties occasioned by this dilemma.

Of course, puppets have an advantage in their dual nature. They are both lifeless objects and imbued with the permanent potential for life. A puppet is a corpse in reverse: it is lifeless, but has the inexhaustible potential for momentary animation. Even though a given performance may end, there can always be another. They can sustain violence and death, and then resurrect at the start of the next show, unbowed by their previous experiences. (Lucky them.) If something falls off, someone glues it back on; if the color fades, someone repaints it. With such resilience, they make admirable surrogates for ourselves on the stage, which becomes a small laboratory of the soul and consciousness.

The puppet's status as a metaphor makes performances ripe with self-referential potential in that regard. Consider the exchange of dialogue between two characters in Trouble Puppet's adaptation of *Frankenstein*:

YRISLAVA: The marionette is the most clever of puppets. She is a vessel. And when she is filled, it breathes through her, gives movement to her limbs. It looks out through her eyes at the world. She sees you.
ELIZABETH: What is it that looks out through her eyes?
YRISLAVA: The same what looks out of your eyeholes. The same what looks out of mine.2

On stage, the sight of two puppets philosophizing about the nature of the puppet—through the manipulation of hooded operators behind them—invites the audience to reflect on the transference of consciousness—of soul or essence—occurring at that moment. In that moment, the boundaries between creator and created, manipulator and manipulated become permeable. Through their reflection invites the audience into a moment of revelation, a transformational opportunity to consider their own nature.

Puppeteer as God, God as Puppeteer

Foreman Brown, cofounder and composer for the Yale Puppeteers, felt deeply the plight of the puppeteer—caught somewhere between hubris and helplessness when confronted with his creations. He expressed it through art on multiple occasions, including his song, "Strings," which laments the difficulty of operating his marionettes from the bridge above the small, lit stage, where the puppets: "tangle in their strings until/They seem possessed of wooden will."3 He goes on to speculate on God's uneasy relationship with his own creations, which Brown also calls "puppets." Human actors are even more troublesome, and he speculates whether God "smiles or sighs" at their stubbornness, pride, and immorality.

A separate poem, "Puppeteer," takes a less wistful, more malevolent view of the situation. Where the puppeteer has "played God," in the past, he anticipates a day where the strain and discomfort of performance will push him too far and he will take angry vengeance: "Ah, how I'll send them swinging through the air!/Ah, how I'll make them leap and grovel then!"4

Together, the two pieces articulate the metaphorical similarities between the puppeteer/puppet and the divine (or universal, if you prefer) /human encounter. The poem "Puppeteer" begins soberly, bemoaning the artist's frustration at the inadequacy of his tools to express a profound vision. It ends with ironic humor, with the aggravated puppeteer threatening to become the petty tyrant of our worst existential fears. "Strings" begins with a wry, tired creator acknowledging (with gentle humor) that his creatures have a will of their own that "thwarts his efforts." But he recognizes that the world stage plays a more tragic story, with actors more troubled than his marionettes. This ending is the sadder of the two, I think. In "Puppeteer," his audience sees the empty threat for what it is—an emotional release. In "Strings," the narrator has privileged information (he knows what God knows), but is powerless. He has some microcosmic influence (on his own bridge, holding someone else's strings), but none in the wider world, where he also is just a puppet and prone to his own failings and limitations.

Though the song's tone is playful, it also reflects a deep-seated human anxiety that the universe is largely outside of our control, and we are entirely in its power. There is fear that the gods are petty and cruel, anguish that the uncaring cosmos holds no justice or mercy. Something hides in the shadows below the stage of our lives and pulls our strings; anyone might find themselves suddenly uprooted and "swinging through the air," might dread being made to "leap and grovel" by circumstances beyond their will. Ironically, according to Gross, even as the puppet submits to the manipulation of the operator, the puppeteer must surrender some of his own will and intention in order to create a successful performance. In "Strings," Brown insists on a burden of suffering when the fragile bonds between creator/created are threatened by the marionettes' obstinacy or frailty.

Still, even as we are afraid of *being* manipulated, and of the cosmic forces that pull our strings, we are equally afraid of our little wooden analogues. People commonly express a sort of dread of puppets. The problem is not the moment of performance; even though an audience will accept the thing as a performer, a character with a will of its own, ultimately they know that a human is in charge, pulling the strings or sticking a hand inside the head. The discomfort arises when the figure is encountered off-stage and inanimate. There's always the possibility that the thing *might* move, even without a puppeteer to compel it. Gross describes his encounter with an Italian puppet maker, saying "He reflects on how, even lying still, it feels mysteriously alive to him, full of a frightening kind of presence; it does not need manipulators to gather a quantity of unsettling life."[5] de Ghelderode felt it too: "Each time I find myself left as the only human being amidst a crowd of puppets hanging from their hoods, I feel a prickle of fear, a feeling of unease."[6]

He insists that the fear is common, especially among the same performers who do the manipulating:

> Former puppeteers, men of the people who have long been familiar with the world of puppets, have described to me how on some evenings they have been seized with a sudden panic on hearing a slight sound, a minute creaking, like a signal arising from this silent crowd of characters, like an order given to motionless troupes urging them to commit some underhand deed.

The thing that frightens us most about the puppet is the suspicion that it desires or possesses that which we desire for ourselves: independence, the volition to move an act without the command of an outside manipulator. We do not wish to be dominated or controlled by any external force, but if we imagine the same as true of our puppets, the conclusions are horrifying. For the puppeteer especially, the burden would be untenable. She could neither abandon nor trust her own creations . . . is that it feels like to be a god? Brown simultaneously highlights ongoing existential dilemmas that plague humanity, and the work that puppetry does to articulate and illuminate them. If a performer's creations become "perverse, petulant, and proud of will," can we blame them? Don't we?

Puppet as God/Puppeteer

Puppets prove unruly not only on the creation side of the triad, when they function as surrogates for humans. They also work as potent totems, serving as representatives for supernatural entities, and occasionally taking on certain aspects of a deity's power and influence. Many of the earliest discovered puppet (or puppet-like) objects, small and simple manipulable figures, were ritual objects. They were made to channel divine energies, to create material change through ritual action, and to inspire awe in the audiences who watched as priests or shamans moved them. As they have evolved and grown past this early use; however, they have brought those capabilities with them.

Like gods, they do not die. At least, as long as the physical object is there, it has the potential for animation. Consider the 1845 Italian newspaper columnist who compares Punch to the Dalai Lama: "like the Delhi Lama in Thibet, Punch within the limits of Naples was the great 'Undying One.'"[7]

Mr. Punch, in fact, can be considered the god of his small world. He is the character with the most agency in the narrative, and other characters always emerge the loser in a direct confrontation with him. In many ways, he determines the rules of the universe in which he lives, and then breaks them at will. He gets away with theft, mayhem, and murder; he even bests the Devil at the end. The Christian tradition in which he was nurtured will not allow for him to be other than an inveterate sinner; he does not fit the profile of even the violent, capricious Yahweh as he is not omniscient, nor invulnerable, nor all-powerful. Other characters do occasionally beat him at his own game. Punch does fit the profile for a Trickster God, however, and his lineage is long enough to suggest that he is one of the old gods who evolved into demons when their cultures converted. This old sinner has much in common with the mischief-making gods of ancient Greek, Norse, and Celtic mythology. Like Hermes/Mercury, Loki, Puck, and others like them, Punch is a trickster, a boundary crosser. Lewis Hyde describes the orientation of the trickster with relation to society:

> We constantly distinguish—right and wrong, sacred and profane, clean and dirty, male and female, young and old, living and dead—and in every case trickster will cross the line and confuse the distinction . . . trickster is the mythic embodiment of ambiguity and ambivalence, doubleness and duplicity, contradiction and paradox.[8]

The trickster god's actions might benefit or harm the mortals in his path; he makes choices for his own reasons, none of them altruistic. You can read through the various explanations of the "benefits" that audiences derive from their association with Punch; these no way affect his reasoning or motives. Gross also speaks of Punch as a figure whose power is grounded in self-awareness, "he gains much of his peculiar strength by being a puppet who knows himself to be a puppet."[9] His knowledge of who and what he is frees Punch from the human rules and restrictions that direct the behavior of the other characters.

Conversations on sacredness and puppetry emerge from time to time on the PuptCrit puppetry listserv, an electronic discussion group for puppet performers and scholars. During one exchange I witnessed, Participant Sean K. wrote that a friend of his thought of Punch as being an elemental spirit that grabs a hold of certain people through the ages and "rides" them like a Voodoo god, which makes me think of Glyn Edwards in the U.K., who says that "Punch chooses you," the puppeteer, rather than the other way around. Maybe he's the dwarf god Bes, or the ID monster, or maybe he's an escaped comic demon from a shadow puppet play, or some feisty lower Roman deity incarnated as a theophanic Maccus or Dossenus.[10]

Performers and observers of the tradition alike have observed that Punch seems to exercise a supernatural power over both the puppeteer and the audience. For some, he fulfills deep-seated social needs for inversion of power structures, temporary subversion of norms, and a clear negative moral example. For others, he calls or indwells his chosen servants. The puppet, a vessel for the puppeteer's art, becomes the one who compels the performance.

Puppets will also find occasion to press audiences on theological and existential questions. Any theatre production *may* do this, of course. But for a puppet show do to so boosts the teleological stakes. Consider: the visible actor raises questions about the invisible causes of being and the world, while being manipulated by an exterior force of which, by nature, it can have no awareness. For example, in John Ludwig's *Heaven and Hell Tour,* a skeleton puppet serves as the "tour guide"/master of ceremonies to a series of vignettes that playfully riff on topics related to the afterlife. In the show's last moments, this tour guide asks the audience:

> What if there are no angels or devils? What if people made them all up? But then, if that's true, where do you come in? Its judgment day and you are your own judges! What are you? An angel or a devil? Who are you going to cling to? God? Yourselves? The Band? Is it really all going to be just fine?[11]

After a brief pause, strobe lights and screams explode on the stage. When the chaos resolves, the central character (hommo icci, an everyman) sits bolt upright in his bed in terror. Characters from the vignettes surround him, and a giant—a deity or mother figure with big hands—steps forward to cover him. The skeleton finishes: "Either God doesn't exist, isn't speaking to us, or has been with us the whole time. It all depends on your point of view doesn't it?" The audience is invited to exit to heaven, hell, or the way they came: "the easy way out."[12]

In truth, most puppet performances unfold without such metaphysical musings; the vast majority of those I have seen over the years, the scripts I have read, the documentation of productions I have studied, maintain a focus on telling a story with well-designed and well-manipulated figures. The audience has no need to worry that they are taking the easy way out. But puppet theatre lends itself to existential and theological questioning, to self-referential moments, and to breaking the fourth wall in a way that insistently gestures to the parallel between the puppets and audience members. *Dr. Faustus,* a longstanding favorite for marionette theatre, hopes to control the world but ends up manipulated by his desires and Mephistopheles. The stories of Bunraku often center on characters whose lives fates are subjects beyond their control, played out with the puppeteers in view—veiled and discrete, but present on stage. *Avenue Q* takes up a monetary collection from the audience under threat that "some puppets will get shot" if they do not open their wallets. In the early scenes of Trouble Puppet's *Frankenstein*, another character refers to Victor's experiments as "gruesome puppets, " and Dr. Praetorius shouts as a machine "I made you/ You have to do what I say!"[13] In both moments, the characters punctuated these statements with a glance toward the audience. By its very nature, the genre seems destined to metaphorical and metatheatrical gestures. It both wears out and plays out the existential anxieties that human beings experience. The puppeteer might play God, but as a finite being, she has a lot more in common with her puppets than with the infinite.

Through puppetry, humanity seeks to manipulate the forces that pull our own strings. This is a fraught business, as many puppeteers have realized. We recognize the affinities between ourselves and the figures, and the ironies inherent in being creators/manipulators in a universe where we have incomplete control over our own existence. We also discover the ways in which the wooden actors slip away, push back, and sometimes become our masters.

Notes

1. Elizabeth Van der Elst, *Puppets in Belgium* (Sprimont, BE: Margada, 1997), 9.
2. Connor Hopkins, "Frankenstein: A Trouble Puppet Show" (unpublished playscript, 2010), 15.
3. Foreman Brown, "Strings," Yale Puppeteers Collection, box 54 (Harry Ransom Center, University of Texas at Austin).
4. Foreman Brown, "Puppeteer," Yale Puppeteers Collection, box 54 (Harry Ransom Center, University of Texas at Austin).
5. Kenneth Gross, *Puppet: An Essay on Uncanny Life* (Chicago: University of Chicago Press, 2011), 16.
6. Van der Elst, *Puppets in Belgium*, 9.
7. Cassetta de Buratinni, "Policinella—Punch," *The Penny Magazine,* April 12, 1845, 142.
8. Lewis Hyde, *Trickster Makes this World: Mischief, Myth, and Art* (New York: Farrar, Straus, and Giroux, 2011[1998]), 7.
9. Gross, *Puppet*, 70.
10. Sean K. posting to Puptcrit discussion list, "Sacred Puppetry," April 22, 2008.
11. "Heaven and Hell Tour," directed by John Ludwig (Center for Puppetry Arts Archive, 1988, 1991), VHS.
12. Ibid.
13. Hopkins, "Frankenstein," 8.

CHAPTER EIGHTEEN

Is There God at the End of Bill Viola's "Room for St. John of the Cross"?: The *Via Negativa* as an Aesthetic Experience

Carlos Vara Sánchez

If I'm successful when you see one of my pieces, you'll have more questions than answers.

—Bill Viola[1]

Introduction

The theological *via negativa*, also known as the apophatic way,[2] is a tradition within Christianity which conceives God as something so beyond our comprehension that we can only describe God for what he is not. Bill Viola (b. 1951) has declared himself somehow related to the mystics that followed this way,[3] but how can a video installation such as "Room for St. John of the Cross" be both faithful to St. John's premises—follower of the aforementioned doctrine—while also relying on positive sensorial information?

Bill Viola is considered a pioneer in the field of video art and is still one of the most prominent figures among contemporary artists. He has exhibited his works at some of the most renowned museums and artistic events, including the National Gallery (London), the Metropolitan Museum of Art (New York), the Grand Palais (Paris), and the Venice Biennale. His oeuvre spans from his early single-channel videos to much more complex installations in which the visual, auditory, spatial, and temporal elements become intertwined. One of the reasons why Viola stands out among his contemporaries is his explicit interest in the universal questions about human existence. His basis for this approach can be found mainly in Zen Buddhism, Islamic Sufism, and last but not least, Christian mysticism. In fact, some of his creations constitute outstanding approaches toward spirituality. Taking this into account, Viola is a very appropriate candidate for the study of the possible ways to represent God in popular culture. Although his oeuvre spans more than 30 years, we will focus on "Room for St. John of the Cross," given its explicit relation with the works and thoughts of the Spanish theologian and mystic St. John of the Cross (1542–1591),[4] who was a major exponent of the *via negativa*. The characteristics of this mystical tradition, which emphasize silent and imageless prayer, create an apparent impossibility for a video installation that embraces its ideas. It is our intention to discuss the way Viola tries to overcome these difficulties in order to offer the spectator an apophatic encounter. It is important to specify that we are not suggesting that Viola's only goal is to facilitate an experience of the Christian God, since the ultimate result of the contact with "Room for St. John of the Cross" will depend on the viewers inner beliefs. However, what is true is that this work intends to propose an exposure to the *via negativa* tenets; therefore our interest.

Bill Viola's constant travels,[5] prior to being a worldwide known artist, led him to realize the intrinsic relationship between different spiritual manifestations around the world. He has stated how the discovery of the importance of the sacred, as an element in the structure of consciousness, shaped his conception of what the artist's role should be.[6] Thus, the explicit transcendental nature of much of his oeuvre is not surprising. More specifically, he has stated his interest in the lives of the mystics, from both the Oriental and the Occidental traditions.[7] Attributing it to his previously indicated engagement with the *via negativa*, he is not interested in offering answers to those that visit his works, but questions destined to help them increase their self-knowledge.[8] Paradoxically, in Japan, Viola came in contact with the books of scholars such as Daisetsu Teitaro Suzuki and Ananda Kentish Coomaraswamy. Through their books he discovered Occidental figures such as Meister Eckhart, St. John of the Cross, and Hildegard von Bingen.[9] As a result of this encounter, he started to delve into mystical concepts like the aforementioned *via negativa*. However, we should not be tempted to consider his works (despite their spiritual emphasis), as tools to proselytize a specific religion, since Viola has expressed not having a particular bond with any specific dogma.[10] His concept of religion is not a restrictive one, having shown interest in the possibility "for the individual to directly connect his or her spirit to the Godhead."[11] The importance granted to this nonmediated experience of God is especially clear in a work such as "Room for St. John of the Cross," in which the theological ideas absorbed by the artist are transmuted into aesthetic elements able to convey transcendental, deep, and intense emotions to the spectator.[12]

Viola's relationship with the figure of St. John (given its importance to the present pages), merits a deeper explanation. Viola decided to elaborate "Room for St. John of the Cross" as a result of the vivid impression he felt after coming in contact with a volume of poetry written by the Spanish friar, which had been reprinted in 1968[13] by an American publisher specializing in Beatnik poetry. This book did not contain the existing pages of the explanations of the poems elaborated by the mystic. In consequence, as Kurt Wettengl explains, Viola's interpretation was "realized intuitively by a reader with appropriate preparation and background knowledge, but the many layers of meaning remain hidden without the metaphor-rich interpretation by the author."[14] It was not until the completion of this work that Viola became acquainted with the deep meanings of St. John's theology. However, as we will see when discussing specific details, his artistic intuitions proved to be extremely insightful.

The Work, the Mystic, and the Theology

Formal Description of "Room for St. John of the Cross"

Prior to embarking on the complex journey of analyzing the elements by which Bill Viola's "Room for St. John of the Cross" can be able to deliver an experience of God, according to the *via negativa* tenets, it is essential to become familiar with the work in and of itself. The video installation was first presented at the Museum of Fine Arts in Santa Fe, New Mexico in 1983. In the very same year, on the occasion of the work's exhibition in Paris, the artist himself introduced it on the following terms:

> A small black cubicle stands in the center of a large dark room. There is a small open window in the front of the cubicle where a sort of glow of incandescent light emerges. On the back wall of the space, a large screen shows a projected black-and-white video image of snow-covered mountains. Shot with an unstable hand-held camera, the mountains move in wild, jittery patterns. A loud roaring sound of wind and white

noise saturates the room from two loudspeakers. The interior of the cubicle is inaccessible and can be viewed only through the window. The inner walls are white. The floor is covered with brown dirt. There is a small wooden table in the corner with a metal water pitcher, a glass of water, and a 4-inch color monitor. On the monitor is a color image of a snow-covered mountain. Shown with a fixed camera, it is presented in real time with no editing. The only visible movement is caused by an occasional wind blowing through the trees and bushes. From within the cubicle, the sound of a voice softly reciting St. John's poems in Spanish is barely audible above the loud roaring of the wind in the room.[15]

From a merely descriptive point of view, there are many different dimensions simultaneously at work in the video installation: spatial, acoustic, visual, and symbolic elements. The architectural feature delimits two separated spaces, which impedes looking at the outer area of the room and at the inner cubicle at the same time. This duality experimented by the spectator is reinforced by the other dimensions aforementioned. Depending on where the visitor remains, what is perceived is something completely different. To be in the bigger room is to be confronted by the roaring sound of the wind and the swaying mountains projected in the screen. The loudness of the sound and the frantic nature of the black-and-white imagery generate on the visitor a feeling of uneasiness. However, this sensation disappears suddenly as soon as someone introduces their head through the tiny aperture of the cubicle. What greets them inside is a radically opposed reality. A smooth voice reciting poetry in Spanish is perceived and a small little monitor displaying the steady image of a snow-covered single mountain enthralls us. Sound and image reinforce reciprocally in order to transmit sheer calmness. In conclusion, at first sight, "Room for St. John of the Cross" offers the chance to experience (almost literally), the calm in the eye of the storm.

In the interior of the cubicle, besides the monitor and the gentle voice, there are also some specific elements with a precise to symbolism to be discussed below. Thus, the spectator will discover in this small space, an austere wooden table, a metal pitcher, a glass of water, and a floor covered with something that seems to be soil.

As noted before, Viola employs clear contrasts in this video installation: The central location is uncomfortably small compared to the outer room, and whereas the first is painted white, the second is black and dark. The pictures in the outer room are black and white, violently edited with noticeable cuts, whereas what it is displayed on the tiny monitor in the cubicle is a color image of a single mountain that seems to be a still frame.

All of these elements, along with the contrast between the exterior cacophony and the voice heard in the little central space, are meant to effectively differentiate the two areas, yet connecting them as opposite poles of a single experience.

The title of this work makes evident the existence of a relation with the Spanish friar St. John of the Cross. This connection is explained by Viola when he affirms that "the dimensions of the cubicle, in this video-sound installation ['Room for St. John of the Cross'] correspond roughly to those of the cell in which the Spanish mystic Juan de la Cruz was confined for nine months."[16] Due to the importance of St. John's ideas and life, for a deeper understanding of the work we will introduce some aspects of his biography as well as some notions about his conception of the *via negativa*.

The Life of St. John of the Cross

St. John of the Cross was born Juan de Yepes y Álvarez in 1542, in Fontiveros, Castile. At the age of 21 he entered the Order of the Highly Blessed Virgin of Mount Carmel. After concluding his studies in philosophy and theology at the University of Salamanca (the most important Spanish university at the time), he was ordained as a priest in 1567. This very same year he met with St. Teresa of Jesus (1515–1582), who was at that moment carrying over a reform of the female branch of the Carmelite order,[17] causing St. John to feel the urge to establish an equivalent reform among the male division of the order they both shared. They founded a certain number of monasteries under the rules of the new observance,[18] which would lead to the posterior establishing of the Discalced Carmelite order in 1593. Although there were no initial problems with their superiors, in the end their reforms were banned. St. Teresa accepted the edict but St. John did not, leading him to be "regarded as a rebel"[19] and subsequently arrested.

St. John's incarceration took place in a monastery of the old observance situated in Toledo (Spain) from December 2, 1577 until an unknown date in August 1578. These seven months were a harsh toll to pay because of the severe cold in the winter, the poor conditions of the cell, and the regular torture he had to endure.[20] One night, he finally succeeded to escape from prison, being able to return to his loyal brothers, and resuming his activities for the reformation of the order. St. John did not live to see the sanction of the Discalced Carmelites in 1593 by Pope Clement VIII because of his death on December 14, 1591, in Úbeda (Spain). He was beatified in 1675 and canonized in 1726.

St. John was a man "who devoted himself equally to prayer and work in the community, renovation and conversion work in the convent and other everyday jobs."[21] Although he was not a professional writer, he left behind a very influential number of poems and prose texts, both to be considered from a theological way and for their sheer poetic beauty. His most important ideas, containing his doctrine of the *via negativa*, are found in *Spiritual Song* (*Cántico espiritual*), *Living Flame of Love* (*Llama de amor viva*), *Ascent of Mount Carmel* (*Subida del Monte Carmelo*), and *The Dark Night* (*Noche oscura*). Using his characteristic metaphorical language he expresses in these pages his religious beliefs, some episodes of his life—especially of the imprisonment and the subsequent nocturnal escape—and his very own relationship with God.

St. John of the Cross's *Via Negativa*

During his formative years in Salamanca, St. John received an extensive philosophic and theological education. It is believed that beyond the orthodox philosophy taught at the university, which included authors such as Aristotle and Thomas Aquinas, he also came in contact with some of the prominent works of the apophatic tradition: the texts of Pseudo-Dionysius the Areopagite; the anonymous book, *The Cloud of Unknowing*; possibly Marsilio Ficino's *Corpus Hermeticum*; and the works of Germanic mystics, such as Meister Eckhart, Johannes Tauler, and Henry Suso.[22] Nevertheless, *St. John of the Cross* poetry is perceived as an authentic experience. The supposition of contact between the authors finally comes to borrowings from them. This is the result of having previously read the texts and not from a literal citation.[23]

St. John is representative of a tradition, the *via negativa*, whose tenets are "what human desire seeks, the divine, highest Being, cannot be defined, pronounced, or known because it is radically *transcendent*. . . . Negative theology's emphasis on the unknowableness, the unutterableness, and the deep darkness of transcendent Being elicits the idea that transcendence is best approached via denials, via what according to earthly concepts is *not*. Hence the name *negative theology*."[24]

The main goal of St. John's theology was the "vision of the human path of life leading to perfection in God."[25] Conceiving this journey as a negative way, in which, through unknowing and renouncement one can finally come upon a mystical union. This idea is summarily elaborated in a diagram elaborated by him shortly after his escape from prison (ca. 1580). In the conserved autographed drawing, which we will soon discuss, one can find a four-stanza poem written in the margin that summarizes the road of spiritual and material negation advocated by him. This design is often used as the frontispiece of his theological treatise *Ascent of Mount*

Carmel (*Subida del Monte Carmelo*) and the referred poem is known under the name of *Mount of Perfection* (*Monte de la Perfección*). An excerpt of this poem can be found in Viola's own book, *Reason for Knocking at an Empty House*[26]; the complete text, translated into English, is as follows:

> To come to enjoy it all,
> desire enjoyment in nothing.
> To come to the knowledge of all,
> desire the knowledge of nothing.
> To come to possess it all
> desire the possession of nothing.
> To come to be it all,
> desire to be nothing.
>
> To come to what you enjoy,
> you must go by a way you will enjoy not.
> To come to what you do not know,
> you must go by a way which you know not.
> To come to possess what you do not possess,
> you must go by a way which you possess not.
> To come to be what you are not,
> you must go by a way which you are not.
>
> When you realize about something,
> you cease to throw yourself into all.
> In order to go from the whole to the whole,
> you must put the whole of you into the whole.
> And when you come to possess it all,
> you have to possess it without wanting it.
>
> In this nakedness the spirit
> is at peace, for when
> it does not yearn for anything, nothing
> wears it down, and nothing
> presses it down, because it is
> centred on its humility.[27]

What St. John seeks to transmit is "the active and passive need of purgation, the teaching of negation and dispossessing of appetites, faculties and everything that happens in the human mind. Obtaining this emptiness will be favorable in order to receive God's grace and glory."[28] St. John's *via negativa*[29] underlines the need of "awareness of being abandoned by God."[30] All that could hinder unity with God has to be eliminated during the experience of the "dark night," including "all the certainties of the senses and reason, but also all conceptions of God, truths of the faith, and other human projections on which believers depend."[31] The sketching beside the poem, *Mount of Perfection,* reiterates this idea by offering three ways of living our lives, but only one (the central one) ending with the ultimate union with God. The other two "denote the roads of imperfection are broad and somewhat tortuous and come to an end before the higher stages of the mount are reached."[32] The central path is certainly the apophatic way, the *via negativa,* as in the successive steps along the way we find the words: "Nothing, nothing, nothing, nothing, nothing, nothing, and even on the mountain nothing" ("nada, nada, nada, nada, nada, nada, y aún en el monte nada"). A clear memento of the sacrifices demanded of those who choose to go through that spiritual route. The result of this road is a radical dispossession, since only by emptying ourselves can God's love finally fill us.

It will be necessary to return to other texts written by St. John and his theological ideas, but for now it is time to resume the analysis of Viola's "Room for St. John of the Cross."

An Apophatic Experience of "Room for St. John of the Cross"

Viola's video installation "Room for St. John of the Cross" has been previously introduced from a descriptive point of view. Therefore, now we will go into further detail regarding the intrinsic value of its experience. Considering the aesthetics mechanisms—as much as their theological correlates—that render it that way.

In one of the sketches drawn by Viola during the process of designing his work, there is a very insightful annotation with respect to the idea underlying this video installation:

> A room within a room—Inside, calm, serene, still. Outside, chaotic, turbulent. The cubicle represents the self. The piece represents the state of self-knowledge. The center is calm and strange, a solid retreat from the turbulence of the outside, where all is loud and jumbled. The self is realized through solitude, which becomes a solid defense to the outside disorder. The inside mountain is still and fixed—the outside one is turbulent and continually in motion. Calm, stability at the center of the storm. The cubicle is a prison. Outside represents the imagination, inside the reality. Outside world is more interesting that the inside, but the inside is what is accepted (the restrictions). One is held prisoner, but the mind is free to wander. Solitary confinement / spiritual freedom.[33]

According to this, the notion of opposition, which has already been briefly introduced before, is at the core of the work. From the text, one can infer Viola's intention of proffering two clearly different areas for the spectator to experience. Furthermore, there is an implicit sense of process in the whole work, which makes necessary to closely study both areas and the precise frontier defined by the tiny window.

The Purgative Outside

The room is the unavoidable first contact with "Room for St. John of the Cross," since the observer is not allowed to introduce his head through the window and into the cubicle without being previously confronted by the bursting sound and the shaking images of the mountains. Therefore, the dark big room is supposed to be the first stage of the experience of self-knowledge that the work intends to offer.[34] Viola employs the terms "chaotic, turbulent, storm" when describing it. These words certainly resemble some verses of Saint·John's *Mount of Perfection,* in which it is said that "to come to the pleasure you have not, / you must go by a way in which you enjoy not" (vv. 9–10). However, it is another poem from the Spanish mystic that offers the complementary insight to understand the complexities of Viola's intention in this initial exposure to the video installation. We are alluding to *The Dark Night* (*Noche oscura*), which not incidentally is one of the four poems[35] that can heard in the interior of the cubicle.

On a dark night,
with yearnings inflamed by love
Oh sheer joy!
I left unnoticed
being my house in deep repose.

In darkness and safe,
disguised by the secret ladder,
Oh sheer joy!
in darkness and concealed,
being my house in deep repose.

In this merry night
in secret, so no one could see me
I didn't looked at anything
since my only light and guide
was that which in my heart burned.

This guided me
more brilliant than the light of noon,
to where I was awaited
by the one I knew well
who waited where no one else was.

Oh night that guided me!
Oh night more gentle than dawn!
Oh night that gathered
lover with beloved,
beloved into lover converted!

Upon my blooming breast
which wholly for him I kept,
there he laid asleep,
as I caressed him
there in cedars fanning's breeze

The blow from the crenel,
as I spread his locks,
with his tranquil hand
my neck was wounded
all my senses suspended.

I remained and I forgot myself,
my face I leaned on the beloved,
everything ceased and I lay
leaving my cares
among the lilies forgotten.[36]

The fourth stanza seems crucial in our intent to understand the mechanisms of "Room for St. John of the Cross," as it underlines the guiding role of the night. Although there may seem to be an opposition between St. John's poem and what Viola features in his work, this conflict disappears when unearthing some specifics of the experience of the "dark night" as the Spanish mystic understands it. Firstly, a distinction should be made between the "active night" and the "passive night." The former corresponds with what is described in the poem *Mount of Perfection* and the latter with what *The Dark Night* narrates. In the words of Bert Blans, "'The Ascent of Mount Carmel' [in which *Mount of Perfection* is included] sees the night as the moment of going forth, through personal effort: actively. 'The Dark Night' discusses the same poem and the same subject, but as *something undergone*, a being met by the Lover: hence a passive night."[37] These two phases are to be understood in the broader context of the classical purgative, illuminative, and unitive ways in Christian spirituality. In his theological work *The Dark Night of the Soul*—not to be confused with the brief poem previously cited, *The Dark Night*—St. John explains how when the "purgative contemplation is most severe, the soul feels very keenly the shadow of death and the lamentations of death and the pains of hell, which consists in its feeling itself to be without God."[38] Therefore, the harsh imagery of the dark in the video installation could be contemplated as "the door to the illuminative way and the beginning of manifest mystical life."[39]

In consequence, this space should be considered as offering both the experience of the active night and the passive night as two phases within the purgative way. Since the God of the *via negativa* cannot be described positively, the visitor (if he intends to follow the path drawn by St. John) is compelled to acknowledge the darkness and danger that surrounds him and to take an active path that he will not enjoy. Only by doing this can one finally achieved the emptiness that would be filled in the subsequent phases. Despite Viola having recognized not being aware of the sheer complexity of the theological thinking of St. John at the time he was designing the work,[40] he intuited the inner meaning of the purgative aspect of the dark night as well as the duality of the passive and the active nights.

In conclusion, this area of "Room for St. John of the Cross" is aimed to prepare the encounter with the transcendent God of the *via negativa*—which cannot be positively shown—by proffering the possibility of embracing his absence in an active way to the spectator. Then, having accepted this radical loneliness among the mountains and the storming sound, go through the passive experience of the "dark nigh" in order to continue this journey of self-discovery under the guidance of Viola's interpretation of St. John's life and work.

The Ascetic Boundary

The boundary between the two main areas is physically nothing but a minuscule window, but whether because of its symbolic meaning and its particular place and size merits further explanation. Its significance reverberates with the already described drawing elaborated by St. John in the same page that he wrote *Mount of Perfection*. Three possible paths are depicted in the sketch, but only the central one leads to the ultimate union with God. In contrast with the other two, this middle way is characterized by being the narrowest, which represents the difficulties to be experienced by those who choose to undertake this road. Having realized this, the position and size of the window seems fully intentional, given its tiny dimensions and its unhelpful low situation. If the spectator intends to gaze at the interior of the room he will be forced to adopt an uncomfortable posture. No matter how hard he tries to contort his body, he will only be able to introduce his head inside the cell while the rest of him shall remain in the external room. These physical difficulties caused by Viola's architectural feature seem to imitate the ideas of Saint John and the whole apophatic mystical tradition, which speaks about the need of "liberating that self from the limitedness of the corporeal and emptying the self of self-will. By going inward, one escapes."[41]

For this reason, the window could be considered as something that adds a physical dimension to the process of the apophatic emptying already initiated in the outer space of the video installation. This aim is fulfilled by obliging the viewer to strive to reach the calmed cubicle. Hence, the aperture is both a remainder and a metaphor of the ascetic effort needed to endure by those who choose to take the narrow central path.

The Unitive Space

The small cube is the third and final step of the complex process that is "Room for St. John of the Cross." After the purgative experience of the night elicited in the bigger space and the physical effort required by the oddly placed window, the spectator ultimately faces the heart of the video installation. But, once again, as soon as someone puts their head trough the aperture, they are forced to confront a paradox that needs to be solved. Although the first feeling experienced will probably be one of calm—given the contrast with the outer audiovisual turbulence—this sensation will not last. A mixed feeling will appear. On the one hand, the small space quickly becomes claustrophobic and together with the incapacity to completely enter the area can generate anxiousness. On the other hand, the peaceful mountain displayed and the serene voice reciting poetry send an opposed message. As we have seen above, in Viola's words, this is supposed to be a calm retreat from the outside turbulences. But how to make oneself comfortable in a place like this?

To understand Viola's idea, it is crucial to note that this area not merely represents the cell in which St. John stayed for several months, but most importantly it symbolizes the spiritual state in which he conceived some of his most memorable poems[42] while deprived of liberty. The possibility for someone to compose verses full of love while held captive and being frequently tortured certainly shows a vast capacity to separate corporal circumstances from the inner self. And this particular state of mind is what Viola seeks to symbolize and (as much as possible) transmit to the spectator. In consonance with this, to describe St. John's spiritual vigor, he has used the metaphor of the typhoon's calm center in the middle of the storm, emphasizing his aim to represent his faith and strength in order to elicit a similar experience for the visitor.[43] Viola also said that this space represented the self, the quietude. According to this, the room should be interpreted in spiritual terms.

All the material elements—the wooden table, the water pitcher, and the glass—speak of someone whose physical needs are far less important than their spiritual ones. This place cannot retain who has climbed the *Mount of Perfection*, because "In this nakedness the spirit / is at peace, for when / it does not yearn for anything, nothing / wears it down, and nothing /presses it down, because it is / centred on its humility" (vv. 23–28). This final step consists in realizing how a prison cannot incarcerate someone's soul. The faith and the strength referred by Viola are symbolized in the sound and image on the monitor that we perceive inside the room. These elements can be understood as the mental activity of St. John while being held prisoner. His body certainly suffered, but he endured the torment and resumed his reformist labor as soon as he escaped. The small screen shows a mountain rising up surrounded by a forest and a meadow, whose quietness largely contrasts with the peaks shown outside. Adding to this the effect of the poetry heard in the cubicle, it feels as if there could be another reality within this small room. Like if there were a place where the mind could go if it finally relinquished its usual way of processing the world. This is fully intentional by Viola, since he acknowledges his belief in "another dimension that you just know is there, that can be a source of real knowledge, and the quest for connection with that and identifying that is the whole impetus for me to cultivate these experiences and to make my work."[44]

Thus, we are at the gates of the unitive experience. A state in which the ultimate union with God happens. St. John's poem, *Living Flame of Love*, is an expression of this utterly indefinable experience, the unitive experience with the transcendent God that remains far beyond the reach of words. The first stanza expresses this impossible estate: "I entered into unknowing / and there I remained unknowing / transcending all knowledge."[45] These verses explain the futility of human knowledge to describe the essence of God, for he reveals himself as something that cannot be grasped or learned, because "he who masters himself / will, with knowledge in unknowing, / always be transcending."[46] This final leap cannot be revealed in the work. Accordingly to the *via negativa*, it is an inward experience as Edward Howells explains:

> To go forward in the "night" by means of faith, hope, and love is to receive an emptying of these faculties—a sense of loss of the familiar things that one identifies with God's presence—but then to be given

new spiritual powers of intellect, memory and will, such that God's deep being, which touches the soul in the soul's "substance" and "center," ceases to be dark and becomes recognizable as light. Thus, the emphasis is on how the mind is transformed by grace to be able to discern God's mystical presence inwardly.[47]

This path followed through Viola's "Room for St. John of the Cross" has led to a point where the visitor is left on the verge of the proximity with the Most High, but this final leap toward the transcendent is an internal one, and there the work cannot help anymore. His function was to situate one in vicinity with the undefinable apophatic God, but the last movement— when contemplating the mountain and listening to the poetry—is as untransferable as much as personal. The God of the *via negativa* cannot be shown, it has to be found inside oneself after a specific path characterized by a progressive emptying and refusal. This final union can only happen through faith, hope, and love, but as the Bible reminds us: "So faith, hope, love abide, these three; but the greatest of these is love."[48] Viola shares this opinion about the utter importance of love in order to reach for God: "When the eyes cannot see, then the only thing to go on is faith, and the only true way to approach God is from within. From that point the only way God can be reached is through love. By love the soul enters into union with God."[49]

Through love the space that meant to be a cell is transformed into a place to experience God. This is achieved not by showing an image— which would break the tenets of the *via negativa*—but allowing the visitor to live a process of spiritual ascent that culminates in this room.

Conclusion

Our intention was to discuss the possibility of rendering an experience of the apophatic way in a contemporary work of art, in order to discover if it is possible to experience God—as it is conceived by the *via negativa*— through a specific video installation. Of course, this text does not defend that every spectator that visits Viola's "Room for St. John of the Cross" will have a transcendental encounter with God. As has been said in the introduction, it depends on the viewers inner beliefs. It is not even necessary to say that this work is not directed to a particular faith. Our sole interest was to study the aesthetic mechanisms employed by Viola and how they relate to St. John's life and work.

Having clarified this issue, it is time to gather conclusions. From the very first moment "Room for St. John of the Cross" revealed itself as a work with a clear contrast between its two spaces. Paying closer attention to the details shown in each area and consulting St. John's poetry, the possibility of considering the video installation as a process took form. The explicit interest in the *via negativa* stated by Viola allowed an interpretation of the work in the light of this theological idea that evoked a possible interpretation. According to this, the work can be conceived not only as an aesthetic creation, but as an explicitation of the whole *via negativa* as it was understood by St. John. In this case the outer room would represent the purgative stage, the place where the "dark night," with its passive and active aspects, has to be experienced. A necessary phase of feeling abandoned prior to undertake the active search of God. Once this is accomplished, the visitor has to endure the need of leaving their material and physical necessities behind, which is symbolized in the aperture and its uncomfortable position. The final stage is the one that occurs in the interior of the small room, which represents St. John's cell. In this austere place the observer is confronted by the paradox of someone who was spiritually free while physically captive. At this point, the work reveals its inner secret: The ultimate experience of God is something internal that cannot be shown or put into words. It demands faith, hope, and, above all, love. Only when emptied of desires can someone be filled by God's love. This was what St. John meant when he wrote seven times "nothing" in the way that leads to the Highest.

"Room for St. John of the Cross" is an accurate intuition of the *via negativa* elaborated as a video installation by Bill Viola. As a result, we can affirm that the work has the potential to succeed in leading the visitor through a process that ends by showing that the apothatic God, although it cannot be shown or understood, can be effectively felt.

Notes

1. Bill Viola, *Reflections*, ed. Anna Bernardini (Milan: Silvana Editoriale, 2012), 63.

2. "The Catholic tradition is marked, moreover, by two different approaches to the mystical life. First, there is the *via negativa*, the apophatic way, which stresses that because God is the ever-greater God, so radically different from any creature, God is best known by negation, elimination, forgetting, unknowing, without images and symbols, and in darkness. God is 'not this, not that.' All images, thoughts, symbols, etc. must be eliminated . . . Secondly, there is the *via affirmativa*, the kataphatic way, which underscores finding God in all things. It emphasizes a definite similarity between God and creatures, that God can be reached by creatures, images, and symbols, because He has manifested Himself in creation and salvation history. The incarnational dimension of Christianity, too, forces the mystic to take seriously God's self-revelation in history and in symbols.

Because Christ is God's real symbol, the icon of God, God is really present in a positive way." Harvey D. Egan, S.J., "Christian Apophatic and Kataphatic Mysticisms." *Theological Studies* 39, no. 3 (1978): 403.

3. "I relate to the role of the mystic in the sense of following a *via negativa*—of feeling the basis of my work to be in unknowing, in doubt, in being lost, in questions and not answers." Bill Viola, *Reasons for Knocking at an Empty House: Writings 1973–1994*, ed. Robert Violette, introduction by Jean-Christophe Amman (London: Thames and Hudson, 2002), 250.

4. "Viola bases his installation ['Room for St. John of the Cross'] not only on the poems but also on the biography of St. John of the Cross." Kurt Wettengl, "Room for St. John of the Cross," in *Bill Viola Europäische Einsichten | European Insights*, ed. Rolf Lauter (Munich: Prestel Verla, 1999), 252

5. Viola has been traveling around the world since 1974. This year he arrived to Florence where he stayed for one-and-a-half years. After this European stay, he began a period that led him to live for a variable time in places such as Salomon Islands, Java, Bali, Australia, Japan, and Tunisia.

6. "This was such a significant discovery for me—'the sacred as an element in the structure of consciousness.' It is within us all. The intuitive awareness and unwavering belief in this other world interwoven with our own, this other place, the 'separate reality', or whatever it has been called, has been the fuel for the fire of almost every artist who has left his or her mark on the earth." Viola, *Reasons for Knocking*, 174.

7. Bill Viola, *Vedere con la mente e con il cuore*, ed. Valentina Valentini (Rome: Gangemi Editore, 1993), 92–93.

8. According to Michael Duncan's words: "Sensory perception is for Viola a spiritual activity, one that leads to a heightened awareness of both nature and culture." Michael Duncan, "Bill Viola: Altered Perceptions," *Art in America* 86, no. 3 (1998): 63.

9. Viola, *Reasons for Knocking*, 283.

10. "My mother did instill in me a deep spiritual sense of the world beyond the specifics of her religion." Lewis Hyde, "Conversation," in *Bill Viola*, ed. D. A. Ross et al. (New York: Whitney Museum of American Art, 1997), 143.

11. Viola, *Reasons for Knocking*, 283.

12. As an example of the nature of reactions triggered by Viola's works, we can offer Jean-Christophe Ammann experience when encountering for the first time "Room for St. John of the Cross": "I well remember the shock I felt on seeing *Room for St. John of the Cross*, 1983, at the Museum of Modern Art in New York. . . . That day I could look at nothing else. I forgot the much advertised Frank Stella exhibition just one floor below. I returned to my hotel through the streets of New York, which seemed for all the deep world like deep ravines in a mountain range, carrying my heart the trembling treeleaves on that bleak and lofty plateau." Jean-Cristophe Ammann, introduction to Viola, *Reasons for Knocking*, 15–16.

13. Wettengl, "Room for St. John of the Cross," 253.

14. Ibid., 258.

15. Suzanne Page, ed., *Bill Viola* (Paris: ARC, Musée d'art moderne de la ville de Paris, 1983), 76.

16. Ibid., 24.

17. Teresa de Ávila advocated for "More freedom and time for spiritual meditation, personal discipline and mental prayer." José Nieto, *Místico, poeta, rebelde, santo: En torno a Juan de la Cruz* (Madrid: FCE, 1982), 53. (Trans. by the author.)

18. On November 28, 1568 in Duruelo (Spain), St. Teresa and St. John of the Cross founded the first monastery.

19. Wettengl, "Room for St. John of the Cross," 252.

20. Edward Howells, "Spanish Mysticism and Religious Renewal: Igna-tius of Loyola, Teresa of Avila, and John of the Cross," in *The Wiley-Blackwell Companion to Christian Mysticism*, ed. Julia A. Lamm (Malden, MA: Wiley-Blackwell, 2012), 432.

21. Wettengl, "Room for St. John of the Cross," 253.

22. Anna Serra Zamora, "Iconología del *Monte de Perfección:* Para una teoría de la imagen en San Juan de la Cruz" (Ph.D. diss., Universitat Pompeu Fabra, 2010), 37–40.

23. Ibid., 40.

24. Ilse N. Bulhof and Laurens ten Kate, eds., *Flight of the Gods: Philosophical Perspectives on Negative Theology* (New York: Fordham University Press, 2000), 5.

25. Wettengl, "Room for St. John of the Cross," 254.

26. Viola, *Reasons for Knocking*, 117.

27. Translation by the author. The original text in Spanish is as follows: "Para venir a gustarlo todo / no quieras tener gusto en nada. /Para venir a saberlo todo / no quieras saber algo en nada. / Para venir a poseerlo todo /no quieras poseer algo en nada. / Para venir a serlo todo / no quieras ser algo en nada. // Para venir a lo que gustas / has de ir por donde no gustas. / Para venir a lo que no sabes / has de ir por donde no sabes. / Para venir a poseer lo que no posees / has de ir por donde no posees. / Para venir a lo que no eres / has de ir por donde no eres. / Cuando reparas en algo / dejas de arrojarte al todo. / Para venir del todo al todo / has de dejarte del todo en todo, / y cuando lo vengas del todo a tener / has de tenerlo sin nada querer. / En esta desnudez halla el / espíritu su descanso, porque no / comu-nicando nada, nada le fatiga hacia / arriba, y nada le oprime / hacia abajo, porque está en / el centro de su humildad." Ms 6296, *Obras de San Juan de la Cruz y Santa Teresa de Jesús*, 1759, Biblioteca Nacional de España, f. 7.

28. Zamora, "Iconología del *Monte de Perfección*," 79.

29. "In the works of St. John we find ourselves at the confluence of a great mystical tradition to which many prior writers had contributed—each uniquely, but only in part—to the culmination of that unified and disciplined whole sys-tematically, and for the first time coherently, articulated in the thought of one writer: St. John of the Cross." Geoffrey K. Mondello, *The Metaphysics of Mysticism: A Commentary on the Mystical Philosophy of St. John of the Cross*, accessed February 23, 2014, http://www.johnofthecross.com/.

30. Bert Blans, "Cloud of Unknowing," in *Flight of the Gods: Philosophical Perspectives on Negative
Theology*, ed. Ilse N. Bulhof and Laurens ten Kate (New York: Fordham University Press, 2000), 72.

31. Ibid., 72–73.

32. St. John of the Cross, *The Essential St. John of the Cross*, trans. E. Allison Peers (Radford, VA: Wilder Publications, 2008), 23.

33. "Further notes for 'Room for St. John of the Cross.'" San Francisco Museum of Modern Art, accessed February 24, 2014, http://www.sfmoma.org/media/features/viola/indepth_BV05.html.

34. Wettengl, "Room for St. John of the Cross," 260.

35. Along with *The Dark Night, Verses on a Moving Contemplation* (*Coplas hechas sobre un éxtasis de harta contemplación*), *Songs of the Soul Which Strives to See God* (*Coplas del alma que pena por ver a Dios*), and *Other Verses with a Divine Meaning* (*Otras coplas a lo divino*) are the four poems chosen by Viola to be recited in his video installation.

36. Translation by the author. The original text in Spanish is the following: "En una noche oscura, / con ansias, en amores inflamada / ¡oh dichosa ventura! / salí sin ser notada / estando ya mi casa sosegada. // A oscuras y segura / por la secreta escala, disfrazada, / ¡oh dichosa ventura! / a oscuras y en celada, / estando ya mi casa sosegada. // En la noche dichosa, / en secreto, que nadie me veía, / ni yo miraba cosa, / sin otra luz ni guía / sino la que en el corazón ardía. // Aquésta me guiaba / más cierta que la luz del mediodía, / adonde me esperaba / quien yo bien me sabía, / en parte donde nadie parecía. // ¡Oh noche que guiaste! / ¡Oh noche amable más que el alborada! / ¡oh noche que juntaste / Amado con amada, / amada en el Amado transformada! // En mi pecho florido, / que entero para él solo se guardaba, / allí quedó dormido, / y yo le regalaba, / y el ventalle de cedros aire daba. // El aire de la almena, / cuando yo sus cabellos esparcía / con su mano serena / en mi cuello hería / y todos mis sentidos suspendía. // Quedeme y olvideme, / el rostro recliné sobre el Amado, / cesó todo, y dejéme, / dejando mi cuidado / entre las azucenas olvidado." "Noche oscura," Juan de la Cruz.

37. Blans, "Cloud of Unknowing," 72.

38. St. John of the Cross, *Dark Night of the Soul*, ed. T. N. R. Rogers, trans. E. Allison Peers (Mineola, NY: Dover, 2003), 67.

39. Ernest E. Larkin, *The Three Spiritual Ways*, New Catholic Encyclopedia, vol. XIV (San Francisco: McGraw-Hill, 1967), 836.

40. Viola himself explains it during an interview: "And so I realized that the most important work I have ever created ['Room for St. John of the Cross'] came about by my creating it at a time when I did not know what I was doing." M. L. Syringe, ed., *Bill Viola: Unseen Images* (Düsseldorf: Städt Ksthalle, 1994), 98.

41. Ronald R. Bernier, "Screening God: Bill Viola and the Theological Sublime" (M.A. diss., University of Scranton, 2010), 29.

42. "*The Spiritual Canticle* of St. John of the Cross—the first 36 stanzas of which he composed while a prisoner in Toledo (1577–1578)." Ann W. Astell and

Catherine Rose Cavadini, "The Song of Songs" in *The Wiley-Blackwell Companion to Christian Mysticism*, ed. Julia A. Lamm (Malden, MA: Blackwell, 2013), 35.

43. "That particular piece ['Room for St. John of the Cross'] has to do with the idea of the calm center inside the storm. When a typhoon comes through, the center is very clear and still. And that, to me, represents the position of great people—like St. John of the Cross—who, in history, have shown in a kind of chaotic period, they can have a strong center. And of course, the center is the self. And it's not only to show that St. John has a strong center, but that each of us, all of us can also have this strong center in our heart. That's the most important connection. And so in *Room for St. John*, there's kind of like a balance between kind of chaotic, violent world and inner calm world. And so St. John's room represents his faith, his strength—and therefore, our faith and our strength—to understand the world, and to live in the world." "Further notes for 'Room for St. John of the Cross,'" San Francisco Museum of Modern Art, accessed February 24, 2014, http://www.sfmoma.org/media/features/viola/indepth_BV05.html.

44. Hyde, "Conversation," 143.

45. St. John of the Cross, *The Collected Works*, 53.

46. Ibid., 54.

47. Howells, "Spanish Mysticism" 434.

48. 1 Corinthians 13:13 [RSV].

49. Bill Viola, *Reasons for Knocking*, 249.

About the Editors and Contributors

Editors

Stephen Butler Murray is president and professor of systematic theology and preaching at Ecumenical Theological Seminary in Detroit, Michigan. He previously served as senior pastor of The First Baptist Church of Boston, Massachusetts, as American Baptist chaplain to Harvard University, and as denominational counselor and lecturer in ministry at Harvard Divinity School. He was the chaplain and served on the faculty at Endicott College, Skidmore College, and Suffolk University, and was an administrator at Yale University's Dwight Hall Center for Public Service and Social Justice. A past president of the North American Paul Tillich Society, he is the author of *Reclaiming Divine Wrath: A History of a Christian Doctrine and Its Interpretation* (2011) and co-edited *Crossing by Faith: Sermons on the Journey from Youth to Adulthood* (2003) with David L. Bartlett and Claudia Ann Highbaugh. He is a graduate of Yale Divinity School and received his Ph.D. in systematic theology from Union Theological Seminary in New York City.

Aimée Upjohn Light is assistant professor of theology at Duquesne University and specializes in interreligious work and feminist theologies. Dr. Light received her Ph.D. from Yale University in philosophy of religion and is the author of *God at the Margins: Making Theological Sense of Religious Plurality* (2014), co-editor of Palgrave's forthcoming series Interreligious Studies in Faith and Practice, and editor of the forthcoming book *Identity and Exclusion* (2015).

Contributors

David E. Beard is associate professor of rhetoric in the Department of Writing Studies at the University of Minnesota Duluth. While raised Catholic, he is at best lapsed into agnosticism, though his life and work with his friend David reminds him that these questions always bear consideration.

Andris Berry has spent a decade working in the film business on commercials, television, and movies in the various roles of production assistant, production coordinator, art department, truck driver, banjo player, songwriter, and gang boss. He is currently writing a book entitled *Notes from the Desire Factory*, based on his experiences in Hollywood. He enjoys spending time with his wife and two children.

Steven Berry (D.D., D.Min.) is spiritually a congregational/Franciscan who seeks to bring the Gospel to people in pertinent and prophetic ways. A friend of spiritual greats Henri Nouwen, Walter Wink, and Richard Wurmbrand, Steve promotes an Integral Worldview through his preaching, teaching, writing, filmmaking, and political activism. He believes that churches must become radicalized in the ways of Jesus if they are to have any relevance in the 21st Century.

Robert Brancatelli, Ph.D., is the founder of Fordham Road Collaborative in New York City, a consulting group dedicated to the advancement of personal and organizational mission in the tradition of Ignatian spirituality. The author of numerous articles and several books, he currently teaches business ethics at Fordham University.

Paul H. Carr led a branch of the AF Research Laboratory, where he is emeritus. He holds undergraduate and master's degrees from the Massachusetts Institute of Technology and a Ph.D. from Brandeis University. His 80 scientific papers and 10 patents contributed to filters used in cell phones, TV, and radar. The Templeton Foundation awarded him grants for his philosophy classes at University of Massachusetts Lowell. This inspired his book, *Beauty in Science and Spirit*.

Carmen Celestini is currently a Ph.D. student at the University of Waterloo, in the religious studies department. The focus of her research is on the overlapping belief systems of Christians and conspiracy theorists and their potential impact on the American political sphere.

Rebecca A. Chabot is currently a doctoral candidate in the joint doctoral program in religious and theological studies at the University of Denver and Iliff School of Theology. Her dissertation is on the social ethics of professional club soccer when soccer is understood as a religion. She has a M.Div. from Boston College School of Theology and Ministry and a B.A. in theology from Creighton University.

Brian Cogan is associate professor and chair of the Department of Communications at Molloy College. Cogan is the author, co-author, and editor of a ton o' books, including *The Encyclopedia of Punk*. He recently released his first novel, *Our Revolutionary Sweetheart*. He is no one to be trifled with.

Amitabh Vikram Dwivedi is an assistant professor of linguistics in the School of Languages and Literature at Shri Mata Vaishno Devi University, India. His research interests include language documentation, descriptive grammar, and the preservation of rare and endangered languages in South Asia. He has contributed articles to many English journals. His most recent publications are *A Grammar of Hadoti* (2012) and *A Grammar of Bhadarwahi* (2013), and *A Grammar of Dogri* is forthcoming.

David Gore is associate professor of rhetoric in the Department of Communication at the University of Minnesota Duluth. David has been called to serve his Mormon community as a Bishop.

Rebecca Whitten Poe Hays is the co-editor of *C. S. Lewis Remembered* (2006), *The Good, the True, and the Beautiful* (2007), and the annual proceedings of the Christianity in the Academy Conference. She is currently pursuing a PhD in Old Testament at Baylor University. Bridging her M.Div. degree and an undergraduate degree in English literature, her research interests involve the rhetorical power of story to communicate theological and ethical teaching.

Andriette Jordan-Fields is pursuing her Ph.D. in religion and theological studies concentrating in social ethics at the University of Denver and Iliff School of Theology. She earned a B.S. in political science from Tuskegee University, a M.P.A. from Northeastern University, and M.A. in social change from Iliff School of Theology. Her research and teaching interest lie at the intersection of ethics, feminist/womanist studies, black church, critical race theory, and postcolonial studies with an overall approach to study of social ethics that engages comprehensive issues of moral agency, cultural memory, ethical accountability, and social justice. Andriette is the 2011-2012 and 2013-2014 Elizabeth Iliff Warren Fellowship recipient.

Joyce Ann Konigsburg is a research/teaching assistant and Ph.D. student at Duquesne University in Pittsburgh, Pennsylvania. Her academic interests include systematic theology, relationality, interreligious work, theological anthropology, science and religion, and sociology of religions. In addition to a M.A. in theology, she earned a B.S. in computer science and in telecommunications and previously held executive-level positions at several information technology companies.

Paula J. Lee is a campus minister and teaches religious studies at a college preparatory academy in Denver, Colorado. Previously she served as an associate pastor and hospital chaplain. She is currently completing her Ph.D. in religion and psychological studies through the joint Ph.D. program at the University of Denver and the Iliff School of Theology.

Jeremy G. Mallory is a senior associate with Massey & Gail LLP in Chicago and has taught Constitutional Law as a Lecturer-in-Law at The University of Chicago Law School. He received his Ph.D. from The University of Chicago Divinity School in 2004 and a J.D. from the Law School in 2007.

Jeff Massey is professor of English language and literature (medieval-classical-linguistical) at Molloy College. Massey has published various articles (and comics) on topics ranging from Anglo-Saxon philology to Victorian mimesis and is the co-editor of *Heads Will Roll: Decapitation in the Medieval and Early Modern Imagination*. He has never read Proust.

Jason Neal is head of community outreach for the Dallas Beer Guardians and is a regular contributor to BigDSoccer.com as well as cohost of The Back of the Net Soccer Podcast.

Guido Oliana is a Comboni missionary. He spent 17 years in Uganda, 7 in the United States, and 5 in Kenya, where he lectured in the faculty of theology in Catholic University of Eastern Africa. At present he is lecturing theology in Juba (South Sudan). He holds a doctorate in liturgical theology (St. Anselm, Rome) and a doctorate in systematic theology (faculty of theology, Milan). His academic interests are in the areas of the theology of Paul Tillich, on whom he wrote his doctoral dissertation in systematic theology, liturgical-sacramental theology, Christology, theology of religious pluralism, and theological method in general.

B. J. Parker is a Ph.D. candidate in the religion department at Baylor University. Before beginning his Ph.D., he completed an M.A. in religion at Baylor, his M.Div. at the McAfee School of Theology of Mercer University, and his B.A. in biblical studies at Atlanta Christian College. B. J.'s current research explores the experience of suffering portrayed in the book of Psalms, as well as the convergence of religion and popular culture.

Carolyn D. Roark is the founding editor of Ecumenica. A scholar whose work has been focused on religion and performance, social pedagogy, and performing objects, her writing has appeared in *Theatre History Studies, Youth Theatre Journal, Ollantay, Puppetry International,* and other publications. She has served as Focus Group Representative for Religion and

Theatre at ATHE, as well as co-convener of the Articles-in-Progress workshop for MATC. She has a mild obsession with puppets.

Carlos Vara Sánchez holds a B.Sc. in biology, an Ms.C. in neuroscience, and an M.A. in humanities. Currently, he is working on his doctoral thesis at Barcelona's Pompeu Fabra University, studying the video installations of Bill Viola as a way of contrasting the philosophical and neuroscientific approaches to the role of the temporal experience in aesthetic perception. His publications and research interests span a wide range of issues on the boundaries between philosophy, art, and neuroscience.

Jann Cather Weaver, a practicing art photographer and published liturgist, is professor emerita of worship and theology and the arts at United Theological Seminary of the Twin Cities in St. Paul, Minnesota. She received her Ph.D. in theology and the arts from the Graduate Theological Union of Berkeley, California, and served as associate dean of community and student life at Yale Divinity School from 1993 to 2001. Jann was ordained by the United Church of Christ in 1982, serving congregations in Missouri and Wisconsin.

Nicholas R. Werse is a graduate of Palm Beach Atlantic University and George W. Truett Theological Seminary and is currently a Ph.D. candidate in Baylor University's Department of Religion where he is studying the Hebrew Bible. His research interests in biblical studies and North American religious movements converge in the exploration of modern biblical interpretation. His past publications focus upon the Hebrew prophetic literature, biblical methodologies, and church history.

Index

Adams, Douglas, 62–63
Adams, John, 80
Adebayor, Emmanuel, 11
advertising: authenticity and, 104–105; constant innovation and, 111; consumerism and, 104; effective, 106; emotional connections and, 107, 109–110; goal of, 103–104, 112; good, 105; language of, 103–104; message repetition in, 111; religion and, 103; religious/sacred language of, ix, 109, 112–113; slogans, 103, 108. *See also* attention; branding, faith in
African culture, 225; Christianity and, 226. *See also* African dances; African drums; African languages
African dances, ix, 226, 233–241; Acholi, 233; anthropological meaning of, 238; as cultural vector, 234; as discourse of the body, 234; as expressions of African genius, 234; as language, 233–234, 237; as narrative *poiesis,* 237; as symbols of holistic interpretation of life, 233–234; basic functions of, 234; communicating emotions through, 233; corporative engagement of, 226; dance of death, 237–238; *dingding* dance, 233; drumming and *poiesis,* 238; forms, 233; gentle dance of Banyankole, 233; Jesus Christ and, 237–238; jumping dances of Karimojong, 233; meeting between peoples and, 234; memorial power of, 234–239; rites of passage and, 233;
royal dance (*bwola*), 233; theological meaning of, 238; tribe member bonds and, 233
African drums, ix, 230–233, 238, 240–241; ancestor worship and, 231; as carrier of primordial word, 232; calling the community with, 231; clan drumbeats and rhythms, 231; dancing and *poiesis,* 238; forbidden in church services, 232; identified with primordial word, 232; Jesus Christ and, 232–233; memorial power of, 232–233; rhythmic musicality of, 226, 230–233; symbols of divine power, 231–232; therapeutic uses of, 231–232; use in celebration of sacraments, 232
African languages, ix, 226, 227–230, 240–241; African liturgical preaching, 227–228; communicating power of, 226, 227–230; rituals and, 229–230
African liturgical inculturation, 239–241
Alexander, Eben: God and near-death experience of, 192, 193, 199
Alvarez, Julia, 182
Anointed Fighter website, 33–34
anti–Catholicism, 80, 81
Antiochian Orthodox Basilica of St. Mary (Livonia, MI), 136
Apple Corporation: iPad Air Super Bowl commercial, 178–179
Apsara, 209
Aristotle, 42, 258